ASPEN PUBLIS

Siegel's

TORTS

Essay and Multiple-Choice Questions and Answers

BRIAN N. SIEGEL
J.D., Columbia Law School

LAZAR EMANUEL
J.D., Harvard Law School

Revised by

Arthur Best
Professor of Law
University of Denver
Sturm College of Law

Wolters Kluwer
Law & Business

AUSTIN   BOSTON   CHICAGO   NEW YORK   THE NETHERLANDS

Aspen Publishers
Attn: Permissions Department
76 Ninth Avenue, 7th Floor
New York, NY 10011-5201

To contact Customer Care, e-mail customer.care@aspenpublishers.com, call 1-800-234-1660, fax 1-800-901-9075, or mail correspondence to:

Aspen Publishers
Attn: Order Department
PO Box 990
Frederick, MD 21705

The authors gratefully acknowledge the assistance of the California Committee of Bar Examiners, which provided access to questions on which many of the essay questions in this book are based.

Printed in the United States of America.

1 2 3 4 5 6 7 8 9 0

ISBN 978-0-7355-7887-6

About Wolters Kluwer Law & Business

Wolters Kluwer Law & Business is a leading provider of research information and workflow solutions in key specialty areas. The strengths of the individual brands of Aspen Publishers, CCH, Kluwer Law International and Loislaw are aligned within Wolters Kluwer Law & Business to provide comprehensive, in-depth solutions and expert-authored content for the legal, professional and education markets.

CCH was founded in 1913 and has served more than four generations of business professionals and their clients. The CCH products in the Wolters Kluwer Law & Business group are highly regarded electronic and print resources for legal, securities, antitrust and trade regulation, government contracting, banking, pension, payroll, employment and labor, and healthcare reimbursement and compliance professionals.

Aspen Publishers is a leading information provider for attorneys, business professionals and law students. Written by preeminent authorities, Aspen products offer analytical and practical information in a range of specialty practice areas from securities law and intellectual property to mergers and acquisitions and pension/benefits. Aspen's trusted legal education resources provide professors and students with high-quality, up-to-date and effective resources for successful instruction and study in all areas of the law.

Kluwer Law International supplies the global business community with comprehensive English-language international legal information. Legal practitioners, corporate counsel and business executives around the world rely on the Kluwer Law International journals, loose-leafs, books and electronic products for authoritative information in many areas of international legal practice.

Loislaw is a premier provider of digitized legal content to small law firm practitioners of various specializations. Loislaw provides attorneys with the ability to quickly and efficiently find the necessary legal information they need, when and where they need it, by facilitating access to primary law as well as state-specific law, records, forms and treatises.

Wolters Kluwer Law & Business, a unit of Wolters Kluwer, is headquartered in New York and Riverwoods, Illinois. Wolters Kluwer is a leading multinational publisher and information services company.

Introduction

Although law school grades are a significant factor in obtaining a summer internship or entry position at a law firm, no formalized preparation for finals is offered at most law schools. For the most part, students are expected to fend for themselves in learning how to take a law school exam. Ironically, law school exams may bear little correspondence to the teaching methods used by professors during the school year. At least in the first year, professors require you to spend most of your time briefing cases. This is probably not great preparation for issue-spotting on exams. In briefing cases, you are made to focus on one or two principles of law at a time; thus, you don't get practice in relating one issue to another or in developing a picture of an entire problem or the entire course. When exams finally come, you're forced to make an abrupt 180-degree turn. Suddenly, you are asked to recognize, define, and discuss a variety of issues buried within a single multi-issue fact pattern. Alternatively, you may be asked to select among a number of possible answers, all of which look inviting but only one of which is right.

The comprehensive course outline you've created so diligently, and with such pain, means little if you're unable to apply its contents on your final exams. There is a vast difference between reading opinions in which the legal principles are clearly stated and applying those same principles to hypothetical essay exams and multiple-choice questions.

The purpose of this book is to help you bridge the gap between memorizing a rule of law and **understanding how to use it** in an exam. After an initial overview describing the exam-writing process, you see a large number of hypotheticals that test your ability to write analytical essays and to pick the right answers to multiple-choice questions. **Read them—all of them!** Then review the suggested answers that follow. You'll find that the key to superior grades lies in applying your knowledge through questions and answers, not through rote memory.

GOOD LUCK!

Table of Contents

Essay Answers

Multiple-Choice Questions

Multiple-Choice Answers

Index

Preparing Effectively for Essay Examinations[1]

To achieve superior scores on essay exams, a law student must (1) learn and understand "blackletter" principles and rules of law for each subject; (2) analyze how those principles of law arise within a test fact pattern; and (3) clearly and succinctly discuss each principle and how it relates to the facts. One of the most common misconceptions about law school is that you must memorize each word on every page of your casebooks or outlines to do well on exams. The reality is that you can commit an entire casebook to memory and still do poorly on an exam. Our review of hundreds of student answers has shown us that most students can recite the rules. The students who do **best** on exams are able to analyze how the rules they have memorized relate to the facts in the questions, and they are able to communicate their analysis to the grader. The following pages cover what you need to know to achieve superior scores on your law school essay exams.

The "ERC" Process

To study effectively for law school exams you must be able to "ERC" (*E*lementize, *R*ecognize, and *C*onceptualize) each legal principle covered in your casebooks and course outlines. *Elementizing* means reducing each legal theory and rule you learn to a concise, straightforward statement of its essential elements. Without knowledge of these elements, it's difficult to see all the issues as they arise.

For example, if you are asked, "What is self-defense?" it is **not** enough to say, "Self-defense is permitted when, if someone is about to hit you, you can prevent him from doing it." This layperson description would leave a grader wondering if you had actually attended law school. An accurate statement of the self-defense principle would go something like this: "When one reasonably believes she is in imminent danger of an offensive touching, she may assert whatever force she reasonably believes necessary under the circumstances to prevent the offensive touching from occurring." This formulation correctly shows that there are four separate, distinct elements that must be satisfied before the argument of self-defense can be successfully asserted: (1) the actor must have a *reasonable belief* that (2) the touching that she seeks to prevent is *offensive* and that (3) the offensive

---

1. To illustrate the principles of effective exam preparation, we have used examples from Torts and Constitutional Law. However, these principles apply to all subjects. One of the most difficult tasks faced by law students is learning how to apply principles from one area of the law to another. We leave it to you, the reader, to think of comparable examples for the subject matter of this book.

touching is *imminent*, and (4) she must use no greater force than she **reasonably believes necessary under the circumstances** to prevent the offensive touching from occurring.

Recognizing means perceiving or anticipating which words or ideas within a legal principle are likely to be the source of issues and how those issues are likely to arise within a given hypothetical fact pattern. With respect to the self-defense concept, there are four *potential* issues. Did the actor reasonably believe the other person was about to make an offensive contact with her? Was the contact imminent? Would the contact have been offensive? Did she use only such force as she reasonably believed necessary to prevent the imminent, offensive touching?

Conceptualizing means imagining situations in which each of the elements of a rule of law can give rise to factual issues. **Unless you can imagine or construct an application of each element of a rule, you don't truly understand the legal principles behind the rule!** In our opinion, the inability to conjure up hypothetical fact patterns or stories involving particular rules of law foretells a likelihood that you will miss issues involving those rules on an exam. It's *crucial* (1) to *recognize* that issues result from the interaction of facts with the words defining a rule of law and (2) to develop the ability to *conceptualize* or *imagine* fact patterns using the words or concepts within the rule.

For example, a set of facts illustrating the "reasonable belief" element of the self-defense rule might be the following:

> One evening, A and B had an argument at a bar. A screamed at B, "I'm going to get a knife and stab you!" A then ran out of the bar. B, who was armed with a concealed pistol, left the bar about 15 minutes later. As B was walking home, he heard someone running toward him from behind. B drew his pistol, turned, and shot the person advancing toward him (who was only about ten feet away when the shooting occurred). When B walked over to his victim, he realized that the person he had shot was dead and was not A, but another individual who had simply decided to take an evening jog. There would certainly be an issue whether B had a reasonable belief that the person who was running behind him was A. In the subsequent wrongful-death action, the victim's estate would contend that the earlier threat by A was not enough to give B a reasonable belief that the person running behind him was A. B could contend in rebuttal that, given the prior altercation at the bar, A's threat, the darkness, and the fact that the incident occurred soon after A's threat, his belief that A was about to attack him was "reasonable."

An illustration of how the word "imminent" might generate an issue is the following:

> X and Y had been feuding for some time. One afternoon, X suddenly attacked Y with a hunting knife. However, Y was able to wrest the knife away from X. At that point, X retreated about four feet away from Y and screamed: "You were lucky this time, but next time I'll have a gun and you'll be finished." Y, having good reason to believe that X would subsequently carry out his threats (after all, X had just attempted to kill Y), immediately thrust the knife into X's chest, killing him. Although Y certainly had a reasonable belief that X would attempt to kill him the next time the two met, Y would probably not be able to assert the self-defense privilege because the element of "imminency" was absent.

A fact pattern illustrating the actor's right to use only that force that is reasonably necessary under the circumstances might be the following:

> D rolled up a newspaper and was about to strike E on the shoulder with it. As D pulled back his arm for the purpose of delivering the blow, E drew a knife and plunged it into D's chest. Although E had every reason to believe that D was about to deliver an offensive impact on him, E probably could not successfully assert the self-defense privilege because the force he utilized in response was greater than reasonably necessary under the circumstances to prevent the impact. E could simply have deflected D's blow or punched D away. The use of a knife constituted a degree of force by E that was not reasonable, given the minor injury he would have suffered from the newspaper's impact.

"Mental games" such as these must be played with every element of every rule you learn.

Issue-Spotting

One of the keys to doing well on an essay examination is issue-spotting. In fact, issue-spotting is *the* most important skill you will learn in law school. If you recognize a legal issue, you can find the applicable rule of law (if there is one) by researching the issue. But if you fail to see the issues, you won't learn the steps that lead to success or failure on exams or, for that matter, in the practice of law. It is important to remember that (1) an issue is a question to be decided by the judge or jury and (2) a question is "in issue" when it can be disputed or argued about at trial. The bottom line is that *if you don't spot an issue, you can't raise it or discuss it.*

The key to issue-spotting is to learn to approach a problem in the same way an attorney does. Let's assume you've been admitted to practice and a client enters your office with a legal problem involving a dispute. He will recite his facts to you and give you any documents that may be pertinent. He will then want to know if he can sue (or be sued, if your client seeks to avoid liability). To answer your client's questions intelligently, you will have to decide the following: (1) what principles or rules can possibly be asserted by your

client; (2) what defense or defenses can possibly be raised to these principles; (3) what issues may arise if these defenses are asserted; (4) what
arguments each side can make to persuade the fact finder to resolve the issue
in his favor; and (5) finally, what the *likely* outcome of each issue will be.
***All the issues that can possibly arise at trial will be relevant to your
answers.***

How to Discuss an Issue

Keep in mind that ***rules of law are the guides to issues*** (i.e., an issue arises
where there is a question whether the facts do, or do not, satisfy an element
of a rule); a rule of law ***cannot dispose of an issue*** unless the rule can
reasonably be ***applied to the facts***.

A good way to learn how to discuss an issue is to study the following
mini-hypothetical and the two student responses that follow it.

Mini-Hypothetical

A and B were involved in making a movie being filmed at a local bar. The
script called for A to appear to throw a bottle (which was actually a rubber
prop) at B. The fluorescent lighting at the bar had been altered for the
movie—the usual subdued blue lights had been replaced with rather bright
white lights. The cameraperson had stationed herself just to the left of the
swinging doors serving as the main entrance to the bar. As the scene was
unfolding, C, a regular patron of the bar, unwittingly walked into it. The
guard who was usually stationed immediately outside the bar had mo-
mentarily left his post to visit the restroom. As C pushed the barroom
doors inward, the left door panel knocked the camera to the ground
with a resounding crash. The first (and only) thing C saw was A (about 5
feet from C), who was getting ready to throw the bottle at B, who was
at the other end of the bar (about 15 feet from A). Without hesitation, C
pushed A to the ground and punched him in the face. Plastic surgery was
required to restore A's profile to its Hollywood-handsome pre-altercation
look.

Discuss A's right against C.

Pertinent Principles of Law:

1. Under the rule defining the prevention-of-crime privilege, if a person
   sees that someone is about to commit what he or she reasonably believes
   to be a felony or misdemeanor involving a breach of the peace, he or she
   may exercise whatever degree of force is reasonably necessary under the
   circumstances to prevent that person from committing the crime.

2. Under the defense-of-others privilege, if a person reasonably believes
   that someone is about to offensively contact a third party, he or she may
   use whatever force is reasonably necessary under the circumstances to

prevent the contact. Some jurisdictions, however, limit this privilege to situations in which the actor and the third party are related.

First Student Answer

Did C commit an assault and battery upon A?

An assault occurs when the defendant intentionally causes the plaintiff to be reasonably in apprehension of an imminent, offensive touching. The facts state that C pushed A to the ground. Thus, a battery would have occurred at this point. We are also told that C punched A in the face. It is reasonable to assume that A saw the punch being thrown at him, and therefore A felt in imminent danger of an offensive touching. Based on the facts, C has committed an assault and battery upon A.

Were C's actions justifiable under the defense-of-others privilege?

C could successfully assert the defense-of-others and prevention-of-crime privileges. When C opened the bar doors, A appeared to be throwing the bottle at B. Although the "bottle" was actually a prop, C had no way of knowing this fact. Also, it was necessary for C to punch A in the face to ensure that A could not get back up, retrieve the bottle, and again throw it at B. Although the plastic surgery required by A is unfortunate, C could not be successfully charged with assault and battery.

Second Student Answer

Assault and battery:

C committed an assault (causing A to be reasonably in apprehension of an imminent, offensive contact) when A saw that C's punch was about to hit him, and battery (causing an offensive contact upon A) when (1) C knocked A to the ground, and (2) C punched A.

Defense-of-others/prevention-of-crime defenses:

C would undoubtedly assert the defense-of-others privilege (when defendant reasonably believed the plaintiff was about to make an offensive contact upon a third party, he was entitled to use whatever force was reasonably necessary to prevent the contact) and the prevention-of-crime privilege (when one reasonably believes another is about to commit a felony or misdemeanor involving a breach of the peace, he may exercise whatever force is reasonably necessary to prevent that person from committing a crime).

A could contend that C was not reasonable in believing that A was about to cause harm to B because the enhanced lighting at the bar and camera crash should have indicated to C, a regular customer, that a movie was being filmed. However, C could probably successfully contend in rebuttal that his belief was reasonable in light of the facts that (1) he had not seen the camera when he attacked A, and (2) instantaneous action was required (he did not have time to notice the enhanced lighting around the bar).

A might also contend that the justification was forfeited because the degree of force used by C was not reasonable, because C did not have to punch A in the face after A had already been pushed to the ground (i.e., the danger to B was no longer present). However, C could argue in rebuttal that it was necessary to knock out A (an individual with apparently violent propensities) while the opportunity existed, rather than risk a drawn-out scuffle in which A might prevail. The facts do not indicate how big A and C were, but assuming C was not significantly larger than A, C's contention will probably be successful. If, however, C were significantly larger than A, the punch may have been excessive (because C could presumably have simply held A down).

Critique

Let's start by examining the First Student Answer. It mistakenly treats as an "issue" the assault and battery committed by C upon A. Although the actions creating these torts must be mentioned in the facts to provide a foundation for a discussion of the applicable privileges, there was no need to discuss them further because they were not the issue for which the examiner was testing.

The structure of the initial paragraph of the First Student Answer is also incorrect. After an assault is defined in the first sentence, the second sentence abruptly describes the facts necessary to constitute the commission of a battery. The third sentence then sets forth the elements of a battery. The fourth sentence completes the discussion of assault by describing the facts pertaining to that tort. The two-sentence break between the original mention of assault and the facts that constitute assault is confusing; the facts that call for the application of a rule should be mentioned *immediately* after the rule is stated.

A more serious error, however, occurs in the second paragraph of the First Student Answer. Although there is an allusion to the correct principle of law (prevention of crime), the **rule is not stated**. As a consequence, the grader can only guess why the student thinks the facts set forth in the subsequent sentences are significant. A grader reading this answer could not be certain whether the student recognized that the issues revolved around the **reasonable belief** and **necessary force** elements of the prevention-of-crime privilege. Superior exam-writing requires that the pertinent facts be **tied** directly and clearly to the operative rule.

The Second Student Answer is much better than the First Student Answer. It disposes of C's assault and battery upon A in a few words (yet tells the grader that the writer knows these torts are present). More important, the grader can easily see the issues that would arise if the prevention-of-crime privilege were asserted (i.e., "whether C's belief that A was about to commit a crime against B was reasonable" and "whether C used unnecessary force in punching A after A had been knocked to the ground"). Finally, it also utilizes all the facts by indicating how an attorney would assert those facts that are most advantageous to his or her client.

Structuring Your Answer

Graders will give high marks to a clearly written, well-structured answer. Each issue you discuss should follow a specific and consistent structure that a grader can easily follow.

The Second Student Answer basically utilizes the *I-R-A-A-O format* with respect to each issue. In this format, the *I* stands for *Issue*; the *R* for *Rule of law*; the first *A* for *one side's Argument*; the second *A* for *the other party's rebuttal Argument*; and the *O* for your *Opinion as to how the issue would be resolved*. The *I-R-A-A-O* format emphasizes the importance of (1) discussing **both** sides of an issue and (2) communicating to the grader that, where an issue arises, an attorney can only advise his or her client as to the **probable** decision on that issue.

A somewhat different format for analyzing each issue is the *I-R-A-C format*. Here, the *I* stands for *Issue*; the *R* for *Rule of law*; the *A* for *Application of the facts to the rule of law*; and the *C* for *Conclusion*. *I-R-A-C* is a legitimate approach to the discussion of a particular issue, within the time constraints imposed by the question. The *I-R-A-C format* must be applied to each issue in the question; it is not the solution to the entire answer. If there are six issues in a question, for example, you should offer six separate, independent *I-R-A-C* analyses.

We believe that the *I-R-A-C* approach is preferable to the *I-R-A-A-O* formula. However, either can be used to analyze and organize essay exam answers. Whatever format you choose, however, you should be consistent throughout the exam and remember the following rules:

First, *analyze all of the relevant facts*. Facts have significance in a particular case *only as they come under the applicable rules of law*. The facts presented must be analyzed and examined to see if they do or do not satisfy one element or another of the applicable rules, and the essential facts and rules must be stated and argued in your analysis.

Second, you must communicate to the grader the *precise rule of law* controlling the facts. In their eagerness to commence their arguments, students sometimes fail to state the applicable rule of law first. Remember, the *R* in either format stands for *Rule of law*. Defining the rule of law *before* an analysis of the facts is essential in order to allow the grader to follow your reasoning.

Third, it is important to treat *each side of an issue with equal detail.* If a hypothetical describes how an elderly man was killed when he ventured upon the land of a huge power company to obtain a better view of a nuclear reactor, your sympathies might understandably fall on the side of the old man. The grader will nevertheless expect you to see and make every possible argument for the other side. Don't permit your personal viewpoint to affect your answer! A good lawyer never does! When discussing an issue, always state the arguments for each side.

Finally, don't forget to *state your opinion or conclusion* on each issue. Keep in mind, however, that your opinion or conclusion is probably the *least* important part of an exam answer. Why? Because your professor knows that no attorney can tell his or her client exactly how a judge or jury will decide a particular issue. By definition, an issue is a legal dispute that can go either way. An attorney, therefore, can offer the client only his or her best opinion about the likelihood of victory or defeat on an issue. Because the decision on any issue lies with the judge or jury, no attorney can ever be absolutely certain of the resolution.

Discuss All Possible Issues

As we've noted, a student should draw *some* type of conclusion or opinion for each issue raised. Whatever your conclusion on a particular issue, it is essential to anticipate and discuss *all of the issues* that would arise if the question were actually tried in court.

Let's assume that a negligence hypothetical involves issues pertaining to duty, breach of duty, proximate causation, and contributory negligence. If the defendant prevails on any one of these issues, he or she will avoid liability. Nevertheless, even if you feel strongly that the defendant owed no duty to the plaintiff, you *must* go on to discuss all of the other potential issues as well (breach of duty, proximate causation, and contributory negligence). If you were to terminate your answer after a discussion of the duty element only, you'd receive an inferior grade.

Why should you have to discuss every possible issue if you are relatively certain that the outcome of a particular issue would be dispositive of the entire case? Because at the commencement of litigation, neither party can be **absolutely positive** about which issues he or she will prevail upon at trial. We can state with confidence that every attorney with some degree of experience has won issues he or she thought he or she would lose, and has lost issues on which victory seemed assured. Because one can never be absolutely certain how a factual issue will be resolved by the fact finder, a good attorney (and exam writer) will consider **all** possible issues.

To understand the importance of discussing all of the potential issues, you should reflect on what you will do in the actual practice of law. If you represent the defendant, for example, it is your job to raise every possible defense. If there are five potential defenses, and your pleadings rely on only three of them (because you're sure you will win on all three), and the plaintiff is somehow successful on all three issues, your client may well sue you for malpractice. Your client's contention would be that you should be liable because if you had only raised the two additional issues, you might have prevailed on at least one of them, and therefore liability would have been avoided. It is an attorney's duty to raise **all** legitimate issues. A similar philosophy should be followed when taking essay exams.

What exactly do you say when you've resolved the initial issue in favor of the defendant, and discussion of any additional issues would seem to be moot? The answer is simple. You begin the discussion of the next issue with something like, "Assuming, however, the plaintiff prevailed on the foregoing issue, the next issue would be . . . ." The grader will understand and appreciate what you have done.

The corollary to the importance of raising all potential issues is that you should avoid discussion of obvious nonissues. Raising nonissues is detrimental in three ways: First, you waste a lot of precious time; second, you usually receive absolutely no points for discussing an issue that the grader deems extraneous; and third, it suggests to the grader that you lack the ability to distinguish the significant from the irrelevant. The best guideline for avoiding the discussion of a nonissue is to ask yourself, "Would I, as an attorney, feel comfortable about raising that particular issue or objection in front of a judge?"

Delineate the Transition from One Issue to the Next

It's a good idea to make it easy for the grader to see the issues you've found. One way to accomplish this is to cover no more than one issue per paragraph. Another way is to underline each issue statement. Provided that time permits, we recommend that you use both techniques. The essay answers in this book contain numerous illustrations of these suggestions.

One frequent student error is to write two separate paragraphs in which all of the arguments for one side are made in the initial paragraph, and all of the rebuttal arguments by the other side are made in the next paragraph. This organization is *a bad idea*. It obliges the grader to reconstruct the exam answer in his or her mind several times to determine whether all possible issues have been discussed by both sides. It will also cause you to state the same rule of law more than once. A better-organized answer presents a given argument by one side and follows that immediately in the same paragraph with the other side's rebuttal to that argument.

Understanding the "Call" of a Question

The statement *at the end* of an essay question or of the fact pattern in a multiple-choice question is sometimes referred to as the "call" of the question. It usually asks you to do something specific such as "discuss," "discuss the rights of the parties," "list X's rights," "advise X," "give the best grounds on which to find the statute unconstitutional," "state what D can be convicted of," "recommend how the estate should be distributed," and so forth. The call of the question should be read carefully because it tells you exactly what you're expected to do. If a question asks, "what are X's rights against Y?" or "what is X liable to Y for?" you don't have to spend a lot of time on Y's rights against Z. You will usually receive absolutely no credit for discussing issues or facts that are not required by the call. On the other hand, if the call of an essay question is simply "discuss" or "discuss the rights of the parties," then *all* foreseeable issues must be covered by your answer.

Students are often led astray by an essay question's call. For example, if you are asked for "X's rights against Y" or to "advise X," you may think you may limit yourself to X's viewpoint with respect to the issues. This is *not correct*! You cannot resolve one party's rights against another party without considering the issues that would arise (and the arguments the other side would assert) if litigation occurred. In short, although the call of the question may appear to focus on the rights of one of the parties to the litigation, a superior answer will cover all the issues and arguments that person might *encounter* (not just the arguments he or she would *make*) in attempting to pursue his or her rights against the other side.

The Importance of Analyzing the Question Carefully Before Writing

The overriding *time pressure* of an essay exam is probably a major reason why many students fail to analyze a question carefully before writing. Five minutes into the allocated time for a particular question, you may notice that the person next to you is writing furiously. This thought then flashes through your mind: "Oh my goodness, he's putting down more words on the paper than I am, and therefore he's bound to get a better grade." It can be stated **unequivocally** that there is no necessary correlation between the number of words on your exam paper and the grade you'll receive. Students who begin their answer after only five minutes of analysis have probably seen only the most obvious issues and missed many, if not most, of the subtle ones. They are also likely to be less well organized.

Opinions differ as to how much time you should spend analyzing and outlining a question before you actually write the answer. We believe that you should spend at least 12 to 18 minutes analyzing, organizing, and outlining a one-hour question before writing your answer. This will usually provide sufficient time to analyze and organize the question thoroughly **and** enough time to write a relatively complete answer. Remember that each word of the question must be scrutinized to determine if it (1) suggests an issue under the operative rules of law or (2) can be used in making an argument for the resolution of an issue. Because you can't receive points for an issue you don't spot, it is usually wise to read a question **twice** before starting your outline.

When to Make an Assumption

The instructions for a question may tell you to **assume** facts that are necessary to the answer. Even when these instructions are **not** given, you may be obliged to make certain assumptions about missing facts in order to write a thorough answer. Assumptions should be made only when you are told or when you, as the attorney for one of the parties described in the question, would be obliged to solicit additional information from your client. On the other hand, assumptions should **never be used to change or alter the question.** Don't ever write something like "if the facts in the question were . . . , instead of . . . , then . . . would result." If you do this, you are wasting time on facts that are extraneous to the problem before you. Professors want you to deal with **their** fact patterns, not your own.

Students sometimes try to "write around" information they think is missing. They assume that their professor has failed to include every piece of data necessary for a thorough answer. This is generally **wrong**. The professor may have omitted some facts deliberately to see if the student **can figure out what to do** under the circumstances. However, in some instances, the professor may have omitted them inadvertently (even law professors are sometimes human).

The way to deal with the omission of essential information is to describe (1) what fact (or facts) appears to be missing and (2) why that information is important. As an example, go back to the "movie shoot" hypothetical we discussed above. In that fact pattern, there was no mention of the relative strengths of A and C. This fact could be extremely important. If C weighed 240 pounds and was built like a professional football linebacker, while A tipped the scales at a mere 160 pounds, punching A in the face after he had been pushed to the ground would probably constitute unnecessary force (thereby causing C to forfeit the prevention-of-crime privilege). If the physiques of the parties were reversed, however, C's punch to A's face would probably constitute reasonable behavior. Under the facts, C had to deal the "knockout" blow while the opportunity presented itself. The last sentences of the Second Student Answer above show that the student understood these subtleties and correctly supplied the essential missing facts and assumptions.

Assumptions should be made in a manner that keeps the other issues open (i.e., they lead to a discussion of all other possible issues). Don't assume facts that would virtually dispose of the entire hypothetical in a few sentences. For example, suppose that A called B a "convicted felon" (a statement that is inherently defamatory—i.e., a statement that tends to subject the plaintiff to hatred, contempt, or ridicule). If A's statement is true, he has a complete defense to B's action for defamation. If the facts don't tell whether A's statement was true or not, it would *not* be wise to write something like, "We'll assume that A's statement about B is accurate, and therefore B cannot successfully sue A for defamation." So facile an approach would rarely be appreciated by the grader. The proper way to handle this situation would be to state, "If we assume that A's statement about B is not correct, A cannot raise the defense of truth." You've communicated to the grader that you recognize the need to assume an essential fact and that you've assumed it in a way that enables you to proceed to discuss all other issues.

Case Names

A law student is ordinarily *not* expected to recall case names on an exam. The professor knows that you have read several hundred cases for each course and that you would have to be a memory expert to have all of the names at your fingertips. If you confront a fact pattern that seems similar to a case you have reviewed (but you cannot recall its name), just write something like, "One case we've read held that . . ." or "It has been held that . . . ." In this manner, you have informed the grader that you are relying on a case that contained a fact pattern similar to the question at issue.

The only exception to this rule is in the case of a landmark decision (e.g., *Roe v. Wade*). Landmark opinions are usually those that change or alter established law.[2] These cases are usually easy to identify, because you will probably have spent an entire class period discussing each of them. *Palsgraf v. Long Island Rail Road* is a prime example of a landmark case in Torts; in Corporations, *Meinhard v. Salmon* is worth remembering. In these special cases, you may be expected to recall the case by name, as well as the proposition of law it stands for. However, this represents a very limited exception to the general rule that counsels against wasting precious time trying to memorize and reproduce case names.

How to Handle Time Pressures

What do you do when there are five minutes left in the exam and you have only written down two-thirds of your answer? One thing *not* to do is write something like, "No time left!" or "Not enough time!" This gets you nothing but the satisfaction of knowing you have communicated your personal frustrations to the grader. Another thing *not* to do is insert in the exam booklet the outline you may have made on a piece of scrap paper. Professors will rarely look at these.

First of all, it is not necessarily a bad thing to be pressed for time. The person who finishes five minutes early has very possibly missed some important issues. The more proficient you become in knowing what is expected of you on an exam, the greater the difficulty you may experience in staying within the time limits. Second, remember that (at least to some extent) you're graded against your classmates' answers and they're under exactly the same time pressure as you. In short, don't panic if you can't write the "perfect" answer in the allotted time. Nobody does!

The best hedge against misuse of time is to *review as many old exams as possible*. These exercises will give you a familiarity with the process of organizing and writing an exam answer, which, in turn, should result in an enhanced ability to stay within the time boundaries. If you nevertheless find that you have about 15 minutes of writing to do and 5 minutes to do it in, write a paragraph that summarizes the remaining issues or arguments you would discuss if time permitted. As long as you've indicated that you're aware of the remaining legal issues, you'll probably receive some credit for them. Your analytical and argumentative skills will already be apparent to the grader by virtue of the issues that you have previously discussed.

---

2. In Constitutional Law and Criminal Procedure, many cases will qualify as "landmark" cases. Students studying these subjects should try to associate case names with the corresponding holdings and reproduce both in their exam answers.

Typing and Writing

Make sure that the way you write or type your answer presents your analysis in the best possible light. In other words, if you write, do so legibly. If you type, remember to use many paragraphs instead of just creating a document in which all of your ideas are merged into a single lengthy block of print. Remember, your professor may have a hundred or more exams to grade. If your answer is difficult to read, you will rarely be given the benefit of the doubt. On the other hand, a paper that is easy to read creates a very positive mental impact upon the professor.

If you decide to use bluebooks and handwriting instead of a computer, it is usually a good idea to write only on the odd-numbered pages (1, 3, 5, etc.). You may also want to leave a blank line between each written line. These things will usually make the answer easier to read. If you discover that you have left out a word or phrase, you can insert it into the proper place by means of a caret sign (∧). If you feel that you've omitted an entire issue, you can write it on the facing blank page. A symbol can be used to indicate where the additional portion of the answer should be inserted.

The Importance of Reviewing Prior Exams

As we've mentioned, it is *extremely important to review old exams*. The transition from blackletter law to essay exam can be a difficult experience if the process has not been practiced. Although this book provides a large number of essay and multiple-choice questions, *don't stop here*! Most law schools have recent tests online or on file in the library, by course. If they are available only in the library, we strongly suggest that you make a copy of every old exam you can obtain (especially those given by your professors) at the beginning of each semester. The demand for these documents usually increases dramatically as "finals time" draws closer.

The exams for each course should be scrutinized *throughout the semester*. They should be reviewed as you complete each chapter in your casebook. Sometimes the order of exam questions follows the sequence of the materials in your casebook. Thus, the first question on a law school test may involve the initial three chapters of the casebook; the second question may pertain to the fourth and fifth chapters; and so forth. In any event, *don't wait* until the semester is nearly over to begin reviewing old exams.

Keep in mind that no one is born with the ability to analyze questions and write superior answers to law school exams. Like any other skill, it is developed and perfected only through application. If you don't take the time to analyze numerous examinations from prior years, this evolutionary process just won't occur. Don't just *think about* the answers to past exam questions; take the time to *write the answers down*. It's also wise to look back at an answer a day or two after you've written it. You will invariably see (1) ways to improve your organizational skills and (2) arguments you missed.

As you practice spotting issues on past exams, you will see how rules of law become the sources of issues on finals. As we've already noted, if you don't *understand* how rules of law translate into issues, you won't be able to achieve superior grades on your exams. Reviewing exams from prior years should also reveal that certain issues tend to be lumped together in the same question. For instance, where a fact pattern involves a false statement made by one person about another, three potential theories of liability are often present—defamation, invasion of privacy (false, public light), and intentional infliction of severe emotional distress. You will need to see if any or all of these legal remedies apply to the facts.

Finally, one of the best means of evaluating if you understand a subject (or a particular area within a subject) is to attempt to create a hypothetical exam for that subject. Your exam should contain as many issues as possible. If you can write an issue-packed exam, you probably know that subject well. If you can't, then you probably haven't yet acquired an adequate understanding of how the principles of law in that subject can spawn issues.

As Always, a Caveat

The suggestions and advice offered in this book represent the product of many years of experience in the field of legal education. We are confident that the techniques and concepts described in these pages will help you prepare for, and succeed at, your exams. Nevertheless, particular professors sometimes have a preference for exam-writing techniques that are not stressed in this book. Some instructors expect at least a nominal reference to the *prima facie* elements of all pertinent legal theories (even though one or more of those principles are *not* placed into issue). Other professors want their students to emphasize public policy considerations in the arguments they make on a particular issue. Because this book is intended for nation-wide consumption, these individualized preferences have *not* been stressed. The best way to find out whether your professor has a penchant for a particular writing approach is to ask him or her to provide you with a model answer to a previous exam. If a model answer is not available, speak to second- or third-year students who received a superior grade in that professor's class.

One final point. Although the rules of law stated in the answers to the questions in this book have been drawn from commonly used sources (casebooks, hornbooks, etc.), it is still conceivable that they may be slightly at odds with those taught by your professor. In the area of corporations law, there are differences from jurisdiction to jurisdiction, and your professor will probably advise you to follow the Model Business Corporations Act, Delaware law, or the laws of the state in which you are located. In instances in which a conflict exists between our formulation of a legal principle and the one taught by your professor, ***follow the latter***! Because your grades are determined by your professors, their views should always supersede the views contained in this book.

Essay
Questions

Question 1

A and B had exchanged words in the past. One day they passed each other on a crowded street. Within the hearing of several passersby, A called B a "wimp." B said, "I'll show you who's a wimp; let's see what kind of a man you are." They squared off and began a furious fistfight and wrestling match. A appeared to be winning when C, B's brother, came upon the scene. C pulled a knife and thrust it at A. A's brother, D, then came up and saw C attacking A with a knife. D pulled a pistol and shot at C. D missed, but hit and wounded E, an innocent passerby who had just stepped out of a store. D did not have a license to carry a firearm. B and C fled after D's shot.

D picked up C's knife, which C had dropped while fleeing. D took it home. It had a value of $25. When C later found out that D had his knife, he went to D's house. C walked up to D's door and knocked. D answered the door and told C to "get off my land." When C refused, D let his dog, Homer, loose. Homer chased C off D's property, but the dog never bit C.

Discuss the tort liabilities of the various parties.

Question 2

Driver bought a car for $65,000. The car had interior gold fixtures, a slide-out bar, a computer system, and other "special" accessories. To protect the car from vandalism and theft, Driver equipped it himself with a system he designed. The system was simple: Anyone opening a car door would receive a severe electric shock and cause an alarm to sound. Only Driver knew how to disarm the system.

Baker, a commercial photographer, saw the car parked at a downtown curb. He induced his friend, Art Archer, to get into the car so he could take a picture of Art at the wheel. Art was reluctant but finally agreed. Art took hold of the handle of the door on the sidewalk side. As Art tried to open the door, he received a shock. The shock would not ordinarily have injured a healthy person, but Art had a serious heart condition. The shock caused Art to stagger back, collapse on the sidewalk, and die.

As Art fell, his wife Sue Archer, who had witnessed the incident, ran to help him but was knocked down when he fell against her. As a result of this experience, she was unable to sleep, and frequently experienced headaches, nausea, and vomiting.

Neither Art nor Baker knew that the car had been wired to induce electrical shocks. Neither had seen a sign on the front windshield which could be read from the sidewalk and which stated, "Beware, this car is equipped with a protective device—DO NOT TOUCH!"

Suits are brought against Driver and Baker for damages resulting from the death of Art and the injury to Sue Archer.

What result? Discuss.

Question 3

Peter, a movie producer, leased the Calumet Saloon in a small Western town in order to film an indoor barroom scene for his next movie. The leading man, Dan, was to enter the barroom and take a shot at Jim, who was holding a whisky bottle in his hand. This was to be followed almost immediately by a second shot by Dan which would appear to hit Jim. Shortly before the scene was started, a prop man accidentally inserted live ammunition into Dan's gun, instead of the blanks he meant to insert. The first bullet from Dan's gun pierced Jim's cowboy hat. Jim now realized that the second shot would wound or kill him. The script called for a big, noisy, shouting crowd around the bar. Jim called out to Dan, "Don't shoot, don't shoot," but the noise prevented Dan from hearing him. Jim raised his arm to throw the bottle he was holding at Dan. Because this gesture was not in the script, Dan was alarmed by Jim's conduct.

At this very moment, Fred entered the saloon. He was a regular customer there, and had no connection to the movie production. He hadn't noticed a prominent sign by the door stating that the Calumet Saloon would be closed all day. When Fred pushed open the swinging door, the door knocked over an extremely expensive movie camera (valued at $125,000) belonging to Peter. The camera shattered into many pieces.

As Fred entered, he saw Jim raising his arm to throw the bottle at Dan. To prevent Jim from throwing the bottle, Fred knocked Jim to the floor and punched him in the face.

What are Jim's rights, if any, against Dan and Fred? Discuss.

What are Dan's rights, if any, against Jim? Discuss.

What are Peter's rights, if any, against Fred? Discuss.

Question 4

A storage shed on the suburban yard of Construction Co. (Conco) caught fire on a Sunday morning. Dennis, an accountant at Conco's downtown office, happened to be bicycling by on a personal errand. He contacted the local volunteer fire department and broke into the yard office through a closed window. He then located the ignition keys for eight pieces of heavy equipment and moved the equipment onto an adjacent field, breaking some pavement as he drove the equipment over it. The equipment consisted of trucks and bulldozers. Dennis was able to move them all before the fire reached them.

Unknown to Dennis, the adjacent field belonged to Frank, a wholesale florist. The field appeared to be unused, but in fact, Frank had planted it throughout with valuable tulip bulbs. Bulbs valued at $9,000 were destroyed under the weight of the heavy equipment.

After the firefighters had extinguished the fire, Frank asked Dennis to come to his office to discuss the damage. Dennis agreed. As soon as Dennis entered the office, Frank told Dennis, in the presence of four of Frank's employees, that Dennis would have to remain at the office until he summoned the president of Conco and the president arrived at the office. When the president arrived an hour later, Frank told Dennis he could leave, and Dennis left.

What are Frank's rights against Dennis and against Conco? Discuss.

What are Dennis's rights against Frank? Discuss.

Question 5

The Babel Hotel, an extended-stay hotel whose guests usually stayed for lengthy periods, caught fire. Abel, who was staying at the hotel for an extended period, started to leave his room. He realized that his next-door neighbor, Miss Cool, an invalid who usually kept her door unlocked, might need help. He entered her apartment and picked Cool up. By this time, the flames had engulfed the entire hallway outside Cool's room.

A city ordinance required hotels to have four fire exits on each floor, but there were only two on each floor of the Babel Hotel. Unable to get out of the apartment into the hallway, Abel (with Cool on his shoulder) finally jumped out of Cool's bedroom window. He intended to land on the roof of the adjoining building. When he did, the roof collapsed under his weight. Abel and Cool fell through the roof to the floor of a restaurant. Pierre, the owner of the restaurant, quickly ordered three of his employees to move Abel and Cool into the street. This aggravated the severe back injury Abel had sustained in the jump and fall. Cool sustained multiple injuries.

Discuss Abel's rights, if any, in suits against Babel, Pierre, the owner of the adjoining building, and the city.

Question 6

Henry and his pregnant wife, Wendy, went to Baseball Stadium to watch a baseball game. The parking lot and stadium are owned by Baseball, Inc. Henry paid the parking fee and parked. In opening her door, Wendy hit a car parked alongside, causing some paint to chip off. Kevin, the owner of the car, jumped out and screamed at Wendy, "You moron, why don't you look what you're doing? I ought to kick your butt." The shock of Kevin's words caused Wendy to faint. Henry ran up and punched Kevin in the mouth, knocking out two teeth. Kevin and Henry then began to scuffle.

John, an onlooker, tried to break up the fight but was knocked to the ground and injured. John doesn't know who hit him. The local police and two security guards employed by Baseball, Inc., arrived after about five minutes. The local police took both Henry and Kevin to jail. The two security guards carried Wendy to the stadium infirmary to rest until she could recover consciousness. About 20 minutes later, Wendy began to moan loudly. Because the heavy game traffic would have prevented an emergency ambulance from reaching the infirmary, she was taken to a nearby hospital by the local police. At the hospital, it was discovered that Wendy had suffered a miscarriage.

Discuss Henry's and Wendy's potential rights and liabilities.

Question 7

Farmer (F) was burning weeds on his land, which was adjacent to a public highway. This was a customary practice for farmers in the area. The wind was erratic, and from time to time heavy smoke was blown across the highway.

Husband (H) and wife (W) were traveling along the highway in a car owned by W. H was driving the car at about 50 mph. As they approached the area of the smoke, they could see that the smoke was constantly shifting its direction, blowing one way and then another. As they proceeded, the wind changed in their direction, and heavy smoke from the burning brush enveloped the car. H was unable to see, and he immediately applied the brakes. Before he could stop, he ran into T, a driver going in the opposite direction. T's car had crossed over the center line. The impact was substantial. H and W were injured and the car was damaged. A few moments later, a bus owned by Coach Co. (C) and driven by one of its drivers crashed into W's car and caused further damage and injury to H and W.

The driver of the bus claimed he had not seen the car ahead of him, but admitted he had seen the smoke crossing the highway as he approached. He told the police that he had reduced his speed to about 35 mph when he approached the smoke and claimed that when he saw the car, he tried to stop, but it was too late to avoid hitting it. The speed limit on this road was 45 mph.

What are the rights of H and W against F, C, the driver of the bus, and T?

Question 8

Alan and Anne Parenti are the parents of Alice, age 6, and Sandy, age 7. One evening they left the two children with Barbara, a 14-year-old babysitter. This was the first time they had asked Barbara to take care of the children. In fact, they had never met Barbara before. Barbara arrived at the house about 20 minutes late, and the Parentis had only enough time to tell her the children's bedtime hour. They assumed she could manage the rest.

After they left, Barbara was joined by her boyfriend. He and Barbara ignored the children. They failed to notice the children leave the house to go to Farmer's adjacent property to play in Farmer's barn. Farmer had told the children many times that they could play on the swing in his yard, but that they were not to go into his barn. On two previous occasions, he had chased them out of the barn. This evening, the children saw, just inside the door of the barn, a charcoal grill containing live coals. They decided to play "make believe" cooking and piled some loose hay on the grill. The hay began to burn. In the resulting fire, the barn was completely destroyed and Alice and Sandy were burned.

Discuss the rights of Farmer against the Parentis and Barbara, and Alice and Sandy against Farmer.

Question 9

Chuck entered a highway without looking to see if it was safe and collided with an automobile owned by Ace Auto Rentals (Ace) and rented to and driven by Bruce. Bruce was not able to avoid the collision because he was driving recklessly fast. Unknown to Ace, Bruce had no driver's license.

Chuck's car caught fire as a result of the collision. Dave, a passenger who had met Chuck through an online ad and was sharing expenses and driving responsibilities with Chuck on a cross-country trip, escaped without injury. Chuck was trapped in the burning car. Peter, a bystander, tried to pull Chuck out of the car. Peter was severely burned. Chuck died of his burns.

What are Peter's rights, if any, against Ace, Dave, and Chuck's estate? Discuss.

Question 10

Abel and Baker were working on a scaffold lawfully erected over a public sidewalk. Contrary to an express rule of his employer, Abel was not wearing a hard hat.

Trying to park her automobile near one of the supports of the scaffold, Diana saw that she had maneuvered it into such a position that there was a risk she would knock down the scaffold if she were to back up without someone to guide her. She appealed for help to Sam, a stranger who was passing by. Sam refused to help. Angered, Diana proceeded to back her car up without assistance and knocked a support out from under the scaffold, causing Abel and Baker to fall.

Abel fractured his skull severely. If he had been wearing his hard hat, he would have suffered only a slight concussion with minimal disability.

Baker sustained a fracture of a vertebra, but he was able to walk away and felt only slight pain. The fracture could have been easily diagnosed by X-ray, and a doctor of average competence could have treated it successfully. Instead of visiting a physician, Baker worked the rest of the day. Driving his car home later that day, Baker stopped at an intersection for a light. Before the light turned, his car was struck from the rear by a car driven by Ed. The collision caused only slight damage to Baker's car, but it was sufficiently severe to aggravate the fracture in Baker's back, paralyzing Baker.

Diana and Sam settled Baker's claim against them and received general releases from him. Abel sued Diana and Sam. Baker sued Ed. Assume that Diana, Sam, and Ed raise all appropriate defenses.

What rights, if any, does Abel have against Diana and Sam? Discuss.

What rights, if any, does Baker have against Ed? Discuss.

Question 11

Dan, the operator of a large moving van, was approaching an intersection on a four-lane street at noon when his engine died and the vehicle came to a complete halt. Dan had nothing to do with the failure of the engine. Unable to move the vehicle, he left it standing unattended in the road while he went to secure help. The van was stalled just immediately before the intersection (but not within it) in the fast lane of the two lanes on his side of the road. There was ample room for cars in the right lane to pass the van.

After Dan left to find help, Vick approached the intersection in a car and came to a halt in the right lane parallel to the van. As Vick approached the intersection, the van obscured his vision to the left, but he decided to proceed into the intersection anyway. As he did so, he struck a motorcycle approaching from the left on the intersecting street. The cyclist, Peter, saw Vick's car emerging from behind the van. He could have brought his cycle to a halt in time to avoid being struck were it not for the fact that his brakes were bad. By the time Vick saw Peter it was too late to stop. It is conceded that both Vick and Peter would have seen each other in abundant time to avoid the accident if Dan's van had not obstructed their views.

Discuss Peter's rights against Dan and Vick (1) assuming a Motor Vehicle Code provision makes it unlawful to leave a vehicle unattended on a public road and (2) assuming there is no such statutory provision.

Question 12

Acme Construction Co. had contracted to add two lanes to a heavily used highway in a rural area. To establish the proper grade, Acme had to engage in blasting, because there was a lot of solid rock at or close to the surface.

Acme placed signs at the side of the road, at the approaches to the blasting area, warning motorists as follows: "Blasting in progress. Stop all radio transmission." Baker, a motorist using his two-way radio, failed to observe the sign; a premature detonation resulted, caused by the transmission from his radio. In the ensuing explosion Baker was injured when a boulder hit his car. Baker's radio was rendered inoperative.

Charles, a motorist who stopped at the scene of the accident and then hurried off to summon medical assistance, was killed when his car swerved from the road and hit a tree. Charles was not wearing his seat belt at the time. The car was so mangled that it was impossible to tell whether Charles would have been killed even if he had been wearing his seat belt. It was also impossible to tell whether Charles would have escaped fatal secondary impact after his car hit the tree if he had been wearing his seat belt.

Discuss the rights of Baker and the rights of those with standing to sue for Charles's death under the pertinent wrongful death statute.

Question 13

ABC Department Store retained Joe to paint the front of its building. When Joe arrived, he asked for a ladder so that he could inspect the facade to determine if any sandblasting was necessary. Malcolm, the store manager, gave Joe a ladder which ABC had purchased from Bigstore a little more than four years before. At the time of the purchase, the ladder was delivered in a box that had the following statement in large block letters:

CAUTION: THE NORMAL OPERATIONAL LIFE OF A SPELDING LADDER IS THREE YEARS.

The ladder was manufactured by the Spelding Company, which had found that the hinges frequently wore out after three years. Malcolm never saw this warning. The previous manager (who was retired) had taken the ladder out of the box and discarded the box. Sure enough, while Joe was making his inspection, one of the legs of the ladder collapsed. Joe fell and landed on Mr. Jones, a passerby. Joe broke his own collarbone and Mr. Jones suffered a broken shoulder and right arm. Mrs. Jones (who was walking beside Mr. Jones when this occurred) began running up and down the sidewalk screaming, "Get a doctor! Get a doctor!" In her frenzy, she slipped and broke her left ankle.

Discuss the possible tort claims of Mr. Jones, Mrs. Jones, and Joe.

Question 14

Mary White, owner of White's Diner, watched a television advertisement about the "new and improved" Cookwell Electronic Oven. The announcer stated that the Cookwell "could be used with your own cookware and is the best and safest electronic oven on the market."

To test its economic desirability and efficiency, White leased the Cookwell from Black's Appliances. Black negligently omitted a manual from the manufacturer which contained on the cover page the following warning:

WARNING! DO NOT USE METAL DISHES OR METAL COOKWARE.

No such warning appeared on the oven itself.

Mary White used a tin plate to cook some food in the Cookwell during a busy lunch hour. The microwaves bounced off the tin dish. This caused a hole to burn through the oven's outer surface. This enabled electronic impulses to escape. Both Mary and one of her patrons, John Green, who was eating near the oven, suffered blindness. In addition, White's Diner had to be shut down until a new oven could be installed.

What are the rights of White and Green? Discuss.

Question 15

Nerv was an extremely nervous person. He discussed his problems with his friend Phil, a licensed pharmacist who owned and operated a drug store. Phil recommended "Dreamy," a new tranquilizer manufactured by Drugco. Dreamy did not require a prescription. Dreamy had been extensively tested by Drugco. Four months previously, it had been approved for sale without prescription by the Food and Drug Administration (FDA). Nerv purchased a bottle of Dreamy and began taking it in accordance with the instructions. The label on the bottle stated, "Normal dosage: two pills every 12 hours—safe for adult use—not habit forming."

The day after the purchase, Nerv took two Dreamy pills upon arising, had breakfast, and then got in his car and headed for the golf course. While driving on a public street, Nerv suddenly became dizzy and lost control of his car. The car swerved onto the sidewalk, hit Jane, seriously injuring her, and then ran into a pole, seriously injuring Nerv.

Subsequent analysis revealed that Nerv's dizziness was caused by an allergic reaction to Dreamy, but that only 5 people out of 10,000 would have such a reaction. None of this had been discovered during the extensive pre-marketing tests, which led to approval by the FDA. It was also learned that during the four months since Dreamy was first marketed, two other persons had had reactions similar to Nerv's, and that Drugco had conducted further tests and had ordered new labels, which would contain the following legend: "CAUTION—Dizziness may result from normal dosage."

Discuss the rights of Jane against Nerv and Drugco.

Discuss the rights of Nerv against Phil and Drugco.

Question 16

Mag, Inc., publishes a magazine and operates a laboratory for testing the merchandise of its advertisers. Mag authorizes the use of a symbol that says "Mag Seal of Approval" when Mag's tests indicate the product is safe and wholesome.

Mag examined samples of Tint, a hair coloring produced by Tintco, Inc. Mag's tests indicated that Tint was effective and satisfactory. Mag authorized Tintco to use Mag's Seal of Approval in advertising Tint and on Tintco's labels placed on containers of Tint. Neither Tintco nor Mag was aware that when Tint is brought into direct contact with Balm, an infrequently used prescription scalp medicine, Tint causes hair to turn purple.

Gloria, a contestant in a beauty contest, used Tint on her hair while it was still wet with Balm. As a result, Gloria's hair turned purple and she had to withdraw from the contest. She had been regarded as the favorite. To Gloria's embarrassment, the purple discoloration persisted until her hair grew out.

Discuss Gloria's rights against Tintco and Mag.

Question 17

While in a variety store owned by Black, Alan, a high school student, noticed a sign on the wall reading "FREE—PLEASE TAKE ONE." Directly below the sign was a display of LED flashlights. He put one of the flashlights in his pocket and walked out of the store. Black rushed out of the store after Alan shouting, "Come back here with that flashlight, you thief!" The street was crowded, and Alan, confused and humiliated by the noisy accusation, eluded Black and ran home.

Later that day, Carl, a customer who resembled Alan, went into the restroom of Black's store. Thinking Carl was Alan, Black locked the restroom door and called the police. There was an open window in the restroom. Intending to climb through the window, Carl mounted the one chair in the room. Carl should have realized that the window was out of reach, but he tried anyway. As he put his weight on the back of the chair, the chair tipped over. Carl fell to the floor and broke his leg.

Several days later, Alan learned that the "FREE—PLEASE TAKE ONE" sign referred to advertising bulletins which were usually beneath the sign and not to the flashlights. He immediately offered to return the flashlight, but Black refused to accept it.

Discuss the rights of Alan and Black against each other and the rights of Carl against Black.

Question 18

Peter carelessly left his wallet containing $100 lying on the cashier's counter in Jim's restaurant and walked away. Jim saw the wallet but neglected to call it to Peter's attention. Immediately thereafter, David, another restaurant patron, paid his bill and picked up Peter's wallet by mistake, thinking it was his own.

As David was leaving the restaurant, Peter saw the wallet in David's hand and recognized it as his own. Before Peter could call out, David boarded a bus owned by Busco. Peter followed and managed to board the bus just as it started to move. He skinned his knee in so doing. He yelled, "Stop, thief!" and worked his way around other passengers to where David stood.

Peter's loud accusation angered David, who now noted he was carrying someone else's wallet. David retorted, "Don't you call me a thief! Take your wallet and get out of here." He hurled the wallet at Peter. It struck Peter's face, glanced off and flew out the bus window. When the bus stopped for traffic, Peter jumped out and ran back. He was unable to find his wallet.

Discuss Peter's rights against Jim, David, and Busco.

Discuss whether David has any rights against Peter.

Question 19

Twenty years ago, Resco erected a building in what was then an unsettled area. Resco conducts experimental work in connection with cattle virus disease. The area surrounding the Resco property has now become a thriving cattle and dairy district.

Cattle ranchers in the area tried to induce Zoe, a cattle auctioneer, to establish a local market. Zoe was reluctant to do so because of his fear that the virus might escape from Resco's property and infect cattle.

Some of the ranchers called on Prex, the president of Resco. They told Prex of their desire to establish a market in the area and asked him to make a statement which would dispel Zoe's fears.

Prex called a conference and, without having made any investigation and without naming Zoe, stated that there was "no danger at all" of any virus escaping from the Resco premises and that only an "idiot" could conclude otherwise. This statement was printed in *News*, a local newspaper, and received wide attention. As a result, Zoe was frequently referred to in the community as an "idiot." This caused him considerable embarrassment.

Persuaded that Prex's statement concerning the safety of the Resco operation was correct and wanting to escape further embarrassment, Zoe established a market in the area for the auction of cattle. Shortly thereafter, without any negligence on the part of Resco, the virus escaped from Resco's premises and infected cattle in the area.

To stop the spread of the infection, public authorities ordered the slaughter of all infected or exposed cattle and Zoe had to abandon his market with great financial loss.

Discuss Zoe's rights against Resco, Prex, and *News*.

Question 20

Norm is a well-known author who gave a lecture at a private college. During the question period following the lecture, one of his answers about the leaders of the "Social Justice" movement was as follows: "One of the top leaders of Social Justice at this college is a high school dropout who was once arrested for peddling dope." In response to this diatribe, pandemonium broke loose in the lecture hall. Polly, the secretary of the relatively small and obscure Social Justice club at the college, rushed to the platform and would have struck Norm had she not been forcibly restrained.

The daily student newspaper, the *Spector*, reported the episode but inaccurately stated that Polly had hit Norm, that "blood gushed from his temple," and that Norm had said Polly had been convicted of peddling dope.

This information was obtained by the newspaper from several persons who attended the lecture. Polly read the article and claims that she has not been able to sleep as a result, that she has had to revisit a psychiatrist who had discharged her before the episode as cured from a nervous ailment, that she was unable to take her examinations at the end of her senior year, and that her graduation has been delayed one year.

Discuss Polly's rights against Norm and the *Spector*.

Question 21

White, a Marine Corps officer, was convicted of murder 25 years ago in a highly publicized trial. The only evidence against him at the trial was the testimony of two former Marines that Vietnamese prisoners of war had been killed while in the custody of troops commanded by White during a battle. Eight years later, one of these witnesses confessed that he and the second witness had lied at the trial of White to avoid punishment for their own misconduct. When investigation confirmed the truth of the confession, White received a pardon, was released from prison, and entered a religious order where he lived in seclusion under vows of silence and poverty.

Early this year, White developed a serious illness. He reluctantly left the order and entered a hospital for treatment.

News, a daily newspaper in the city in which the hospital is located, has prepared a feature article that fully and truthfully recounts the trial, the imprisonment, and the events leading to the pardon of White. The author and editors have relied solely on information available in public records. *News* has notified White that it intends to publish the article. White objects to the prospect of unwelcome publicity. White and *News* have been warned by White's doctors that the emotional stress White may suffer if the story is published will impede his recovery.

If the story is published, on what theory or theories can White base an action for damages against *News*? Discuss.

If White seeks an injunction to prohibit publication of the proposed story, what defenses should *News* offer, and how should the court rule on them? Discuss.

Question 22

Upon their retirement, Bill and Jane Mason purchased a mobile home from Dealer for $95,000. They made a down payment of $20,000 and financed the balance of the purchase price with Finance Company. The Masons moved their mobile home into a space rented from Dream Park, to which they paid monthly rental.

Several months later, at the request of Finance Company, the trailer was removed from Dream Park by Repo Co., an entity specializing in repossessions. Bill protested the removal. As the trailer was being pulled away, Bill suffered a broken leg when he refused to step down and fell from the step of the trailer. He has since been hospitalized. Bill advised the Repo Co. employees that they were making a mistake, but they curtly responded, "That's what they all say, buddy."

Because of the mental distress she suffered when she learned about all this two hours later, Jane has been hospitalized and is under the care of a physician.

Repo Co. had repossessed the Masons' trailer by mistake, believing it was the property of Stranger. Stranger had defaulted on a debt to Finance that was secured by a mortgage on a trailer that was similar to the Masons' trailer. The Masons were in fact current on their payments to Finance Company.

The fair rental value of the Masons' trailer is $3,000 a month. A small section of the trailer was dented while it was in Finance's possession. It would cost $1,500 to repair the dent, but the damage is neither serious nor noticeable. The Masons' clothes and other personal possessions are missing from the trailer. The Masons replaced their personal property at a cost of $5,000.

Discuss the rights of Bill and Jane against Finance Company.

Question 23

Disco, a discount retailer, opened a new store. To publicize the event, Disco placed the following advertisement in local newspapers:

> Announcing the Grand Opening of Disco's New Store—January 10—Bargains Galore—Win the Door Prize—A Week in Paris for Two—Drawing Time 4 P.M.—You Must Be Present to Win.

Ellen, age 15, read the advertisement and came to the opening. When she entered the store she received a numbered slip of paper. She was directed to write her name on the paper and to deposit it in a box inside the store. She complied with those directions. At 4 P.M. she was announced the winner of the door prize and was asked to come to a platform at the front of the store. Ellen did so. She was introduced as "Ellen, lucky winner of Disco's door prize."

Disco had arranged with a local newspaper to send a reporter and a photographer to report the event. They took Ellen's photograph and published it with a story announcing that Ellen had won a trip to Paris for two.

During the next few days, many of Ellen's schoolmates told her they had seen the photo and asked when she was leaving for Paris and who was going with her.

A week after the drawing, Ellen returned for the tickets and expense money. Mana, Disco's owner, explained that Disco had never intended to give the winner anything and that the advertisement and drawing were merely promotional stunts. Ellen felt humiliated when, in response to her schoolmates' continuing inquiries, she had to explain that she would receive nothing as a door prize.

Discuss Ellen's rights against Disco.

Question 24

One day, Ben, beneficiary of a trust administered by Bank, went to Bank and said to the bank manager in a loud voice: "Although I do not believe it to be true, I have heard that one of the people in the trust department has used trust funds to take trips to Hawaii." About 14 customers overheard Ben's remarks.

Four employees work in the trust department, including Arthur. None of the trust department employees had ever been to Hawaii or misused trust funds. Arthur became extremely upset at Ben's remark.

While Ben was talking to the bank manager, his friend Ed, who had accompanied him to the bank, spoke with Jane, a secretary in the trust department, about how to prepare a will.

Jane told him that it was easy: Just type it, sign it, and have it notarized. Jane had obtained these instructions from an attorney, Larry, several weeks before at a cocktail party. Ed died three weeks after making his will in accordance with these instructions, leaving all of his property to his brother, Bill. However, his will was held to be invalid because it was not properly witnessed and his property passed instead to his children.

Discuss the tort liability of Ben, Bank, Jane, and Larry.

Question 25

Able is in the real estate investment business. He is trying to have the zoning ordinance of City amended to permit his company to erect an apartment building. Opposition to the amendment is headed by Mrs. Bird, a well-known socialite, and by Cross, the owner of several small apartment houses and office buildings.

Able hired detectives to follow Mrs. Bird. In accordance with Able's instructions, they followed Mrs. Bird on public streets, tape-recorded her statements whenever she appeared in public to discuss the amendment, and looked with binoculars from adjacent premises into the windows of her home. These activities ceased after one month, but in the meantime, they had embarrassed and humiliated Mrs. Bird so that she requires psychotherapy.

Cross was interviewed on television station XYTV concerning the proposed zoning amendment. During the live interview, Cross stated: "I can't believe the City Council will approve Able's idiotic and stupid proposal. The guy had to be flying on something to propose that one." Able was greatly disturbed by the broadcast but is unable to establish any actual monetary loss as a result of it.

Following the broadcast, Able advised various suppliers with whom he did business that he would not do business with anyone who had anything to do with Cross. Some of these suppliers, who were tenants at will of Cross, terminated their tenancies. Others, whose leases will expire shortly, have notified Cross that they will vacate at the end of their respective terms.

Discuss Mrs. Bird's rights against Able, Able's rights against Cross and XYTV, and Cross's rights against Able.

Question 26

In 2008, when he was 19 years old, Yorick Young bought a counterfeit driver's license from Fred Forger. A few months later, Young went to a bar with some friends to drink alcoholic beverages and to socialize. He gained admission to the bar by using the counterfeit license (it showed a date of birth that would have made Young more than 21 years old). The legal drinking age in Young's state is 21. While Young was in the bar, a fire broke out and Young was injured. The fire started because the manager of the bar placed some candles too close to some posters and other paper decorations.

The following statute has been in effect since 2005:

> False Identification Documents—Prohibitions
>
> (1) As used in this section, the term "identification document" means any document or card issued to an individual by a government agency containing the name of a person and a description of the person, and includes, without being limited to, a driver's license or an identification card.
>
> (2) It is unlawful to knowingly manufacture, sell, or distribute a false or fraudulent identification document.

Young seeks damages for his injuries from Forger claiming that Forger acted negligently in providing the counterfeit license.

Discuss what effect (if any) the statute should have in Young's effort to establish negligent conduct by Forger. Also, assuming that Forger's conduct could be found negligent, discuss the causation aspects of Young's claim.

Question 27

Pat Parker pays a monthly fee for access to a small parking lot. The lot has spaces for ten cars. To enter the lot, a driver inserts a card into a card-reading device near a gate. The system opens the gate and records the time that a particular card was used. Anyone entitled to use the lot may park in any available space.

On April 3, 2009, Parker drove into the lot and parked early in the morning. Late in the evening that day, Parker went to the lot. Parker's car was the only car in the lot. It had been badly damaged, apparently as a result of another car having been driven into it. The gate to the lot was working properly and had not been damaged.

Parker can prove that between the time she parked the car in the lot and the time she discovered it had been hit, seven other individuals used their cards to open the gate. Six of those individuals each obtained access once. One of those individuals, named Oscar Often, obtained access seven times on April 3. That means that he drove in seven times and also drove out seven times, since his car was not present at the end of the day.

Parker is considering suing Often for the damage to her car. Discuss the applicability (if any) of each of the *res ipsa loquitur* and market share liability doctrines to Parker's potential case.

Question 28

Bruce Baker, a 13-year-old student at a private school, was experienced in gymnastics. He was also interested in performing in and helping to produce plays. For a play that was to be performed in the school's gym, he devised and constructed a pulley mechanism to allow an actor to appear to fly above the other actors. He made the apparatus from a climbing harness, fabric webbing, a pulley, and a cable hung from the gym's ceiling. During the first rehearsal, Baker climbed a tall ladder that another student was holding and connected himself to the webbing through a loop on the harness. He shouted that everyone should watch him and be sure not to stand under him. He then jumped from the ladder and hovered above the gym floor for a few minutes. Unfortunately, the apparatus then failed and Baker fell to the floor. He suffered serious injuries. As he fell, he knocked over another student, Chris Carter. Carter also suffered serious injuries. Carter was not an actor or other participant in the play. He was walking through the gym to get to a locker room in order to get ready for soccer practice.

Carter has sued Baker on a negligence claim. The jurisdiction in which the case will be tried has adopted the pure form of comparative negligence.

Baker has requested a jury instruction that applies the child's standard of care to his conduct. Carter has argued that the child's standard should not be used because of the nature of Baker's activity. Carter has argued also that the child's standard of care should not be used because the jurisdiction's adoption of comparative negligence has made it obsolete. Discuss Carter's two arguments.

Assuming that a jury could conclude that Baker had been negligent, discuss the causation issues in Carter's claim.

Question 29

At a private swimming and tennis club, Thelma Thirsty was standing near a soft drink vending machine near the swimming pool, waiting to buy a can of Coca-Cola. George Grabber was in front of Thirsty, putting money into the machine and then pushing a button to select a drink. For some reason, Grabber suddenly grabbed the machine with both hands and attempted to shake it. He was standing barefoot in a puddle of water. When he grabbed the machine, Grabber received a severe electric shock. His muscles convulsed and his body jerked with great force against Thirsty. Thirsty was thrown down and her head hit the ground with great force. She was injured.

The machine was made by Vending Company. It was equipped with a thick electrical cord, meant to be plugged into an electrical outlet. The cord extended 15 feet from the back of the machine, so the machine could be plugged into an outlet right behind it or could be plugged into an outlet some small distance away. At the time Thirsty was injured, the cord on the machine was partially underneath the machine. Its insulation had become worn away through contact with the metal base of the machine, apparently because the machine was occasionally moved and its bottom metal surface had scraped the cord.

Grabber received his shock because the damaged cord and the metal frame of the machine touched each other. The accident would *not* have happened if Grabber had touched the machine with only one hand, if the cord had been shorter or thicker, if the bottom of the machine had been shaped differently, if the machine had not been moved so much, or if someone had inspected the cord under the machine and discovered the worn insulation. A thicker cord would have added some cost to the machine and might not have been flexible enough to allow ideal positioning of the machine in cramped locations. If the bottom of the machine had been shaped differently, the machine might have been less stable and the risk that it might fall on a person would have been greater.

Thirsty has sued Vending Company for damages on a strict liability design defect theory. Discuss the significant issues in the case.

Question 30

Last month, Alan Able clipped a "free visit" coupon from a newspaper advertisement that entitled him to a free visit at a health club and fitness center called Kinetic Fitness Center (KFC). He went to KFC, presented the coupon, and asked if he had to pay a fee. The person at the desk told Able that there was no fee, but that he would have to sign a "sign-in" list so that Kinetic Fitness Center could keep track of who used its coupons. The "sign-in" list had a printed paragraph at the top and lines for about 20 signatures below that paragraph. Able asked whether KFC had any treadmills, and then signed on one of the lines.

Able changed into exercise clothes in a locker room, and then went to an area of the facility where there were a large number of exercise machines. A short while later, Able was found dead on the floor against a wall near a treadmill. The cause of death was a head injury. Able had suffered from concussions in the past, and was more susceptible to head injuries than typical individuals. Able knew about this weakness. Able also knew that he sometimes became dizzy when he exercised.

The back of the treadmill was positioned only about three feet from the wall where Able was found. Most exercise facilities place treadmills further away from walls because a person who uses a treadmill may be propelled backward off the treadmill if he or she slips or loses balance. A person who is propelled off a treadmill may hit something like a wall or another machine if a wall or another machine is too close to the back of the treadmill.

KFC chose the location of its treadmill in part because its entire facility was fairly small. KFC paid less rent for its small facility than it would have paid for a larger place. The savings on rent increased KFC's profits and also allowed KFC to charge customers fees that were lower than typical fees charged by KFC's competitors.

No witness can be found who saw what happened to Able. The following descriptions are among the possible explanations for how Able suffered his fatal injury. Able might have (1) slipped or become dizzy while using the treadmill and been propelled backward off the treadmill and into the wall, or (2) fallen while walking among the exercise machines and hit his head on the floor, or (3) been pushed into a wall or machine by another person. The treadmill Able was near was not in motion when Able was found, but it is equipped with a timer that turns the machine off after the period of time selected by the user has expired.

The entire text of the sign-in list's printed paragraph reads:

MEMBER SIGN-IN. I understand that Kinetic Fitness Center ("KFC") reserves the right to revoke my membership for failure to respect KFC's rules and policies. I UNDERSTAND THAT I AM NOT ENTITLED TO A REFUND FOR MEMBERSHIP FEES OR DAILY VISIT FEES FOR ANY REASON. I understand that KFC endeavors to provide adequate numbers of exercise machines for the number of members expected to be present, but that KFC does not guarantee availability of any specific machine at any time. I agree that KFC will have no responsibility for any injury I may suffer as a result of any negligence by KFC. I agree that offers by KFC to provide discounts on future fees in exchange for referring new members to KFC are administered in KFC's sole discretion. DISPUTES ABOUT ENTITLEMENT TO MONETARY BENEFITS IN CONNECTION WITH MEMBERSHIP REFERRALS ARE SUBJECT TO RESOLUTION ENTIRELY BY KFC AND ANY DECISIONS BY KFC WITH REGARD TO SUCH DISPUTES WILL BE FINAL. Weight loss and improvements in physical fitness cannot be guaranteed. The primary determinant of success in an exercise program is the participant's consistent dedication to the program.

Discuss the significant issues in a suit by Able's estate against KFC seeking damages for Able's death on the theory that KFC was negligent to place its treadmill so close to a wall and that this negligence caused Able's death.

Essay Answers

Answer to Question 1

A v. B (Assault and Battery):

A can sue B for assault and battery. An assault occurs when one person intentionally causes another person to be in apprehension of a harmful or offensive contact. A battery occurs when one person intentionally inflicts harmful or offensive bodily contact on another. Here, the assault upon A arguably occurred when B threatened to hit A, and the battery when B actually struck A. B would assert two defenses: (1) **consent** (arguing that A "squared off" against him), and (2) **self-defense** (if A threw the first punch). When a person reasonably believes that someone is about to cause an imminent, offensive contact upon him, he can exercise whatever force is reasonably necessary under the circumstances to prevent the contact. In most jurisdictions, an individual cannot validly consent to a criminal act, especially if it involves a breach of the peace. These jurisdictions permit two people who fight against each other to recover from one another. In such a jurisdiction, B's consent defense would fail. Whether B will prevail on the self-defense claim would depend on whether A was the initial aggressor. The facts are not clear as to who threw the first punch. It seems more likely that B was the initial aggressor because A merely called B a wimp, while B's statement, "I'll show you who's a wimp; let's see what kind of a man you are," is considerably more aggressive and may well have been accompanied by a raised fist. If all A did initially was to insult B, B cannot claim self-defense, as words alone do not generally constitute an assault. If A was in fact the initial aggressor, B's self-defense claim will probably prevail. B was entitled to defend himself with his fists against A's fists.

Conclusion:

More facts are needed to identify the initial aggressor. If B was the initial aggressor, A can recover against B for nominal damages, compensatory damages (for mental suffering and physical injury), and possibly **punitive damages** (if B's conduct were found to be outrageous or malicious). If A was the initial aggressor, B can claim self-defense and avoid liability. The defense of consent would be available to B only in those jurisdictions which recognize that defense in a fight between two individuals.

B v. A (Assault and Battery):

The discussion above under *A v. B* would be applicable here as well. Additionally, if A utilized more force than was necessary to protect himself against B (the facts indicated that A was "winning"), the **self-defense** privilege would **not** be available to him, even if B was the initial aggressor.

We don't know whether A used excessive force. The fact that A was "winning" does not necessarily mean that A's use of force was excessive.

A v. C (Assault):

A will bring an action for assault against C based on C's knife attack upon him. The elements of an assault are present: C intentionally caused A to be apprehensive of a harmful and offensive contact when he thrust the knife at A. We can't tell from the facts whether A also has a claim against C for battery (did the knife touch or cut A?). C's possible defenses are (1) that he was acting in defense of B, and (2) that he was effecting a citizen's arrest. Under the ***defense-of-others privilege,*** a person may use reasonable force to protect another person, even a complete stranger, against attack. However, as in self-defense, the force used must be reasonable; deadly force may not be used to defend against a nondeadly attack. Here, A was using his fists against B. The use of fists does not ordinarily rise to the level of deadly force. On the other hand, C's knife clearly constituted a deadly force. Thus, C would probably lose the defense-of-others privilege and would be liable to A. Furthermore, if B was the initial aggressor and A did not consent to fight B, C would lose the defense-of-others privilege because most courts would hold that C had stepped into B's shoes. If B was not entitled to use force in self-defense, C would not be entitled to use force on B's behalf.

C is unlikely to succeed in asserting the ***citizen's arrest*** defense. Although a citizen is ordinarily privileged to use force to effect a warrantless arrest when a crime has been committed in his presence, the force employed may not be deadly force unless the person making the arrest is threatened with serious bodily harm or injury. The facts do not seem to support C's right to arrest A. On the facts, B was more likely the instigator of the fight. Also, it's reasonably clear that C's intent was not to arrest A but to come to the aid of his brother.

Conclusion:

C will lose his defense-of-others privilege if B was the initial aggressor. If A was the initial aggressor but his use of force was nondeadly, or if both A and B consented to fight, C will also be unable to assert the defense-of-others privilege. C will probably not prevail on his citizen's arrest claim because he used deadly force and he did not manifest any intent to arrest A. If C loses on his claims of privilege, he will be liable to A for nominal damages, compensatory damages (for mental suffering), and possibly for punitive damages.

B v. D (Assault):

B may be able to assert an action for assault against D, (1) if he reasonably believed that D was aiming the pistol in his direction, and/or (2) if he reasonably believed that D would fire at him after having shot at C. D would assert the privileges of defense-of-others and citizen's arrest. D would prevail on the *defense-of-others claim* only if B was the initial aggressor and D's use of deadly force was not excessive. D would argue that his use of deadly force was not excessive because C was attacking A with a knife, an instrument capable of inflicting death. Whether D will succeed on the citizen's arrest defense will also depend on whether the use of a gun was justified under the circumstances. One could reasonably argue that D should not have fired the gun before warning B and asking him to drop the knife.

C v. D (Assault, Conversion):

C will assert an action against D for two separate instances of assault: (1) the gunshot directed at him during the fight between A and B, and (2) letting Homer loose. On the first assault—the firing of the gun—C will have to show that he was apprehensive that the bullet fired from the gun would strike him. Nothing in the facts shows that C was aware that D had come on the scene or that he had a gun. However, if C was aware of the shooting and therefore could assert an assault claim, D will defend by asserting the privileges of defense-of-others and citizen's arrest (discussed above).

On the other hand, D is responsible for the harm caused by an instrumentality he intentionally releases or sets in motion. The owner of a domestic animal is strictly liable for injuries caused by the animal if the owner knows or has reason to know of the animal's dangerous characteristics. The facts don't show whether D knew that Homer had exhibited any dangerous characteristics. C can also sue D for conversion (intentionally causing a substantial interference with the plaintiff's ownership interest in a chattel) because D took C's knife back to his home. Because the interference by D was probably sufficiently great to require D to pay for the value of the knife, D's actions constitute conversion and not trespass to chattels.

With respect to setting the dog loose, D would argue that he was privileged to use reasonable force to expel C from his land because C was trespassing. This defense is probably tenable because D had warned C to get off his land before he released the dog. He may lose in this defense, however, if C can convince a court that he was in hot pursuit of a chattel (the knife) wrongfully taken from him by D, and was thus privileged to enter D's land. Whether C will prevail on this point will depend on how much time elapsed between D's wrongful possession of the knife and C's attempt to reclaim it. C will also argue that use of a dog to defend one's property is excessive force and precludes assertion of the privilege to defend property. Given that dogs are very frequently used to guard property and in light of the fact that Homer didn't actually harm or even catch C, this argument is unlikely to prevail.

D's wrongful possession of C's knife is probably a conversion, **not a trespass to chattels**, because (1) he has exercised total control over it by taking it and removing it to his own home (indicating that he had no intention to return it), and (2) he acted in bad faith by knowingly taking C's property. D would thus be liable to C for the full value of the knife. D may try to assert the **defense of necessity**—i.e., that he took the knife to prevent C from committing harm either to the community at large (**the defense of public necessity**), or to himself or to A in retaliation for the fight (**the defense of private necessity**). His claim of public necessity will probably not prevail. In cases of public necessity, such as in a fire, the danger to the community must be severe and must threaten a substantial number of people. He may prevail on the private necessity defense, where the threatened danger can be less severe. In that case, he would either have to compensate C for the value of the knife or return the knife and compensate C for the temporary loss of its use.

Conclusion:

C will probably lose on the assault claim based on the shooting. C will probably also lose on the assault claim based on the actions of the dog. We need more facts to determine whether C was justified in going onto D's property to reclaim his knife. In the absence of these facts, we conclude that D was justified in asserting the privilege of defense of property. C will probably prevail on the conversion claim and recover the full value of the knife. If D convinces a court that he acted out of necessity, he will have to compensate C for C's actual loss.

D v. C (Trespass):

As discussed above, D can probably sue C for trespass (intentionally encroaching upon the land of another). However, D will probably recover only **nominal damages** for this tort, since C caused no damage to D's property.

E v. D (Assault and Battery):

E will sue D for battery and possibly assault. Although D was aiming at C instead of E, the transferred intent doctrine would treat D as having intended to harm E. In intentional torts generally, the doctrine of transferred intent provides that so long as the defendant has the necessary intent with respect to one person, he will be held to have committed an intentional tort with respect to any person who happens to be injured by his action. The assault claim may fail, however, because the facts indicate that E had "just" stepped out of the store. Presumably, he did not have an opportunity to be in apprehension of the contact prior to the moment when it occurred.

D would assert the privileges of defense-of-others and citizen's arrest, as discussed above.

E v. A or C or B (Assault and Battery):

It is possible to find on various interpretations of the facts that A, C, and B are all tortfeasors. An intentional tortfeasor is liable for all of the consequences of his actions, whether foreseeable or not. The question, therefore, is whether one or all of these three—A, B, or C—was an intentional tortfeasor on these facts. If A is deemed the original aggressor or if he consented to the fight, he is an intentional tortfeasor and will be liable to E. If B was the original aggressor or if he consented to the fight, he is an intentional tortfeasor and will be liable to E. If C was not privileged to attack A in the defense of B or in the execution of a citizen's arrest, then C is an intentional tortfeasor and would be liable to E.

Answer to Question 2

Estate of Art (EST) v. Driver (D):

All the states now have survival statutes enabling the estate of a decedent to recover from a tortfeasor for the consequences of the tort to the decedent. In many states in which survival actions are authorized, wrongful death actions may also be brought by the spouse or children of the deceased. Where both actions are authorized, the estate's survival claims are limited to recovery for pain and suffering, lost earnings, and medical expenses. If the death is instantaneous, these claims cannot usually be sustained. Assuming in this case that both a survival statute and a wrongful death statute exist, because A's death was instantaneous, EST will defer to an action for wrongful death by A's spouse.

Sue Archer (SA) v. D for injury to A (Battery, Negligence)

Battery: SA will base her wrongful death action against D on the tort of battery (intentional infliction of an offensive touching upon A). She will argue that D committed this tort when he intentionally equipped his vehicle to cause an electric shock to any person opening its doors. Although D almost certainly did not intend to injure anyone (the facts tell us that a healthy person would *not* ordinarily have been injured by the shock), injury is not an essential component of the tort of battery, which requires only an offensive touching.

D would assert the privilege of **defense of property**. Generally, an individual may defend his property in the same way and to the same degree as his person—he may ordinarily utilize the degree of force which he reasonably believes necessary under the circumstances to prevent another from taking or tampering with his property. However, force capable of causing death or serious injury is *not* permissible, except when the owner reasonably believes that the intruder will cause death or serious bodily harm if he is not stopped. Because this device was automatic, and operated in the absence of any probable bodily harm to D, its use was tortious. D will contend that the device he installed was reasonable for this purpose and that it did not constitute deadly force—i.e., a normal, healthy person would not have suffered any permanent injury. SA will contend in rebuttal that an electric shock is not reasonable force under any circumstances, and it is especially unreasonable when used only to prevent access to a car.

If SA prevailed on the battery issue, D would be liable to SA for A's death. It is well established that an intentional tortfeasor is responsible for all injuries his victim suffers, whether foreseeable or not.

Negligence: SA will also assert a wrongful death action against D based on his negligence. The tort of negligence occurs when one person's conduct imposes an unreasonable risk of harm on another person who is injured as a result. SA would argue that in designing his antitheft device, D acted unreasonably by planning and installing a mechanism capable of administering an electric shock. In determining whether D's conduct was reasonable under the circumstances, the court will consider whether similar shock devices are legal. The court will also consider custom and practice as evidence of reasonableness; i.e., is it common for shock devices to be included in antitheft systems? It might conclude that shock devices on a car door are inherently unreasonable because the consequences of using them cannot be foreseen: a passerby might attempt to do a good deed by turning off the headlights; a child might be attracted to the car and try to open the door.

SA will have to show that D's negligence was the ***proximate cause*** of A's injury. SA would argue that the injury to A was reasonably foreseeable as an inevitable result of D's negligence (i.e., it was reasonably foreseeable that someone would try to enter D's car). After all, the device was installed by D exactly because D foresaw that people would try to enter his car. D will contend that A's conduct was a superseding cause—i.e., an intervening cause canceling D's liability. D will probably lose on this point, since both the intervening cause and the kind of harm that resulted were foreseeable. If D is found to have been negligent and the basic injury (i.e., the shock) to A foreseeable, D will be liable for A's death. The unusual magnitude of A's injury (death due to a heart condition) will not preclude liability. A negligent defendant takes his victim as he finds him.

SA will have to prove actual damages as a result of D's negligence. Here, the actual damages are those resulting from A's death. Under most wrongful death statutes, SA could sue for lost economic support, and for some emotional consequences of the death.

SA v. D for injuries to SA (Battery, Negligence):

Apparently, SA was ***not*** injured when she was knocked to the ground by her husband's fall. She will rely on her right to recover for negligent infliction of emotional distress.

If SA is successful in her contention that D committed a battery against A, D will be liable to SA for her injuries as well since, as discussed above, an intentional tortfeasor is responsible for virtually all consequences that flow from his tort, whether foreseeable or not.

SA will also contend that D was negligent as to her. She will allege that D acted unreasonably in installing the shock device on his car and in leaving his door unlocked.

D will contend in rebuttal that (1) SA was not a foreseeable plaintiff (i.e., he could not reasonably foresee the harm to anyone except a person attempting to open the car door), and (2) his actions were *not the proximate cause* of SA's harm (A's intentionally tortious conduct in committing a trespass to D's chattel was an unforeseeable intervening cause). However, SA will respond that she was a foreseeable plaintiff—i.e., she was among the class of persons who might be harmed by D's negligence (a person stunned by an electric shock is likely to stumble backward into anyone, including a passerby; the electric shock received by a person attempting to open the car door might pass through that person to someone standing nearby; or someone who witnessed a family member's death as a result of D's conduct might be severely traumatized). SA should prevail on these issues.

There are three views as to when someone who suffers emotional distress can recover from a negligent tortfeasor.

The traditional view was that an impact must be made upon her person for the plaintiff to sue for *mental distress*. The defendant's conduct did, indirectly, cause an impact on SA. That might be enough to satisfy the impact rule, although almost no states apply that doctrine at present.

Most courts permit a plaintiff to recover for emotional distress if she was in the zone of danger created by the defendant's negligent conduct. The facts here are silent as to how far SA stood from A at the time of the incident. Unless she was touching him or standing within a foot or two of him, it is unlikely that SA will be deemed to have been in the zone of danger.

Finally, some jurisdictions permit a "bystander" such as SA to recover *damages for emotional distress* after weighing the following factors: (1) the relationship of the plaintiff to the victim, (2) whether the plaintiff observed the incident which resulted in injury to the victim, and (3) the extent to which some physical harm to the plaintiff is manifested. Because (1) SA was A's wife, (2) she personally observed the incident, and (3) her mental distress was manifested in physical symptoms (vomiting, nausea, etc.), all of the elements necessary to satisfy this view appear to be met.

D's defenses: D would argue in response to the battery claim that A's actions in ignoring the sign on the front window warning of a protective device and instructing everyone not to touch the car constituted *consent* to the harm which occurred. SA would argue in rebuttal, however, that the sign was not adequate because (1) it was placed only in the front windshield, rather than on the side (where someone attempting to enter the vehicle would be more likely to see it), and (2) the sign did not warn a trespasser that the protective device was something so potentially jarring and injurious as an electric shock. Baker (B) will probably testify that neither he nor A saw the sign and that A did not consent to the harm. SA should succeed on this issue.

D will argue in response to the negligence claim that A assumed the risk of harm based on these same facts. Here, SA will prevail because A clearly did not expressly assume the risk, and a court will not find implied *assumption of risk* unless the defendant can show that the injured party (here, A) (1) actually knew of the risk in question, and (2) voluntarily consented to bear the risk. Again, B will testify that A did not see the sign and did not knowingly consent. D has the burden of showing that A assumed the risk.

D may also try to defend against the negligence claim on the grounds that A was negligent in entering D's car. In most jurisdictions, A's conduct will be evaluated as part of a comparative negligence inquiry, and might reduce or bar recovery depending on the form of comparative negligence the jurisdiction uses and the degree to which a jury assigns fault to A.

SA v. Baker (B) (Negligence):

SA might contend that B failed to act reasonably in persuading A to attempt to enter D's car and that he should be liable to SA because A died as a consequence of B's suggestions. However, words alone do not ordinarily constitute unreasonable conduct when spoken to an adult who is presumably in full control of his faculties and actions.

Conclusion:

SA will probably win the wrongful death action based on battery. She will be able to recover nominal, compensatory, and possibly punitive *damages* for this intentional tort. If she loses on the battery claim, she may prevail on negligence grounds, but proximate cause issues make this less sure than the battery claim. If SA wins on negligence, she will get damages for loss of economic support, lost companionship, and possibly grief.

D will be liable to SA for her mental distress if the court is satisfied with her battery claim. Whether D will be liable for SA's mental distress on a negligence theory will depend on what rule the jurisdiction follows with respect to liability for mental distress.

Answer to Question 3

Jim v. Dan (Assault, Battery, and Negligence)
Assault and Battery:

Did Dan assault or commit a battery upon Jim? An assault occurs when the defendant intentionally causes the plaintiff to be reasonably apprehensive of an imminent, offensive touching. A battery is an intentional harmful or offensive touching. The intent required for both assault and battery is not intent to harm another; instead, it is intent to commit the acts of threatening or making offensive contact. Here, although Dan shot at Jim, Dan never intended to make Jim fearful of injury or of his life; he meant only to play a role in a movie scene with a fellow actor. Therefore, no assault was intended or occurred. Dan also did not intend to inflict harmful physical contact on Jim, because he believed he was only firing blanks. Thus, there was no battery.

Negligence:

Did Dan act reasonably under the circumstances? The tort of negligence occurs when one person's conduct imposes an unreasonable risk of harm on another person who is injured as a result. Here, Jim would need to argue that Dan acted unreasonably in not checking the gun prior to firing it. However, an actor would not ordinarily be expected to check the work of his prop man any more than he would be expected to edit the author's script. Dan should prevail on this issue.

In summary, Jim probably has no right of recovery against Dan.

Jim v. Fred (Assault and Battery):

If Jim saw Fred coming toward him to prevent him from throwing the bottle, Jim will be able to assert a claim of assault against Fred. A battery also occurred when Fred intentionally inflicted harmful and offensive physical contact on Jim by (1) knocking him to the ground and (2) punching him in the face.

Is the "defense-of-others" privilege available to Fred? An individual can ordinarily defend another person with the same degree of force as would reasonably have been available to that other person in his own defense. Although at common law this privilege was limited to the defense of one's family, courts today allow bystanders to use reasonable force to defend strangers against attack. Since Dan had the right to protect himself from Jim's bottle-throwing, Fred would argue that he had the right to subdue Jim in the same way as Dan might have done. Jim will contend in rebuttal that the force utilized by Fred was excessive (i.e., Fred didn't have to punch him in the face; he could have simply held Jim down), and therefore the privilege was nullified. Fred could respond that punching Jim was a reasonable way of assuring that he would be restrained. The facts are silent as to the relative size and strength of Jim and Fred. Assuming they were of approximately equal weight and strength, Fred would assert that he did **not** use excessive force because Jim was obviously violent and dangerous (only a violent person would throw a bottle toward what Fred perceived as the crowd at the bar). However, if the facts showed that Fred was substantially bigger and heavier than Jim, Fred's punch would probably constitute excessive force.

Jim could argue that Fred was mistaken in his assumption that Jim was the aggressor who needed to be subdued, because Jim was in fact defending himself against Dan. Jim would contend that this mistake destroyed Fred's **defense-of-others privilege.** Most courts would hold that Fred had stepped into Dan's shoes and that if Dan would not have been entitled to use force because he was the initial aggressor, Fred would also not enjoy that privilege. But Dan had no knowledge that he was firing real bullets, and if he believed that Jim was attacking him without provocation, he would have been privileged to defend himself against Jim. Therefore, mistake would not be the basis for depriving Fred of the privilege of defending Dan.

Is the "prevention-of-crime" privilege available to Fred? A private citizen can ordinarily use reasonable force to prevent the commission of a felony (a few states permit this only after the felony has been committed). Because throwing a bottle at another person with intent to injure him is probably a felony in most jurisdictions, our discussion with respect to the defense-of-others privilege would be equally apt on this issue as well.

Dan v. Jim (Assault):

Did Jim assault Dan? The facts tell us that Dan was alarmed when Jim raised the bottle to throw it at him. Jim clearly committed an assault on Dan. Because Jim's actions were not in the script, it was reasonable for Dan to fear that Jim meant to strike him. Jim had the intent necessary for assault because he meant to cause Dan to fear the imminent contact.

Dan will probably not be able to recover against Jim, however, because Jim can assert the **self-defense privilege.** Jim will be entitled to claim this privilege as long as (1) he reasonably believed that Dan was about to harm him and (2) the degree of force he used to defend himself was not excessive under the circumstances. It was reasonable for Jim to believe Dan was about to harm or even kill him, because Dan had just shot a bullet into Jim's hat and because the script called for Dan to fire another shot at Jim. Jim did not use excessive force because the room was too noisy for Dan to hear any warnings from Jim and he was too far from Dan to try to take the gun away from him. He was privileged to use the degree of force necessary to prevent the imminent harm. When the threatened harm is death, a person is privileged to use deadly force. A bottle thrown from a distance may constitute a potentially deadly force, but Jim was entitled to use it under the circumstances because there was no other way to prevent the second shot and he was facing the threat of death or serious injury.

In summary, Dan probably has no right of recovery against Jim.

Peter v. Fred (Trespass and Negligence):

Did Fred commit a trespass? A trespass occurs where one intrudes upon the land of another, even if the trespasser mistakenly thinks he is entitled to enter. Because Peter had rented the saloon, and his sign was clearly posted (obviating an argument by Fred based on implied consent), Fred's action in entering the saloon probably constituted a trespass. In many jurisdictions a trespasser is liable for all injuries or losses occasioned by his trespass, whether those losses were accidental or not. Thus, Fred would probably be liable for the value of Peter's camera.

Negligence:

Did Fred act reasonably under the circumstances? If Fred's entry occurred in a jurisdiction which does not hold a trespasser liable for all damages occasioned by his trespass, Peter would sue Fred in negligence. (Peter would argue that Fred acted unreasonably in failing to see the "Closed for Day" sign which was prominently displayed.)

In the negligence action, Fred would argue that a reasonable person in a small Western town would not look for or respond to a warning sign on the door of a saloon which he regularly frequented, particularly when the saloon was routinely open for business at all usual times and had not, to his knowledge, previously been used as a film set or for any other purpose than as a saloon. Whether this argument would prevail would depend on the extent to which the filming of the movie had become common knowledge in the town. To determine whether Fred acted reasonably under the circumstances, we probably need additional facts.

Was Fred's conduct the proximate cause of Peter's loss? If Fred did act unreasonably, then Peter would have to show that Fred's actions were the proximate cause of his loss. While Fred's conduct was clearly the cause of the loss, a resulting issue would be whether the extent of the loss ($125,000) was reasonably foreseeable from the action of pushing open a saloon door. Although Peter would contend that $125,000 was not an excessive measure of damages, by ignoring the sign and pushing the door open, Fred might just as possibly have injured an extra or a cameraman as caused the camera to break. Thus, the harm to the camera was within the general characterization of the type of risk that made Fred's conduct negligent. That finding would satisfy the requirement of proximate cause.

Was Peter contributorily negligent? If Fred is found to have been negligent and the $125,000 in damages foreseeable, Fred has available the affirmative defense that Peter was also negligent. Fred would argue that Peter should have taken greater measures to protect the film site, such as hiring guards to prevent people from entering the saloon, placing more signs in front of the site, or locking or barricading the entry. The success of this defense would depend on what a reasonable person in Peter's circumstances would have done. Additional facts, such as what standard precautions are used in the film industry, are needed. In the majority of jurisdictions, comparative negligence would be applied to reduce or bar recovery if Peter's conduct was found to have been negligent.

In summary, Peter can probably recover in trespass for the value of the camera and any other ***damages*** occasioned by Fred's conduct. On a negligence theory, whether and how much Peter can recover will depend on additional facts.

Answer to Question 4

Frank (F) v. Dennis (D) (Trespass):

Is D liable to F for trespass? The tort of trespass occurs when a person intentionally enters upon someone else's land without permission, or when a person places an object on someone else's land without permission. It's irrelevant that the encroachment may result from a good-faith mistake. Because D intentionally moved the Conco (C) vehicles onto F's land, he will be liable for all the foreseeable damage resulting from his actions. In cases of intentional tort, proximate cause doctrines are applied with great liberality toward defendants. The likelihood that some harm would be caused by moving heavy equipment onto the land would support recovery for the actual damage. Thus, in the absence of a valid defense, D would be liable to F for $9,000, the value of the destroyed bulbs.

Can D escape liability with a claim of necessity? D will defend by claiming that his trespass was privileged as a *public necessity* (i.e., that the damage or inconvenience to F's property was outweighed by the potential loss of life and property to the public as a whole). (D can also argue that there was a private necessity to protect the property of C, but a person who trespasses out of private necessity is still liable for any damage to the owner's property.) When public necessity is applicable, however, the actor is relieved of all liability. D will argue that a public necessity existed because the vehicles at C's plant would have caught fire and exploded, causing injury to anyone in the area, especially the firefighters responding to the fire alarm. F would argue that the yard was located in a suburban area, that little or no threat was posed to the public at large, and that D was acting only to protect the private interest of his employer. Whether D will be found to have acted out of public necessity will depend on facts we don't have, such as the likelihood of explosion, the size of the fire, the presence of flammable materials near the fire, the density of population in the area, etc. Because they can spread quickly and become dangerous to life and property, fires generally pose a risk to the public at large. D (and thus C) will probably prevail.

F v. D (Negligence):

F would probably also sue D for negligence. The tort of negligence occurs when one person's conduct imposes an unreasonable risk of harm on another person who is injured as a result.

Did D act unreasonably under the circumstances? Land on which tulips have been planted would appear to an observer as vacant land which would not be harmed materially by driving vehicles over it. Facing the threat that eight expensive vehicles might be damaged if they were not moved away from the yard onto F's land, D probably did not act unreasonably.

Even if D did act unreasonably under the circumstances, it is not clear that D's actions were the **proximate cause** of F's losses. Proximate cause is a judicial concept in response to the belief that a person who has been negligent should not be responsible for consequences other than those whose likelihood supports a finding that his conduct was negligent. The concept is generally based on foreseeability—i.e., was this particular consequence a reasonably predictable or foreseeable result of the negligence? Considering that F's land was likely to appear barren (i.e., there would be no visible evidence that tulips had been planted under it), D could probably argue successfully that no one could reasonably foresee that there were bulbs planted under the ground or that a $9,000 loss would result. F will contend that one can always foresee the possibility that damage will result when eight heavy vehicles are moved suddenly onto someone's land (e.g., underground pipes or wires would be broken). A jury could decide whether the risk of damage to pavement or utilities was significant, and whether it was similar enough to the kind of damage that actually occurred to support imposition of liability.

In summary, D is likely to prevail in the event F brings a negligence action against him.

If Dennis is liable, is Conco also liable for his intentional acts or negligence? Under the doctrine of **respondeat superior**, if an employee commits a tort while in the scope of his employment, the **employer** will be jointly liable with the **employee**. The question is: Was D acting in the scope of his employment? Because D committed the tort(s) on a Sunday while on a personal errand, at a facility which was not his place of employment, and because the responsibilities of an accountant do not typically include responses to emergencies or the operation of heavy equipment, D probably was acting outside the scope of his employment.

D v. F (False Imprisonment and Intentional Infliction of Severe Emotional Distress):

The tort of false imprisonment (FI) occurs when the defendant has intentionally confined the plaintiff within definite physical boundaries. Here, although D was clearly within definite physical boundaries (the office space), it is arguable from the facts that there was no confinement (i.e., D was not prevented from leaving). However, D will argue that use of words "have to" in the presence of four men loyal to F could be reasonably construed as a threat to prevent his departure—forcibly, if necessary. However, when a plaintiff voluntarily submits to verbal commands unaccompanied by force or threats, false imprisonment is difficult to establish. F will argue that D was simply told to remain there and that no threats were made—his employees just happened to be there. Telling D that he would have to wait for C's president was not in itself a threat; F meant only that the president was the only person with the authority to settle the matter. Furthermore, there is no FI when the plaintiff's confinement results solely from his own desire to clear himself of suspicion in the commission of a tort; here, D may have decided to stay simply out of a desire to clear up the matter of his responsibility for the damage to F's property, as would seem apparent from his agreement to meet with F in the first place. If, nonetheless, an FI were held to have occurred, F might contend that D *consented* to the alleged FI because he voluntarily went to F's office; but this defense would fail because D presumably did so with the belief that he would be free to leave whenever he chose to go. If an FI occurred, it appears that D can recover only nominal damages since he suffered no real loss.

Conclusion:

D will be liable to F for the damages resulting from D's trespass. Additional facts are needed to determine whether D can avoid paying damages under a public necessity defense. C will be free from *respondeat superior* liability. Neither D nor C will be liable on a negligence theory. A false imprisonment claim by D against F will probably fail.

Answer to Question 5

Abel (A) will consider actions against Babel (B) and Pierre (P). A's action against B will be based on B's negligence. A will also consider bringing an action against the city for its failure to enforce its building and fire ordinances.

A v. B (Negligence):

A would argue that by having only two fire exits on Cool's (C's) floor, B acted unreasonably under the circumstances and that A was injured as a result of B's unreasonable conduct.

Did B fail to act reasonably under the circumstances? A would show that B was under a *legal duty* to conform to a level or standard of care sufficient to avoid unreasonable risk to others, and that B breached that standard of care. The duty that the owner of a building owes to others will depend on the jurisdiction. In the case of a hotel, an innkeeper is ordinarily required to exercise reasonable care for the safety of its guests. In this case, the city ordinance will be considered evidence of the minimum standard of care for B.

In some instances, a statute will define reasonable conduct in a particular context. This happens most frequently when safety standards have to be set for a particular industry or occupation. Although the violation here involves a city ordinance and not a statute, it is likely in this case to be construed as establishing negligence *per se* because hotel fire standards are generally set by local ordinance and not by statute. In any event, failure of B to adhere to the ordinance would clearly be very strong evidence of negligence.

Was B's negligence a "but for" cause of A's injuries? A defendant's failure to have acted reasonably must be a "but for" cause of the plaintiff's harm to invoke liability. B will argue that its failure to have two additional fire exits was not the actual cause of A's injuries. It will point out that A's path into the hallway (where all exits would be located) was entirely blocked by the fire by the time A was ready to leave Cool's room. Therefore, the lack of fire exits did not cause A's injuries. Even if there had been as many exits as the ordinance required, A would still have been unable to use an exit.

Was B's negligence the proximate cause of A's injuries? Because B's negligence was not a cause-in-fact (or "but for" cause) of A's injury, legal cause or proximate cause would not be established. Our "but for" analysis is an element in the analysis of causation—the relationship between cause and effect. We must also inquire whether there was an intervening cause of A's injuries—i.e., a force that took effect after B's negligence and that contributed to A's injuries. Additionally, the highly unforeseeable conduct of Pierre would likely be treated as a superseding cause of A's injury, even if there otherwise was a basis for holding B liable for it.

A v. P and His Employees (Assault and Battery):

While P did not actually move A himself, he would be liable for the actions of his employees because they were acting under his direction. A should be able to sue P and his employees for assault (intentionally causing the plaintiff to be in apprehension of an imminent, offensive touching—A's fear of being moved) and battery (intentionally causing an offensive contact upon the plaintiff—by moving A). The defendants could argue that A was a trespasser who could be ejected by the use of reasonable force. However, trespass occurs only when the entry is voluntary. When someone enters an owner's land involuntarily, he is not a trespasser. A intended to land on the roof of the adjacent building. He did not intend to fall through the roof to P's floor. A will also argue that he was privileged to be in P's restaurant under the private necessity doctrine (the interest in saving his life outweighed any risk of business interruption to P). When someone is privileged by private necessity to enter someone else's property, the owner cannot use reasonable force to defeat the exercise of the privilege and is liable for any damages resulting from the use of force.

A v. Owner of Building:

It's not clear from the facts whether B was the owner of the building or what the condition of the roof was. If the roof was not constructed properly or if the owner was aware that it had fallen into disrepair and been weakened, then the owner might be liable to A for creating an unreasonable risk that someone falling or landing on the roof would fall through it and be injured. It's also not clear from the facts whether even a well-constructed roof in good repair would have held up under the combined weight of A and C after they had fallen onto it from above.

Damages: Assuming A were successful in his lawsuit against B, P, and the latter's employees, or any of them, he would be able to recover for any past and prospective lost income, medical bills, and pain and suffering attributable to the incident. A might also be able to get punitive damages from B if a jury found that B's conduct was "reckless" or "willful and wanton." A might get punitive damages from P (and his employees) if a jury found their conduct was outrageous or malicious.

Answer to Question 6

Wendy (W) v. Baseball, Inc. (B) (Negligence):

W can sue B in negligence for her miscarriage, for the pain and suffering that resulted from it, and for the consequences of Kevin's (K's) assault.

Duty: The duty that B, as the owner of the property upon which the injury occurred, owed W will depend on whether this jurisdiction distinguishes among categories of persons who come upon another's land. If it does, then B owed W a duty to make the premises safe and to assist her in the event of an emergency. As a customer who had paid for her ticket to the game and for parking in the lot, W was a business invitee. The owner's duty to invitees is to use reasonable care. This probably requires the owner to exercise control over third persons on the premises; W will argue that B had a duty to take reasonable security measures to protect her from K's assault upon her.

If this jurisdiction has rejected different levels of care, and instead uses a single "reasonable person" standard of liability for persons who rightfully come on the owner's land, then B owed W a duty to exercise reasonable care under the circumstances.

Here, the facts are such that B's duty would be the same whether we use the standard applied to invitees or the reasonable person standard.

Breach of duty: W will argue that B is liable on either of two theories: (1) It failed to make the premises safe for invitees; or (2) it did not satisfy the reasonable person standard by failing to prevent Kevin's conduct, and by failing to provide W with reasonable medical help, including examination by a doctor or trained paramedic.

B will contend that it could not reasonably have prevented K's conduct because his actions occurred spontaneously. To satisfy a higher standard, B would be required to have a security guard at every single parking place in order to prevent an altercation between drivers. Further, because K's conduct consisted of speech, however threatening, B's guards could not be expected to know what was said or that it represented a threat, unless they were standing within earshot of W and K. A court would probably conclude that B had met its duty by posting security guards in the parking lot. Unless additional facts would show that the security guards were somehow delinquent in performing their job—e.g., the guards had left their posts, or they had in fact heard K's threats and done nothing, W is not likely to win on this issue.

B would also argue that it was not B's responsibility to have a doctor and an extensive medical facility at the stadium and that the infirmary where first aid care could be administered was sufficient. B probably did not fail to act reasonably in not having a complete medical facility. W will argue, however, that when she began to groan, it was reasonable to question whether she was pregnant. At that point, B should have taken the reasonable precaution of asking for a doctor on its public address system. It would be reasonable to assume that at least one of the fans at the game was a doctor.

Whether B failed to exercise reasonable care by neglecting to provide W with immediate medical assistance (or at least by sending her to a hospital sooner) would depend upon the state of her pregnancy. If it was obvious that she was pregnant, B probably should have recognized that immediate medical attention was necessary to avert a miscarriage. But if W was in the early stages of her pregnancy, then B probably acted reasonably in simply having W rest in its infirmary until she could regain consciousness and could drive home. We need more facts before we can resolve this issue.

Actual causation: If B breached its duty of care by not preventing K's assault, then its breach would be the actual (or "but for") cause of W's harm.

On the other hand, B's failure to provide immediate medical attention for W would constitute the actual cause of W's harm only if it can be shown that the miscarriage would have been prevented if B had acted more promptly. If B can show that the miscarriage occurred when W fainted and struck the ground, actual causation by B would be absent (unless B failed to act reasonably in not averting K's conduct). Again, more facts would be needed on this issue.

Proximate cause: Even if W can establish that B breached its duty of care and that its breach actually contributed to her injuries, she must still show that B's conduct was the proximate cause of her injuries—i.e., that there was a sufficiently close causal link between B's negligence and her injuries as to impose liability upon B. A court would probably find that it was reasonably foreseeable that failure to prevent an assault on a customer would result in injuries to the customer, and that failure to provide adequate medical attention would either cause new injuries or aggravate existing ones.

Conclusion: B probably satisfied its duty of care to W by providing guards in the parking lot, by carrying her to its infirmary, and by sending her to a hospital.

W v. Police (Negligence):
W would consider suing the police for negligence on the grounds that they acted unreasonably under the circumstances by taking her to the hospital in

a police car rather than an ambulance. She would argue that this negligence caused her miscarriage because she was unable to receive proper medical care en route to the hospital.

Even if she can prove that the miscarriage would not have occurred if she had been taken by ambulance, W would probably lose. A court would probably find that the police did the only reasonable thing under the circumstances—it would not have been reasonable to wait for an ambulance that might not reach them for a long time because of the heavy traffic.

W v. K (Assault, Intentional Infliction of Emotional Distress):

W would sue K for assault and intentional infliction of emotional distress. An assault occurs when the defendant has intentionally caused the plaintiff to be in reasonable apprehension of an imminent, offensive touching. Although words alone are usually not sufficient to constitute an assault, they may be construed as an assault when they are accompanied by an overt act, however slight. K "jumped out" of his car and screamed at Wendy. He suggested that he should "kick your butt." A court could easily find that these overt acts made it reasonable for W to be apprehensive that he would carry out the actions threatened by his words. Indeed, to commit an assault, K did not have to touch W; the intent required for an assault is merely to put another person in **apprehension** of abusive or offensive contact. When an assault has occurred, the plaintiff can recover for the emotional suffering resulting from her apprehension of imminent harmful or offensive conduct.

The tort of **intentional infliction of emotional distress** requires (1) intent or recklessness, (2) a showing that the defendant's conduct was extreme and outrageous, and (3) severe emotional distress on the part of the plaintiff. W will establish K's intent by showing (1) that K wanted to cause her emotional distress, or (2) that K knew with substantial certainty that she would suffer emotional distress, or (3) that K recklessly disregarded the high probability that she would suffer emotional distress. The tort does not occur when the defendant has merely insulted the plaintiff or hurt her feelings. K went far beyond insults, however. A woman faced by a man who screamed at her and suggested kicking her butt would certainly consider his conduct to be extreme and outrageous. The court is likely to find that K's conduct was outrageous. The threat of physical violence against any woman would foreseeably cause her intense anxiety. Here, if W's pregnancy was obvious to the ordinary observer, K's conduct was especially egregious because it would cause W to fear for the welfare of her unborn child. Resolution of this issue would depend upon how pregnant W appeared to be.

K's defenses: K would argue that he was acting in ***defense of his property.*** In general, a person may use reasonable force to defend his property. Here, although K arguably used words and not force, a court might find that he acted unreasonably in the face of what was merely an act of minor negligence which caused little damage to K's car. Because K's car was already parked when W parked her car, W may be able to show that K had parked his car in such a way as to make it impossible for another driver to open the door of his car without touching K's car.

Conclusion: W will probably recover from K for assault. Her claim of infliction of emotional distress will probably succeed as well, especially if she was visibly pregnant. If W were successful upon either theory, she would be able to recover for the miscarriage as well as emotional suffering; an intentional tortfeasor is generally liable for all of the consequences of his act. She may be able to recover punitive damages if K's conduct is found to be particularly outrageous or malicious.

K v. Henry (H); H v. K (Assault and Battery):

In deciding between H and K, we need to determine whether H was justified in punching K in the mouth. H will argue that he was privileged in punching K in the mouth because ***he was acting in defense of W***. The success of this defense will depend upon whether H reasonably believed that W was in imminent danger of serious injury (i.e., whether K seemed agitated enough to kick or strike W after she fainted and on whether H used reasonable force in acting to protect W). Whether H will prevail on this point will depend on facts not revealed to us, such as what K did after W fainted. If he moved toward her aggressively, then H probably acted reasonably. If he merely stood still or recoiled in surprise, then H probably acted unreasonably.

H may argue that he acted in self-defense. There is nothing in the facts to show that K threatened H. On the contrary, H ran toward K and threw the first punch. It would be more persuasive if K asserted the privilege of self-defense. Although K was guilty of an assault on W, he had not shown any hostility toward H, and H did not act reasonably in striking him. Once H had hit him and knocked out his teeth, K was entitled to use reasonable force to defend himself.

John (J) v. H or K (Assault and Battery):

J would argue that he was attempting to effect a warrantless arrest for a breach of the peace committed in his presence, and that therefore ***his action was privileged.*** He should be able to recover from either H or K or both.

K v. W (Trespass to Chattels, Negligence):

K will try to recover from W for the damage to his car, either on a trespass to chattels theory or on a negligence theory. Trespass to chattels is intentional interference with another person's use or possession of property. Here, W probably did not have the required intent; at most, she acted negligently in opening her car door without exercising reasonable care to avoid K's car. Thus, K's claim will depend on ordinary negligence. Whether W acted reasonably under the circumstances may depend on additional facts. Was she in advanced pregnancy? If so, she may have had difficulty getting out of her car and so scraped K's car in spite of exercising as much care as she was able to. Also, W may be able to show that K was contributorily negligent—he may have parked his car in such a way as to make it impossible to open the door of a car parked alongside his without scratching his car. If W was negligent and K was not contributorily negligent, K can recover for the actual damage to the car. If W was negligent but K was contributorily negligent, K's recovery would depend on the allocation of negligence between W and K and the effect of the jurisdiction's system of comparative negligence.

Answer to Question 7

H and W v. F (Public Nuisance, Negligence):

Public nuisance: H and W (Plaintiffs) will sue F on the theory that F had created a public nuisance. They will claim that F's conduct interfered with their ability to use a public highway, a right common to the general public. In determining whether F's conduct amounted to a public nuisance, the court will consider these factors: the type of neighborhood; the nature of the act; the proximity of the act to the victims; the frequency, duration, and timing of the act; and the extent of the damage that resulted. Here, the neighborhood would appear to be a rural farming area with a sparse population. This would give F more leeway in the activities he conducted on his own land. However, because his conduct was deliberate, and he had an opportunity to put the fire out when he saw the volatility of the smoke, a court might find F's conduct unreasonable under the circumstances, especially because he was aware that his land was adjacent to the public highway. The facts don't tell us a number of things that would make our decision easier: How often did F light these fires? Was this an unusual wind storm, or were these storms constant in this area? How long had this fire been burning? Had similar fires by F or by other farmers in the area caused damage to cars on the highway previously? A court might also inquire whether burning weeds was reasonably necessary to F's livelihood. Whether a court would find that F had caused a public nuisance will depend on these factors.

Even if a court did hold that F's conduct was a public nuisance, Plaintiffs would have to show that the injury to them was different in kind, not in degree, from the injury, or potential injury, to the public at large. Plaintiffs would have to argue that there was a particular moment unique to them when the smoke from the burning of the weeds was thick enough and close enough to affect them in a way no other car on the highway would have been affected. Whether a court would find their injury sufficiently different in kind is not clear. Plaintiffs probably have a better chance to recover from F on a negligence theory.

Negligence: Plaintiffs would contend that F was negligent in burning weeds on land adjacent to a highway when the wind was blowing in the direction of that highway.

Duty: Landowners generally have a duty to prevent unreasonable risk of harm to persons off their land when a hazardous condition on the land has been artificially created by the owner. Many of the cases illustrating this duty involve land adjacent to a public highway, as in this case. Plaintiffs would argue that the act of burning weeds next to a public highway under the wind conditions described in the fact pattern would come under this principle, and that F had a duty to prevent the risk that drivers on the highway would find their vision obstructed by the smoke created by his fire.

Breach of duty: Plaintiffs would contend that F failed to act with due care (i.e., reasonably under the circumstances) by permitting smoke from his fire to drift over a pubic highway and obscure the vision of drivers on the highway. Although F could contend that it was "customary" for farmers in the area to burn weeds in that manner, that fact alone would not make F's conduct reasonable. Even if the burning of weeds was customary in the area, F should not have started his fire—or should have put it out—when he saw the volatility of the wind and smoke. Plaintiffs should prevail on this point.

Actual causation: F would contend that the actual cause of the Plaintiffs' harm was not his conduct but T's misconduct in crossing over the center line of the highway. However, unless additional facts show that T was asleep at the wheel, for example, we may reasonably presume that T crossed the center line because he was also blinded by the smoke generated by F's fire. Plaintiffs should prevail on this issue also, because a collision between two cars was reasonably foreseeable in the heavy smoke.

Proximate causation: When there is a subsequent, unforeseeable intervening factor between the defendant's negligence and the plaintiff's harm, the defendant's liability is usually extinguished. F will contend that because there were several intervening factors between his conduct and Plaintiffs' harm (the wind shifted; T was over the center line; the bus driver hit Plaintiffs from the rear), proximate causation is absent. However, Plaintiffs will probably succeed by showing that (1) wind shifts are not "unforeseeable" and were in fact happening regularly this day; (2) F could see that the wind and the smoke were shifting and that the smoke was thick enough to obscure the vision of drivers; (3) T was probably over the dividing line as a consequence of the smoke (rather than T's own negligence); and (4) the negligence of the bus driver, if any, was a contributing (rather than a superseding) cause of their harm.

Plaintiffs' negligence: F would argue that Plaintiffs were negligent in continuing down the highway with knowledge that the wind could shift and blow the smoke over them. Plaintiffs will contend that H acted cautiously under the circumstances, observing the wind as he drove, and that the smoke that enveloped them changed in their direction suddenly. We don't know if there was a shoulder or safety zone on this highway. If there wasn't, it would have been dangerous to stop on the highway, especially in view of the blowing smoke. It is unlikely on these facts that F would succeed in establishing that Plaintiffs were negligent.

In a *comparative negligence* jurisdiction, if Plaintiffs were found negligent, the court would reduce Plaintiffs' recovery in proportion to Plaintiffs' share of the fault. In a "pure" comparative negligence system, Plaintiffs would recover damages even if their fault were found to be greater than F's. In a "49 percent" system or "50 percent" system, Plaintiffs would recover only if their negligence were less than F's (49 percent system) or less than or equal to F's (50 percent system).

More facts may establish that Plaintiffs were negligent, although that is not likely under the circumstances.

H and W against Bus Driver and C (Negligence):

Plaintiffs will sue the driver of the bus and C for their negligence (i.e., the driver acted unreasonably in proceeding into an area of poor visibility). The driver is responsible for his own conduct. C is liable for the driver's conduct under the doctrine of *respondeat superior* (an *employer* is liable for the acts or omissions of his *employees* within the scope of their employment).

Breach of duty: C and the bus driver will contend that the driver acted reasonably under the circumstances—he slowed his bus to 35 mph (10 mph below the legal rate of speed). However, Plaintiffs will argue that the bus driver acted unreasonably in proceeding down a highway which was clearly engulfed in smoke and that he should have stopped altogether. Plaintiffs will find it difficult to make this argument stick, however, because they themselves did the very same thing—they continued to drive ahead knowing that the smoke might engulf them. They will insist, however, that they could not know whether the smoke would reach them, while the bus driver knew for sure that he was driving into the smoke.

Plaintiffs' negligence: C and the bus driver will contend that Plaintiffs were negligent (discussed above under *H and W v. F*).

Conclusion: Plaintiffs may be able to recover from C and the bus driver on a negligence theory. If Plaintiffs are shown by additional facts to have been negligent themselves, their ability to recover will depend on whether this is a contributory negligence jurisdiction or a comparative negligence jurisdiction.

H and W v. T (Negligence):

Did T fail to act with due care? We need additional facts to determine whether T failed to act reasonably under the circumstances. If T was surprised by the sudden wind shift in the same way as H and attempted to stop his vehicle immediately, forcing him to swerve into the other lane, T would not have acted negligently. But if T had been drinking, or if he had fallen asleep at the wheel, then the cause of his swerving might not be his sudden stop.

Damages: Assuming (1) Plaintiffs successfully sued F, C, T, and the bus driver in a joint and several liability jurisdiction, and (2) it was not possible to distinguish between the injuries caused by the impact with the bus and those suffered when the Plaintiffs collided with T's car, Plaintiffs would be entitled to recover the full amount of their actual damages, or any portion thereof, from each of the defendants. Defendant(s) from whom damages are collected may be able to seek contribution from the other defendants, if they paid more than the share represented by their percentages of responsibility. If Plaintiffs' damages are found to be a divisible harm, then liability will be apportioned according to the damages caused by each defendant. Finally, C may have a right of indemnity against the bus driver.

Answer to Question 8

Farmer (F) v. Parentis (Ps) and Babysitter (B) (Negligence):

F will contend that the Ps and B (Defendants) are jointly and severally liable to him in negligence as a result of (1) the Ps' negligent hiring of and negligent supervision over an incompetent babysitter and (2) B's failure to supervise the children, her failure to keep them in the house, and her failure to prevent them from entering F's barn and starting the fire. Alternatively, F will sue B on a negligence theory and claim that the Ps are liable for B's negligence under the doctrine of ***respondeat superior.***

Duty: The defendants had a duty to act with the care that a "reasonable person" would exercise under the circumstances.

Breach of duty: F will argue that the Ps failed to act reasonably under the circumstances by entrusting the children to a 14-year-old teenager whom they had never met before and who had already demonstrated her lack of responsibility by arriving 20 minutes late. However, assuming B appeared to be reasonably intelligent and mature, the Ps will argue that there was no reason to conclude that she was less competent than other 14-year-olds who are normally hired as babysitters.

Of course, we do not have all the facts that a jury would want to consider: How had the Ps learned of B? Had she worked for their friends? Was she the daughter of a neighbor? Had she been recommended by her school or by her church? All of these questions would go to the reasonableness of the Ps' willingness to entrust their children with B. On the facts we have, the Ps may very well lose on this issue.

B's vulnerability as a defendant is increased by her negligence in permitting her boyfriend to enter the house and in allowing herself to be distracted by him from her responsibility to the children. A reasonable babysitter keeps children 6 and 7 years old under her constant supervision. She will read to them, play games with them, sit with them while they watch TV. After she puts them to bed, she will look in on them from time to time.

Although she was only 14, B will be held to a standard of care that is reasonable for a child at her age. Certainly, that standard would require being attentive to children she was hired to watch. A court is likely to find that B acted unreasonably.

Causation: Assuming the Ps and B are found negligent, F must still show that their conduct both actually and proximately caused his loss.

F can show that both the Ps and B combined to act as the ***actual ("but for") cause*** of his loss. If the Ps had not been negligent in hiring B, and if B had not acted unreasonably, the children would not have entered the barn, piled the hay on the grill, and started the fire that caused F's loss. A loss may have more than one actual cause. If the Ps had not hired B, the loss would not have occurred; if B had exercised reasonable care, the loss would not have occurred.

F will argue that the conduct of the Ps and B **proximately caused** his loss because it was reasonably foreseeable that children left unattended might leave the house and wander onto adjoining property. F will argue that children are frequent trespassers; that these children had trespassed on his property before; and that because he was the immediate neighbor, his was the property the children would be most likely to enter. He would also argue that it was foreseeable that the children would cause some damage if they were unattended, given their ages. Defendants will argue that F's act in placing a lighted charcoal grill inside the barn was a superseding cause that should relieve them of liability, and that the precise nature of F's loss was not foreseeable (i.e., that the children would find the hay and put it on the fire). Putting all the facts together, the jury would probably find for F on these issues.

Are the Ps liable for B's negligence? Even if the Ps were not negligent in hiring B, F will nonetheless try to recover from them under the doctrine of **respondeat superior**. Under **respondeat superior**, if an employee commits a tort while in the scope of his employment, the employer will be jointly liable with the employee. A threshold issue here is whether B was the Ps' employee or an **independent contractor**. This would depend on the degree of control that the Ps had over B. The Ps would contend that parents have no real control over a babysitter. By definition, they are not present during the babysitter's work. It is not enough that the employer exercise control over the general manner in which the work is carried out; he must also be responsible for the physical details of the work. However, although the parents may not be present, the physical details of the job of babysitter fall within very narrow boundaries. Babysitters are expected to watch their charges, offer them light snacks, keep them under watchful supervision, and get them ready for bed. Parents generally define these functions for the babysitter. Further, it serves public policy to impose responsibility on the parents rather than on babysitters whom they hire. Parents are better able to pay for the consequential damages to a third party than the babysitter will be. The Ps are likely to be held vicariously liable for B's negligence as B's employers.

Was F negligent? F was probably not negligent under the analysis which follows (*Children v. F*). If he were found negligent in a comparative negligence jurisdiction, his recovery would be reduced in proportion to his fault (unless his negligence exceeded 49 percent or 50 percent in jurisdictions that use those forms of comparative negligence). In a contributory negligence jurisdiction, any negligence by F would bar recovery.

Conclusion: Both the Ps and B were guilty of negligence which resulted in F's damages. F will have the option of recovering all his damages from the Ps.

Children v. F (Negligence):

Although a landowner normally has no duty to trespassers, special principles apply when the trespassers are children. This is because children are less able to appreciate the risks involved in particular circumstances; children trespass more often than adults and the danger to them is therefore more foreseeable; and the courts are generally more sympathetic to children. The Restatement lists the following requirements for liability to trespassing children: (1) the owner has reason to know that the condition causing the risk is in a place where the children are likely to trespass; (2) the owner knows of the condition and has reason to believe it poses a risk of injury to children; (3) the children, because of their youth, do not realize the danger posed by the condition; (4) the benefit to the owner of maintaining the condition is slight when compared to the risk to the children; and (5) the owner fails to use reasonable care to eliminate the danger to the children. We know that F was aware of the children's propensity to enter his land (he had explicitly instructed them to stay away from his barn). He also knew of the dangerous condition because he had created it by setting the grill near the door and lighting the coals, and he should have known that it posed an unreasonable risk of serious injury to the children, who would be attracted by the coals and cannot be assumed to know that the dry hay would quickly ignite.

F will argue that even very young children are able to appreciate the risk of fire in live coals. One of the first lessons most parents teach their children is to avoid the risk caused by fire. F would also argue that the children were aware that the barn was a dangerous place for them, since he had chased them out of it on two prior occasions. He will also argue that the utility to him of being able to use his grill in the barn outweighed the risk that the children would be hurt by it, especially since he did not expect them to be outside and trespassing at night. The children will argue that F failed to exercise reasonable care in anticipating the danger. F would argue that he did not have an obligation to make the barn child-proof, but only to make it reasonably safe. He could not reasonably have anticipated that the children would ignore his previous warnings.

Were the children negligent? Assuming F was negligent, F could argue that the children were negligent to seek to bar their recovery in a contributory negligence jurisdiction or to reduce it in a comparative negligence jurisdiction. The standard of care to which children are held is that of a reasonable child of similar age, intelligence, and experience. Under that standard, we would ask whether a child of seven (the older child) would be aware of the risks involved in placing hay on live coals. Unless he had been instructed by his parents in the dangers associated with grills, or had observed flames rising from a grill after someone placed a dry object on it, he would be unlikely to understand or be aware of the risks. Of course, the facts indicate that the children knew enough to play "make believe cook," suggesting that they were aware they were dealing with fire, but it is not reasonable to conclude that a seven-year-old really understood all the risks.

If the children were negligent, they will not recover in a contributory negligence jurisdiction. In a comparative negligence jurisdiction, their recovery would be reduced by the relative share of their fault.

Conclusion:

The children may be prevented from recovering from F because he had warned them repeatedly to stay out of his barn and because he could not foresee that they would be trespassing at night, when children of their age are usually not outside. However, because courts tend to be sympathetic to injured children, and given the children's youth and F's knowledge of their propensity to trespass, a court could conceivably find against F.

Answer to Question 9
Peter (P) v. Ace (A) (Negligence, Vicarious Liability):

A bystander who goes to the rescue of a person at risk of injury because of the negligence of a third person is entitled to recover from that third person if he himself is injured and if his intervention was reasonably foreseeable. P would contend that A was negligent in leasing a car to Bruce (B), who did not have a license. P will also assert that A is vicariously liable for B's negligence.

Did A act reasonably under the circumstances? A will be found liable to P for negligence if its conduct imposed an unreasonable risk of harm to P. A court will probably find that A did not act reasonably because it failed to verify that B had a valid driver's license. These facts raise the issue of foreseeability. When a rescuer is involved, courts are more apt to treat the intervention of a rescuer as foreseeable. If a defendant's negligence creates a risk that some rescuer will intervene, the rescue is not considered a superseding cause unless the rescuer himself is grossly careless.

Was A's conduct the actual cause of P's harm? P will have to show that A's negligence was the *"but for" cause* of P's injuries. It seems clear that "but for" A's negligent conduct, the accident would not have occurred, because (1) B would not have been driving on the road in the rental car when C's car entered the highway; (2) C would not have been trapped in a burning car; and (3) P would not have gone to C's rescue.

Was A's conduct a proximate cause of P's harm? When the plaintiff's harm can be described as the consequence of an unforeseeable, intervening factor, some jurisdictions hold that the defendant's conduct is not a proximate cause of the plaintiff's injuries. A would contend that the acts of B and C were intervening factors which preclude a finding of proximate cause on these facts. However, A's failure to check for the validity of B's license was negligent *because* it created a risk that poor driving would cause an accident. When the negligence of a defendant (A) is such that the negligence of a third party (B) is foreseeable, the defendant will be liable.

Courts often use a relaxed foreseeability measure when rescuers are concerned, on the grounds that "danger invites rescue," and that where the defendant's negligent conduct created the danger that attracted the rescuer, the defendant should be liable. Thus, A will probably be liable to P for its own negligence.

Is A liable to P for B's negligence? If this jurisdiction has an auto consent statute, the owner of a car (the bailor) will be vicariously liable for any negligence committed by someone using the car with the owner's permission (the bailee). P will have to show that B was negligent. B's negligence has two prongs: (1) He drove the car without a valid license. This is a crime in every jurisdiction and may be treated as proof of negligence. (2) B drove the car at a recklessly high speed, putting other drivers and passersby at risk of harm. B's negligence was a *"but for" cause* of P's injuries (had he not rented the car and driven it, and had he not driven so recklessly, he would not have struck C's car and caused it to burn). As we have seen, B's negligence was the *proximate cause* of P's injuries because (1) the presence of other cars is foreseeable on a highway, (2) negligence by other drivers is always foreseeable, and (3) P was a foreseeable rescuer of a person injured in the accident. A would be liable for B's negligence under an auto consent statute, as long as B's use of the car did not exceed the scope of A's consent to B's use of the car.

Without a consent statute, the mere existence of the bailment will not make A vicariously liable for B's negligence.

P v. Dave (D) (Vicarious Liability):

Is D vicariously liable for the acts of C? P will contend that because B and C were sharing the expenses and the driving, they were engaged in a *joint enterprise*, and so D is liable for the negligent conduct of C (discussed below). Persons who engage in a joint enterprise are vicariously liable for the negligent conduct of the other members of the enterprise. There are usually four requirements for a joint enterprise: (1) an express or implied agreement between the members, (2) a common purpose to be carried out by the members, (3) a common pecuniary interest in that purpose, and (4) an equal right of control in the enterprise. The doctrine of joint enterprise is applied frequently in auto accidents in an effort to make a passenger additionally responsible for the negligent driver's conduct. Here, there was an express agreement between C and D to pursue a common purpose—to drive across the country in C's car and to share expenses. However, they do not seem to have had a common pecuniary purpose, in the sense of a shared business objective. They met through an ad and presumably had different reasons for traveling across country, reasons which may have been purely social. Furthermore, the sharing of expenses is not usually enough to constitute the common pecuniary interest required for a joint enterprise. Finally, where a trip is merely social or does not have a common business purpose, courts are reluctant to find that a passenger had a common right of control with the driver. Thus, D will probably not be vicariously liable for C's negligence.

P v. C's Estate (Negligence):

There appears to be little question that C failed to act reasonably under the circumstances by entering the highway without looking. Causation also seems satisfied; if C had not entered the highway without looking, he would not have hit B. The proximate cause discussion above (*P v. A*) is equally applicable here.

Was P negligent? In the same way as A or B, C's Estate might contend that P was negligent (i.e., it was not reasonable under the circumstances to attempt to pull D from the burning car) and that therefore his recovery should be barred or reduced, according to the jurisdiction's general treatment of negligence by a plaintiff. P should be able to argue successfully that it is not unreasonable to attempt to save someone from what is almost certain death.

Conclusion:

A will be liable to P for its negligence and possibly for B's negligence (if there is an auto consent statute in effect). C's Estate will be liable to P for C's negligence. D will not be liable because there was not a joint enterprise between C and D. P was not negligent and therefore will be able to recover for past and future lost income, medical expenses, and pain and suffering.

P's injuries will probably be found to be an indivisible harm, so that defendants will be jointly and severally liable; each defendant will be liable for P's total damages, although P can only recover that total and no more. If P recovers that amount from a single defendant, that defendant may be able to seek contribution from the others (depending on the jurisdiction), either on an equal-share basis or on a comparative negligence basis.

Answer to Question 10

Abel (A) v. Sam (S) (Negligence):

One is ordinarily under no obligation to come to the aid or assistance of another. Unless there is some special relationship between the defendant and plaintiff, the defendant is not liable for his refusal to help the plaintiff. Thus, S had no duty to assist Diana, even though the likelihood that an accident would occur may have increased as a consequence of his refusal to help. S would have no liability to A.

A v. Diana (D) (Assault, Battery, and Negligence):

Assuming that A could see that D had parked in such a way as to threaten the scaffolding, A would sue D for assault (intentionally causing him to be in apprehension of an imminent, offensive touching). Whether or not he sued for assault, he could sue her for battery (intentional infliction of an offensive or harmful bodily contact). The intent required for both torts is not intent to harm, but intent to commit the act which defines the tort. To be liable, the defendant must know with substantial certainty that a particular effect (i.e., the plaintiff's apprehension or the offensive contact) will occur as a result of her actions. It is not clear from the facts whether D had the requisite intent for the torts of assault and battery. The facts indicate that D knew she would collide with the scaffolding if she did not have assistance in parking, but they do not indicate whether she knew there were people on the scaffolding. Whether she had the necessary intent will depend on whether she knew with substantial certainty that they were there. If she knew they were there, then her act of moving the car when she feared she might hit the scaffolding will be deemed intentional for purposes of A's claims.

A battery can occur as a result of harmful contact not only with the body of another but also with an object so closely associated with that body as to be considered a part of it. Here, D's contact with the scaffolding amounted to a contact with A and Baker. If D knew that people were on the scaffolding, a battery occurred first when she struck the scaffolding and again when A struck the ground. The assault would have occurred either immediately before D hit the scaffolding (but only if A saw D moving the car) or while A was falling (apprehension that he would strike the ground shortly).

Negligence: Alternatively, A would sue D in negligence.

There appears to be little doubt that D failed to act with due care (i.e., she did not act reasonably under the circumstances) when she attempted to park with knowledge that she might strike the scaffolding without the help of someone to guide her. D's negligence clearly was a *"but for" cause* of A's injuries; if she had not parked badly, A would not have been knocked to the ground and injured. There would also seem to be no proximate causation problem because there was no intervening factor between D's conduct and A's injuries.

Defenses: D would argue that A was **negligent** in having failed to wear his hard hat and that A's recovery should be barred or reduced, depending on what system the jurisdiction uses for treating a plaintiff's negligence. A did not act reasonably in violating company policy by not wearing a hard hat while working on a scaffolding. To affect A's recovery, A's actions would need to be either a "but for" cause of A's harm or a substantial factor in causing the harm. Here, the facts are explicit—if A had been wearing his hard hat, he would have suffered only a slight concussion instead of a severe skull fracture. Thus, A's negligence was unquestionably a substantial factor in causing his injuries. Proximate cause is also satisfied because the harm A suffered was precisely the harm he should have protected himself against; A's negligence as to his own safety is a proximate cause of his harm. In a **comparative negligence** jurisdiction, A's recovery would be reduced in proportion to the degree of his fault. In a "pure" comparative negligence system, he could recover reduced damages even if his fault was greater than D's. In a "50 percent" system, he could recover reduced damages only if his fault was not greater than D's. Under contributory negligence doctrines, he would be barred from recovery.

Conclusion: D may be liable to A for battery. Her liability for assault will depend on whether A saw or was aware of her actions. A will be able to recover **compensatory damages** (for mental suffering and physical injury) and, if a court finds D's conduct was sufficiently outrageous, punitive damages. D is liable to A for negligence also, but A's recovery will be either barred or reduced as a result of A's own negligence. If A is able to recover damages, A can recover medical expenses, lost earnings, physical pain, mental distress, and hedonic damages.

Baker (B) v. Ed (Negligence):

The facts are silent as to how or why Ed struck B. Assuming Ed was inattentive, there would seem to be little doubt that Ed acted unreasonably under the circumstances We know that B was stopped for a light. Unless something we are not told caused Ed to hit B's car (e.g., ice on the road; another car behind Ed struck his car and pushed it into B's car), there would appear to be no other conclusion than that Ed was negligent and that his negligence caused the injuries to B.

If Ed acted negligently, his negligence would seem to be a *"but for" cause* of the injuries B suffered; if he had not hit B's car, B's fracture would not have resulted in paralysis. The facts we have suggest that B's initial fracture was not serious and that it could have been treated without serious consequence to B. There is also *no proximate causation* problem because a defendant ordinarily takes the plaintiff as he finds him, and there was no intervening factor between Ed's conduct and the aggravation of B's injury. Ed's liability would, however, be reduced to the extent the fracture which B incurred as a consequence of D's conduct could be distinguished from the fracture and paralysis which Ed caused. When two defendants harm the plaintiff and the harms can be divided and apportioned, the harms are said to be divisible and each defendant is only liable for the damages caused by him or her.

Defenses: If Ed was negligent, he might assert that B was also negligent by not seeing a doctor immediately, by working all day, and by driving home himself. All of those actions could have aggravated his injury and been a contributing cause of his paralysis. However, it's not clear that B acted unreasonably—he felt only slight pain, was able to work all day, and may have felt perfectly capable of driving home. We need more facts to determine whether B was negligent and thus whether his recovery might be reduced or barred.

Conclusion: More facts will be developed at a trial to help us determine whether Ed was negligent and whether B was negligent.

Answer to Question 11

Peter (P) v. Dan (D) (Negligence, assuming the statute is applicable):

P will sue D for negligence, claiming that D's violation of the Motor Vehicle Code was negligence *per se.* Under this doctrine, if the plaintiff can establish that the statute was intended to cover a class of persons which includes himself, that the statute was designed to guard against the kind of harm he suffered, and that the act which violated the statute was the actual cause of his harm, then the defendant is negligent *per se* (i.e., the circumstances themselves establish the negligence without further proof).

Class of persons: Here, P will probably convince the court that the statute sought to protect users of public roads and that he belonged to that class of persons (this assumes that the definition of "public road" in the statute includes a four-lane street—the term used in our facts).

Particular harm: P will argue that the statute was designed to protect against the particular harm he suffered: the consequences of an accident triggered by obstructed vision caused by a vehicle left unattended on the highway. However, D may be able to convince a court that the statute was really designed to protect against individuals who **voluntarily park** their vehicles on public roads, and not against vehicles left stranded because of a malfunction. Whether P or D will prevail on this point would depend on the wording and interpretation of the statute.

Causal relationship: P will argue that D's violation **actually caused** the harm that P suffered. If D had remained with the van and had not left it unattended in the street, either Vick (V) or P might not have proceeded through the intersection. D would have been able to direct other drivers around the van.

P will also argue that D's violation was the ***proximate cause*** of the harm. P's injury was foreseeable because drivers approaching the intersection would very likely attempt to move past the van into the intersection; otherwise all traffic would have come to a stop. Further, we don't know from the facts whether there was a traffic light at the intersection. On the assumption there was no light, it was foreseeable that other drivers would try to pass the van even if their view of oncoming traffic was obstructed. V's conduct would not be a superseding cause, even if V was negligent because of its foresee-ability. Furthermore, P will argue that his faulty brakes and consequent inability to stop before being hit by V should not be considered a supersed-ing cause because it was foreseeable that individuals with vehicles in less than perfect condition (and thus less able to respond adequately to the risk D created) would approach the vicinity.

P will probably prevail on the issue of causation.

Was D's violation excusable? In some states, the statute would be viewed as establishing a rebuttable presumption of negligence. In other states, the statutory violation establishes negligence *per se*, but the defendant has the right to show that his particular violation was excusable under the circumstances. D would use the same arguments to establish excuse or to rebut a presumption of negligence.

D would offer two excuses for his violation: (1) that he was confronted with an emergency not of his own making (his van's failure to operate), and (2) leaving the van was the lesser of two risks—compliance would have created a greater risk of harm to himself and to others than violation of the statute. If D had remained with the van, he might have been hit by oncoming traffic. Because he was unable to remove the van from the thoroughfare on his own, the only reasonable conduct under the circumstances was to find help.

P would counter that D's conduct was not reasonable or excusable. A police car would undoubtedly have arrived sooner or later and the police would have called for a towing service. In the meantime, they would have directed traffic around the van and through the intersection. Also, they would have put traffic cones or lights in the roadway behind the truck. P might also argue that the driver of a large moving van might reasonably be expected to carry a cell phone to use in emergencies. A properly instructed jury might find that D's arguments would support a finding of excuse or would rebut the presumption of negligence.

Defenses: If P establishes D's negligence *per se* and D's violation is not excused, D will assert a ***contributory negligence*** defense.

D would argue that P was contributorily negligent in proceeding into the intersection when he knew that another vehicle might enter the intersection from behind the van. Apart from the issue of P's faulty brakes, we are not given enough information to determine whether P was negligent. Was he speeding? When did he see the van and V's car?

D would also argue that P was negligent in operating his motorcycle with faulty brakes. Whether P acted reasonably under the circumstances will hinge on additional facts: Did P know prior to the accident that his brakes were faulty? Or did the brakes cease to work suddenly as a result of a mechanical problem? If the former, then P was contributorily negligent and his recovery should be either barred or reduced in proportion to his negligence. If the latter, P may not be contributorily negligent. The effect of a finding of contributory negligence would depend on whether the jurisdiction uses a form of comparative negligence or continues to use the minority view, traditional contributory negligence that bars recovery by a negligent plaintiff.

Conclusion: Based on our conclusion that the statute was not intended to cover D's actions in leaving the van because he did not do so voluntarily, D probably is *not* negligent *per se*. Furthermore, even if D was negligent *per se* within the statutory definition, his violation will probably be excused in light of the emergency.

If D is not negligent *per se*, P will still assert a negligence claim against him but would probably lose (see the following discussion).

P v. D (Negligence, assuming no statute):

Without a statute, the issue of whether D was negligent would again hinge on whether he acted reasonably under the circumstances. Here, the standard of conduct would be what a reasonable person would have done in D's position. P would argue that D failed to act reasonably in leaving his vehicle unattended (i.e., D should have remained by it to alert other drivers as to the hazard). However, D would argue that it was reasonable to leave to search for assistance and remove the road hazard more quickly. D would appear to have the better argument.

P v. V (Negligence):

P would argue that V acted unreasonably under the circumstances by proceeding into an intersection when his view was obstructed, without pausing to "inch out." Because we don't know whether there was a light at the intersection and don't know how fast V was going when he entered the intersection, we can't really determine whether V was negligent. All we know is that the accident probably would not have happened if the van had not obstructed V's view.

Of course, if V had not proceeded into the intersection, he would not have hit P, and it was foreseeable that another driver would be approaching the intersection. The element of causation is present.

Defenses: V will argue that P was negligent. The outcome will be the same here as it was in our earlier discussion (see *P v. D*).

Conclusion: We don't know enough to determine whether V is liable to P in negligence. If P knew of his faulty brakes in advance, P's recovery will be either barred or, in a *comparative negligence* jurisdiction, reduced in proportion to his fault. If P can recover *damages* from V, V will be liable for medical expenses, lost earnings, physical pain, mental distress, and hedonic damages.

Answer to Question 12

Baker (B) v. Acme (A) (Abnormally Dangerous Activity and Negligence):

Abnormally dangerous activity (ADA): Under the doctrine of *Rylands v. Fletcher*, when a defendant is engaged in an ADA, he is strictly liable to all foreseeable plaintiffs who are injured or suffer property damage as a consequence of his actions. The factors to be considered in determining if an activity should be characterized as an ADA include (1) the high degree of risk of serious harm to others; (2) the likelihood that the resulting harm will be great; (3) the likelihood that the risk cannot be eliminated by the exercise of reasonable care; (4) the extent to which the activity is a matter of common usage in the community; (5) whether the activity is appropriate in the place where it is being carried out; and (6) whether the value of the activity to the community outweighs the danger threatened by it. B will contend that blasting with explosives is probably the most inherently dangerous of any ADA, and that he should be able to recover for the personal injuries and property damage which he suffered. A will reply that the activity was carried on in a rural area, that it was appropriate to the place where it was being undertaken, and that the utility of adding additional lanes to a heavily used highway outweighed the risk posed by the blasting, which was necessary to carry out the construction because of the rocky terrain. However, most courts would probably find that A's blasting was subject to strict liability. Even though it was conducted in a rural (and thus presumably less populated) area, it did involve a heavily used highway. This put many drivers at risk. The degree of risk was high, and the harm threatened severe. Many courts impose *per se* liability for the use of explosives, rejecting the multifactor test for identifying abnormally dangerous activities. Whether the *per se* rule or a multifactor analysis is applied, A is likely to be found liable on these facts.

Defenses: A will contend that B's **contributory negligence** (CN) in not observing the sign bars recovery. However, under traditional CN doctrines, a plaintiff's negligence ordinarily does not preclude strict liability recovery, especially where the type of CN exhibited by the plaintiff consisted of being merely inattentive and not discovering a risk he should have discovered. In those circumstances, courts usually place responsibility for preventing the harm that results from abnormally hazardous activities upon the person who has subjected others to the abnormal risk. Under CN doctrines, most courts require a comparison between the conduct of the negligent plaintiff and the strictly liable defendant. The results of that comparison will vary depending on the jurisdiction's use of either the pure or the modified form of CN.

Negligence: B would also assert liability by A under a general negligence theory, contending that A had acted unreasonably in creating a situation which would cause a passing car on a highly traveled highway to activate an explosion. A should not have engaged in blasting on a public highway when cars would be using it and should have recognized that a passing motorist might fail to observe or understand its sign. Further, A failed to realize that the mere posting of a sign would not be enough to instruct drivers on the risk of using a radio. Instead A should have had the state close down the highway during the blasting. At the very least, it should have posted guards or lookouts to stop motorists before they entered the blasting area and ask them to turn off their radios.

B will have to show that A's negligence actually and proximately caused his injuries. Here, had A either not engaged in blasting or closed the highway before blasting, B clearly would not have been injured. A's conduct also proximately caused the injuries because it is foreseeable that drivers might not see the sign or might not see it in time to turn off their radios before entering the zone of danger.

Defenses: A will respond that B was negligent by reason of his failure to observe and conform his conduct to the sign. However, B will argue that a reasonable driver would not have (1) observed the signs (they were posted "at the side of the road" and it's not clear how visible they were to drivers going at the speed permitted on public highways); or (2) understood the sign to apply to two-way radios (rather than AM-FM radios). The effect of B's negligence, if any, would be to bar recovery under contributory negligence doctrines and to bar or reduce it under comparative negligence principles.

Conclusion: B should be able to recover for his personal and property injuries from A under either an ADA or negligence theory.

Charles's (C) Survivors v. B (Negligence):

C's survivors would bring an action under the state's wrongful death statute, seeking recovery for economic support, companionship, and grief.

C's survivors would contend that B had failed to act reasonably under the circumstances by failing to observe and obey A's sign. As we have discussed above, however, this argument would probably ***not*** be successful.

B could also argue that C was not a foreseeable plaintiff (i.e., was not within the zone of danger created by B's negligence, if any) because C (apparently) came upon the scene after the explosion and after B's injury. However, because calamity invites rescue, and under the cases relating to rescuers, C will be considered a foreseeable claimant.

B could also argue that C was negligent in (1) causing his car to swerve off the road, and (2) not wearing his seat belt. His survivors will reply that (1) he lost control of the car in his anxiety and rush to get help for B as soon as possible; (2) his failure to fasten his seat belt did not contribute to the accident; and (3) there is no evidence that C's failure to wear a seat belt contributed in any way to his death. The latter two points are significant because the injured party's negligence must constitute a "but for" cause of, or a substantial factor in, the plaintiff's harm before it will bar or reduce recovery.

Survivors v. A (ADA, Negligence):

C's survivors will bring a wrongful death action against A, asserting that A should be strictly liable on an ADA theory as well as liable on a negligence theory. The strict liability theory will probably be unavailing because the plaintiff must ordinarily show that his injuries were sustained as a consequence of the particular type of risk created by the ADA (here, blasting). C's death was a consequence of his volunteering to help B, not A's ADA.

But C's survivors should be able to recover from A under a negligence theory, as discussed above under *B v. A*, on the grounds that A failed to exercise due care by blasting next to a busy highway. They would argue that A's negligence created the danger to B, which in turn led foreseeably to rescue efforts by someone who had seen the accident to B. Courts generally reach to find liability when a rescuer is injured in helping a person injured by the defendant's negligence.

Answer to Question 13

Mr. Jones, Mrs. Jones, and Joe v. Spelding, Bigstore, and ABC (Strict Liability Theories):

Mr. and Mrs. Jones (Jones) and Joe (J) would each sue Spelding (S), Bigstore (B), and ABC under a products liability (PL) theory. If additional facts would show that the hinges were not made by S, the plaintiffs would also sue the manufacturer of the hinges. Under the PL theory, anyone who manufactures or sells a product that is defective, and thereby unreasonably dangerous, is liable for personal injuries sustained as a result of the defect. PL actions can be based on a negligence theory, a warranty theory, or a strict liability theory. Here, none of the plaintiffs was a purchaser of the ladder, so they will not be able to use the warranty theory. The plaintiffs will be limited to their claims for negligence and strict liability.

Who may be a plaintiff: In general, any person who is the reasonably foreseeable user of a defective product will have standing to sue the ***manufacturer or seller*** under a negligence or a strict liability theory. Here, although J was not a purchaser, he was a reasonably foreseeable user. Most department stores would keep ladders on the premises for use in emergencies, and it was foreseeable that ABC, the purchaser from B, would provide the ladder for any workers who came to do repairs to its building. Jones will also probably have standing to sue, because courts have generally been willing to extend PL protection to bystanders when the defect is reasonably likely to cause injury to them. Here, we are dealing with a department store that apparently occupied its own building, and it was foreseeable that pedestrians would pass along the sidewalk in front of the building. We may conclude that all of the plaintiffs have standing to sue.

Who may be a defendant: Permissible defendants here are the seller, the manufacturer, and, if the hinges were not made by S, the hinges manufacturer. The plaintiffs could not sue ABC because a person or enterprise is not liable as seller unless it sold the defective product in the ordinary course of its business. Because ABC was not in the business of selling ladders and merely loaned the ladder to J, it would ***not*** be a proper defendant on this theory.

Was the product in a defective (i.e., unreasonably dangerous in light of its anticipated use) condition when it left S and B? The plaintiffs would argue that the ladder was unreasonably dangerous because (1) a ladder should be expected to function safely for more than three years; (2) the hinges were not strong enough to withstand ordinary use for more than three years; (3) the warning should have been placed on the ladder itself, and not on the box, which was certain to be discarded; and (4) the warning on the box was inadequate. The plaintiffs would argue that S failed to design the product in a reasonably safe way because the ladder had a structural weakness (the hinges) that made it unreasonably dangerous. The defect would be considered a design defect.

Whether the plaintiffs would prevail on this point would depend on additional facts (what use was the ladder designed and marketed for; what sort of hinges are usually used by other manufacturers in that type of ladder; what is the usual life span of a ladder, etc.). The plaintiffs would argue that S should have affixed some type of metallic warning to the ladder itself as to its limited life span; it should have anticipated that someone would discard the box and neglect or forget to advise subsequent users of the ladder's limited life span. (It should be noted, however, that a warning, however conspicuous, will almost never shield a defendant from liability for a design defect.)

S and B could contend that the ladder was **not** in an unreasonably dangerous condition when it left either of them because the box carrying the item conspicuously stated that its operational life was only three years. The ladder became defective only when the prior manager removed and discarded the box containing the ladder. But both S and B probably should have foreseen that the box would be removed and that the warning would not be seen by subsequent users. Additionally, the term "normal operational life" does not suggest anything about hinges and is arguably too vague to advise a potential user that the hinges might break. Furthermore, if the ladder was defective by virtue of its flimsy hinges, any warning, however conspicuous, would not make the ladder "un-defective." The plaintiffs should prevail on this issue.

Will the plaintiffs recover under either a negligence or a strict liability theory? If the ladder is found defective and unreasonably dangerous, the plaintiffs can probably recover from both S and B. For strict liability, the plaintiffs have to show that the item was manufactured or placed in the stream of commerce by the defendant. Here, S manufactured the ladder, and both S and B placed it in the stream of commerce. The plaintiffs must also show that the product, by virtue of its defect, actually and proximately caused their injuries. Here, if the hinges had not been too weak and the warning inadequate, none of the plaintiffs would have been hurt. Furthermore, as discussed above, all of the plaintiffs were foreseeable.

S and B might contend that ABC's subsequent intervening conduct in discarding the box, failing to maintain a record of the purchase date and probable life span of the ladder, and failing to warn J of the ladder's limited life span, was an unforeseeable factor which extinguished their liability to the plaintiffs.

They would contend furthermore that ABC's conduct was the sort of unforeseeable conduct that no warning could have protected against.

With respect to Mrs. Jones, S and B would contend that while it was foreseeable that a defective ladder might collapse, and even that a person using the ladder might fall on a passerby, it was *not* reasonably foreseeable that someone observing the incident would panic, and, as a consequence, slip and break her ankle. But people frequently act irrationally when exposed to extreme stress, and this contention should fail. Witnessing one's spouse in an accident of this sort would be extremely upsetting to most reasonable people. Whether Mrs. Jones can recover for her injuries will be discussed below.

The plaintiffs must show that the defect existed when the product left the hands of the defendant. Because this was a design defect caused by the defective hinges and the ladder was placed in a box which contained the warning of the defect, it's clear that the defect existed when the product was first sold.

If the ladder is found to be defective, the plaintiffs can probably recover from S on a negligence theory. The plaintiffs would argue that S failed to act with due care in designing a product with weak hinges and by putting a warning about the life span of the ladder on disposable packaging that most people would not retain. Causation would be satisfied, as discussed above.

The plaintiffs may be able to recover from B on a negligence theory, if they can show that B had reason to know that the product was unreasonably dangerous and failed to warn customers of the danger. B will argue that its only notice of any defect was the warning on the box and that did not give it reason to suspect that the hinges were inadequate. However, a court could find that the warning was sufficient to give B notice that the ladder was defective in some way, even if it did not specify that the hinges were bad. A retailer would not reasonably be expected to sell a ladder with a limited life span. Ladders are not expected by the public to survive only three years of use.

Can Mrs. Jones recover for her injuries? In general, a plaintiff can recover from a negligent tortfeasor for mental distress experienced out of fear, as long as the plaintiff was in the zone of danger created by the defendant's conduct. Here, Mrs. Jones was clearly in the zone of danger since she was walking right next to her husband. Thus, at least on a negligence theory, Mrs. Jones could recover for her own injuries. On a strict liability theory, a court would probably also allow Mrs. Jones to recover, since her actions were reasonably foreseeable in response to the event she witnessed, an event caused by the defective ladder.

Conclusion: The plaintiffs can probably recover from S and B (and from the hinge manufacturer, if it is not the same as S) in products liability on a strict liability theory. The plaintiffs can probably recover from S (and the hinge manufacturer) on a negligence theory, and probably from B as well.

Jones and J v. ABC (Negligence):

The plaintiffs will argue that ABC acted unreasonably in failing to advise J that the ladder's life span had been exceeded. (Since he was at ABC's premises for a business purpose, ABC owed J a *duty to remedy* any defect of which it should have been aware.) Additionally, Jones will argue that ABC was negligent in not roping off the area around J and the ladder so that passersby would not be injured by his activities.

Was ABC's negligence the proximate cause of the plaintiffs' harm? The plaintiffs will assert that ABC's failure to warn J *actually and proximately caused* their injuries. If ABC had warned him, he would probably not have used the ladder and no one would have been hurt. Jones will argue that they were foreseeable plaintiffs because ABC should have realized that customers or other passersby would be in the vicinity of the repairs.

ABC will argue that it had no duty to Jones because they were not necessarily customers and were not in the store when they were injured; thus, they were not business invitees to whom ABC owed a duty of inspection. This argument will probably fail, however, because ABC had created the danger to Jones by having J work on the facade of the building with a defective ladder. Furthermore, even if ABC does not own the sidewalk in front of its building, it is probably required under the usual city code to keep that area safe for the public.

ABC will also argue that it did not know that the ladder was unsafe because its former manager had discarded the warning without communicating its contents to Malcolm. However, the former manager's knowledge would be imputed to ABC. Further, under the doctrine of *respondeat superior*, ABC would be responsible for the negligence of its employee.

ABC will try to argue that Mrs. Jones's injury was not proximately caused by its negligence. This argument will probably fail, in accordance with our prior discussion.

Thus, ABC will probably be liable to Jones and to J for negligence.

Damages: The successful plaintiffs would be able to recover for their past and prospective lost income and medical bills, as well as for pain and suffering resulting from the incident. Jones might also be able to recover for loss of consortium for the period during which they were incapacitated.

Indemnification: Both ABC and B (if B is liable) might be able to seek indemnity from S as the manufacturer of the defective ladder and the source of the inadequate warning (and from the hinge manufacturer, if it is separate from S). When a defendant is liable only because it failed to discover another tortfeasor's defect, it is usually entitled to indemnity from that tortfeasor. However, they would not be entitled to indemnity if the court found that they should have known of the defect by virtue of the warning on the box and if they had been independently negligent by not keeping an adequate record of the life span of the ladder and failing to notify others of its defect. ABC might also be entitled to indemnity from its former manager.

Answer to Question 14

White and Green v. Manufacturer and Black (Products Liability):

White (W) and Green (G) will contend that the electronic oven manufacturer (M) and Black (B) are liable to them on the basis of products liability (PL). Under a PL theory, both the manufacturer and the seller of a product that is **defective** and thereby unreasonably dangerous are liable for any personal injuries caused by the defect. PL actions can be based on strict liability, negligence, or express or implied warranty. This answer will analyze the plaintiffs' claim on each of these theories.

W and G v. M and B (Strict Liability):

The plaintiffs have to show that a defective product was manufactured or sold by the defendants. Here, while it is clear that M made the oven, B will try to avoid liability on the grounds that it was merely a lessor, not a seller. However, many courts have extended strict liability to lessors of defective products (for example, car rental companies).

The plaintiffs must also show the existence of the defect. When a product contains a nonobvious defect threatening personal injury, the defendant will still be liable if he does not warn about that risk even though the product may be properly manufactured and designed. Here, the plaintiffs will argue that the oven should have been accompanied by a permanently affixed label warning about the nonobvious dangers of using metal cookware in it.

The plaintiffs also must show causation. Here, if M had used a warning label that was permanently attached to the product itself and could not be removed, W probably would not have put a tin plate inside it. If she had, her own conduct would be deemed unreasonable. Although M will try to argue that B's neglect in failing to give W the manual which contained the warning is a superseding cause that should relieve it of liability, a court could find that B's conduct was reasonably foreseeable, and that M should have taken measures to safeguard against just such neglect. M and B will try to avoid liability to G on the theory that he was not a reasonably foreseeable plaintiff—he was not the intended user or consumer of the product; however, a court would probably find it reasonably foreseeable that an oven would be purchased for restaurant use, and that it was therefore somewhat foreseeable that a customer of the restaurant would be exposed to its risks.

The plaintiffs must also show that the product was defective when it left the hands of the defendants. This is clearly the case with respect to B, who had neglected to deliver the manual, but M will contend that the oven was not defective (i.e., unreasonably dangerous) when it left its hands, because it was sold with a manual which clearly warned of the risk. However, because there was a reasonable possibility that a vendor might fail to deliver the manual to a purchaser of the oven, the oven would probably be considered defective when it left M without adequate marking on the oven itself. Furthermore, if the risks associated with use of a metal object in the oven could have been reduced at reasonable cost, use of a warning instead of implementing that risk reduction would render the product "unreasonably dangerous."

Defenses: M and B would try to defend on the grounds that W misused the oven (i.e., by putting a metal plate in it). They will argue that the risk associated with using metal in electronic ovens is well known and should be considered obvious. But a court would probably find that awareness of such a risk requires special knowledge, and that it was reasonably foreseeable that a particular consumer or user would not have that special knowledge. Furthermore, when misuse of a product is reasonably foreseeable (as it was here), the defendant will be held responsible to take reasonable precautions to protect against the misuse. The court is likely to find that M's warning was inadequate because it was not attached to the product and could be easily separated, as indeed it was. The product was defective and unreasonably dangerous as used, and the defendants should be liable.

W and G v. M and B (Negligence):

The plaintiffs would argue that M failed to act reasonably by neglecting to attach a permanent warning about the dangers associated with using metal cookware in the electronic oven to the oven itself. The plaintiffs would also argue that B did not act reasonably by failing to deliver the manual to W along with the oven.

M would argue that B's negligence was a superseding cause and that M's conduct was *not a proximate cause* of the plaintiffs' harm; however, as stated above, B's negligence was foreseeable and the chain of proximate causation was not broken. M and B will both try to argue that G was an unforeseeable plaintiff; they will fail in this argument because it was foreseeable that the oven would be used in W's restaurant, and that, if it was used improperly, impulses would escape and injure W's customers.

If the defendants invoke the defense of contributory or comparative negligence, the plaintiffs will respond in the same way as in the case of strict liability, and with the same result. M and B are probably liable to the plaintiffs on a negligence theory.

W and G v. M (Express Warranty):

W and G will also sue M under an express warranty theory. The plaintiffs will have to show that M made a statement about the oven that turned out not to be true, that this statement formed part of the basis of their bargain, and that the plaintiffs were part of the class to whom the statement was addressed. Here, the plaintiffs will base their claim on the statement the oven "could be used with your own cookware." (They are less likely to base their claim on the statement that the oven was the "best and safest on the market," because M can probably argue successfully that the statement was clearly "puffery" and opinion.) The plaintiffs will argue that the statement they relied on was clearly not true—the oven was not able to accommodate W's cookware. The plaintiffs do not have to show reliance or even privity to recover for breach of an express warranty. W will show that the statement formed part of the basis of the bargain (i.e., was part of her understanding of what she was getting when she purchased the oven). But a plaintiff without privity such as G will not be required to show that the statement was addressed to him or that he was aware of the statement. When express warranties are addressed to the public at large, remote buyers, users, or even passersby are often deemed part of the general class to which the warranty was addressed. Thus, both W and G can recover from M on this theory.

W and G v. B (Implied Warranty of Merchantability):

W and G will also sue B for a breach of the implied warranty of merchantability. The UCC establishes an implied warranty in the sale of goods by a merchant that the goods will be fit for the ordinary purposes for which they are used. B will argue that this doctrine has traditionally been limited to claims against vendors (rather than lessors) and that most courts have required privity between the plaintiff and defendant. However, many courts have extended the implied warranty to lessors of goods. Whether G, a bystander, can utilize this theory will depend on whether he can successfully argue that he should be considered a nonpurchaser user and on the specific UCC provision the state has adopted.

B will argue that the oven was fit for ordinary use, and that W misused the product by putting metal plates in it. However, to be "merchantable," goods must be adequately labeled. Here, the oven was not labeled at all. It did not warn of the dangerous use of metal cookware. The warning on the manual was not sufficient to satisfy the requirements of a reasonable warning label because it could become separated from the oven.

Thus, W can recover from B on an implied warranty theory. It is less clear whether G will be able to recover from B on this theory.

Damages: Whether on strict liability, negligence, or implied warranty, the plaintiffs can recover for their personal injuries. W can also recover for her property damage on all of the theories. W can probably recover damages for her lost business while the diner was closed (i.e., intangible economic harm) only on the warranty theory. In her negligence claim, she may be able to recover for her intangible economic harm if it is treated as a consequence of her physical injury.

W and G v. M (Misrepresentation):

W and G can sue M in a misrepresentation action. A seller of goods who makes any misrepresentation on the label or in public advertising will be strictly liable for any physical injury that results, even if the injured person did not buy the product from the defendant and even when the misrepresentation was not intentional or negligent. This cause of action is very similar to the breach of express warranty claim discussed above. G can use this cause of action if the jurisdiction is one with stricter than average privity or reliance requirements in express warranty claims. If W asserted this cause of action, she would be limited to her physical injuries and would not be able to recover for her property damage or her lost business.

G v. W (Negligence):

G might sue W for negligence, asserting that W did not act reasonably under the circumstances by putting a tin plate into the oven, and that this conduct imposed an unreasonable risk on nearby customers. G would argue that W had a **duty** to him as a business invitee to inspect her premises for hidden dangers, and that W **breached that duty**. G will argue that but for W's negligence, he would not have been hurt, and that W's negligence was the proximate cause of his injuries.

G may not recover from W, however, because W may convince the court that she did not breach her duty to G. She will argue that this was the first time she had occasion to use this oven and that she was not aware that it was dangerous to use metal in it. Thus, she acted reasonably under the circumstances. However, G will argue that it's not reasonable to use an electronic oven without having read the manual describing its use.

Answer to Question 15

This answer will discuss Nerv's claims first, and Jane's claims second.

Nerv (N) v. Drugco (D) (Products Liability):

N will bring a products liability claim against D, based on strict liability and warranty.

Strict liability: In strict liability, N will allege that Dreamy was **defective and unreasonably dangerous**, and that D should be strictly liable as a result. The law concerning medical devices and prescription drugs has been in a state of constant change and development. The basic problem in the case of drugs is that they are of high social utility but can produce serious, unavoidable side effects. Assuming approval by the FDA and adequate labeling, the courts are loath to find liability against the manufacturer. Drugs are different from other products in that their risk cannot be measured equally in all persons—a drug which will cure one person may be dangerous to another. The Third Restatement says that a defective design claim will be successful only if the foreseeable risks of harm are sufficiently great that reasonable health providers would not prescribe the drug for *any* class of patients. These facts raise the "unavoidably unsafe" issue. D will argue that there was no way for it to know the danger which Dreamy created for a few people. Because it did not know the danger, there was no way for it to design around it. Under the circumstances, most courts will not hold the manufacturer liable. The Third Restatement agrees that an unknowable danger does not create a "foreseeable risk of harm."

Express warranty: N may try to sue D for having **breached** an express warranty that Dreamy was "safe for adult use." N would have to show that D's statement about Dreamy was not true, that the statement formed part of the basis of the bargain, and that N was part of the class of persons to whom the statement was addressed. N could easily show that his reliance on the statement was part of the reason he purchased the product, and that as a consumer he was part of the class of persons to whom the statement was addressed. N may, however, have trouble convincing a court that the statement was known by D to be untrue. We are told that D only learned of the dizziness reaction after Dreamy was introduced to the market. D would also point to the context of the statement (the words "safe for adult use" preceded the words "not habit-forming"). This showed that D was not warranting that the product was absolutely safe from all possible reactions, but merely that it was safe in that it was nonaddictive. Nothing in the facts indicates that this is not true. D will probably prevail on this issue.

Implied warranty: N could also sue D for breach of an implied warranty of merchantability.

A breach of the ***implied warranty of merchantability*** occurs when a product which is sold by a merchant is not reasonably fit for the ordinary purposes for which the item is used. N would contend that the Dreamy pills which N sold were not reasonably fit, because dizziness resulted from their use and because the label did not warn of dizziness. D could respond, however, that Dreamy was "reasonably fit" when viewed in light of the small proportion of users who would suffer an allergic reaction to it. Courts are likely to hold that when a product is unavoidably ***unsafe but highly beneficial***, it is inequitable to hold the manufacturer liable on a warranty of merchantability theory when the manufacturer has not been negligent.

N v. Phil (P) (Products Liability):

N would bring a products liability suit against P as the vendor of Dreamy. He could base his suit on a strict liability theory or on a warranty theory.

Strict liability: Same result as above (*N v. D*).

Implied warranty: N could sue P for both a breach of an implied warranty of merchantability and for breach of an ***implied warranty of fitness for a particular purpose***.

On the warranty of merchantability theory, N would probably lose for the same reasons cited above with respect to D. Indeed, a court would be even less likely to find P liable, since he was not in as good a position as D to discover the hidden dangers of Dreamy.

The warranty of fitness for a particular purpose arises when the seller of a product has reason to know of the particular purpose for which the product is required by the buyer and that the buyer is relying upon the seller's skill or judgment in selecting it. Here, N described the purpose for which he desired the drug to P, and he selected Dreamy based upon P's recommendation. However, as noted above, Dreamy probably was fit for N's particular purpose; nothing in the facts indicates that it did not calm N as it was intended to. Furthermore, as above, a court might hesitate to impose liability on P when all the available information did not reveal that the drug would cause an allergic reaction.

Conclusion: N probably cannot recover for his injuries from either D or P, unless additional facts indicate that D had negligently conducted its testing.

Jane (J) v. N (Negligence):

J could assert a negligence action against N, based upon the claim that N had failed to act reasonably by driving after taking a tranquilizer without having previously determined if the drug could have an adverse effect upon him. It is relatively common knowledge that tranquilizers sometimes produce unexpected side effects, such as drowsiness. Whether J will prevail on this issue may hinge on additional facts, such as whether Dreamy bore the warning typically found on tranquilizers to the effect that people should not operate machinery after taking the drug. If N had already begun to experience drowsiness before getting behind the wheel, a court could find that he *failed to exercise due care*. There may also be a relevant statute in effect in this jurisdiction prohibiting a person from driving while under the influence of tranquilizers. N's violation of this statute would mean that he was negligent *per se*, and thus liable, unless he could somehow show that his violation was excused. However, in the absence of these additional facts, N could probably successfully contend that because the label on the bottle stated that it was "safe for adult use," he could reasonably conclude that it was safe for him to drive immediately after taking Dreamy.

Thus, whether J can recover from N may depend on additional facts.

J v. D (Products Liability):

J will probably not be able to recover from D on a strict liability or a warranty theory for the reasons discussed above under *N v. D*. Furthermore, even if D were found liable to N, D could probably convince a court that it should not be liable to J, because she was a *bystander* whose injury was not reasonably foreseeable. This is different from a case involving a defective car, for example. If a car is defective, it is reasonably foreseeable that a bystander will be injured as a result of the defect and the risk that the car will malfunction. The risk posed by the defect in Dreamy was that a user would become dizzy. Nothing D did created the risk of dizziness in J. To impose liability on D for J's injuries would be to impose a rule under which a defendant would be liable for all consequences of its conduct, no matter how far-reaching. This result runs directly counter to the principles that underlie proximate cause.

Answer to Question 16

Gloria (G) v. Tintco (T) (Products Liability):

G should sue T in products liability for breach of an express warranty, breach of the implied warranty of merchantability, and misrepresentation. If she asserted a claim for strict liability, her measure of damages as a frustrated beauty contestant would not be as favorable to her (i.e., she could not recover damages for intangible economic harm) as in these other actions. Also, she probably should not rely on a claim in negligence because the facts do not suggest that T was negligent in testing Tint and because the measure of damages might not be as favorable.

Breach of express warranty: G would sue T for having breached its express warranty that Tint was safe and wholesome, as represented by its publication of the Mag Seal of Approval on the Tint labels. G would have to show that this warranty was not true, that the warranty formed part of the basis of the bargain, and that she was part of the class of persons to whom it was addressed. G would argue that Tint was not safe and wholesome because it caused her hair to turn purple when it came in contact with the scalp medicine she used. Women often use a hair coloring product in combination with other hair products, and it was therefore foreseeable that users of Tint might also use other hair products. A hair coloring product cannot be considered "safe" unless it can be used in conjunction with other hair products without causing injury. G would show that the Seal of Approval was part of the reason she purchased Tint, and that as a purchaser, she was clearly within the class of persons whom the label's warranty was intended to reach.

T will respond that by using the Seal of Approval, it was warranting only that Tint was safe and wholesome when used by itself and not that Tint was free from all possible inter-reaction with other products. T will insist that its warranty was true because Tint does not turn hair purple when used alone. T will also argue that because Balm is only infrequently prescribed, Tint's reaction with Balm could not possibly have been foreseen. We may need additional facts to resolve this issue: What percentage of Tint users experienced hair discoloration, with or without Balm? How frequently was Balm prescribed? When Balm was prescribed, was there an accompanying warning that it not be used with any hair coloring? Was there any industry research on the relationship between hair coloring products and Balm? Between hair coloring products and other scalp medicines?

Breach of implied warranty of merchantability: When the seller of an item is a merchant, there is an implied warranty of merchantability that the product will be reasonably fit for the ordinary purposes for which it is used.

Furthermore, to be merchantable, a product must be adequately packaged and labeled and must conform to any promises or statements of fact that are on the label. Although T is not a retailer and therefore not a "merchant" in the traditional sense, most states have extended the implied warranty of merchantability to manufacturers and hold that the warranty extends to remote purchasers.

Here, G would argue that Tint was not merchantable because (1) it was not adequately labeled to warn of possible inter-reactions with other scalp products, and (2) it did not conform to the label's promise (i.e., the Mag Seal of Approval) that the product was safe and wholesome. Her arguments as to safety and wholesomeness would be the same as expressed above (express warranty).

T will argue that Tint was fit for its ordinary purpose: coloring hair. T will also argue that Tint was adequately labeled because T did not, and could not be expected to, know of the specific reaction with Balm. Whether T will prevail on this point will depend on whether T's testing was adequate (the facts do not suggest that T was negligent in the testing or production of Tint) and on whether the Tint label bore any other warnings or disclaimers about possible inter-reactions with other products. T will make the same arguments with respect to safety and wholesomeness as above (express warranty).

Thus, whether G will prevail on an implied warranty theory will depend on additional facts.

Misrepresentation: G could sue T in an action for misrepresentation. A seller of goods who makes any misrepresentation on a product label or in public advertising will be strictly liable for any physical injury that results. This cause of action would be very similar to the express warranty claim discussed above, but has the disadvantage for G of not permitting damages for intangible economic harm (see Damages below). A claim for misrepresentation may be more effective than a claim for express warranty or for implied warranty, however, if the jurisdiction is one with stricter than typical privity requirements for an implied warranty action or stricter reliance requirements for a claim in express warranty.

Damages: If G prevails in an action based on a breach of an express or implied warranty, she will be able to recover damages for her physical injury (the continued discoloration of her hair), her emotional distress resulting from the injury (humiliation because of disfigurement), and her economic loss. Economic loss would include (1) medical expenses (i.e., if she consults a doctor for advice and treatment), (2) lost income (i.e., if she is unable to work due to the discoloration), and (3) lost profits caused by G's with-drawal from the beauty contest she was favored to win (i.e., the prize money and, possibly, contracts for product endorsements and public appearances that usually go to a beauty contest winner). Because she would be consid-ered a remote purchaser, G will be more likely to recover these lost profits, which are usually considered an intangible economic loss, under an express warranty claim than under an implied warranty claim, especially if the court decided that the discoloration did not constitute physical injury (an unlikely finding).

G v. Mag (M) (Express Warranty, Negligent Misrepresentation):

G would probably sue M for breach of an express warranty and negligent misrepresentation.

Express warranty: The essence of G's claim against M on this theory would be the same as expressed above (*G v. T*, Express Warranty). M would try to argue that it was not properly a defendant, because it neither manufactured nor sold Tint. However, some courts have found endorsers liable if the plaintiff can show that the endorser issued a representation as to the quality of a product and that the representation was not true. On these facts, M held itself out to be an endorser of products. It operated a laboratory specifically for the testing of products. It represented to the public by issuing its seal that it had tested a particular product and that it was safe. Whether G can recover against M will depend on the scope and reasonableness of M's tests and whether it was reasonably justified in stating that Tint was safe and whole-some.

If M is liable in express warranty, G's measure of damages will be as above (Damages).

Negligent misrepresentation: G will try to sue M for negligent misrepre-sentation. She would have to show that M's statement (embodied and implicit in its Seal of Approval) was not true and that she relied justifiably on the misrepresentation. G will also have to show that M made the misrepresentation in the course of its business and that it had a pecuniary interest in the transaction. Here, a substantial part of M's business presum-ably consists of selling advertising space, and its Seal of Approval is a way to attract advertisers. Even if M did not receive direct pecuniary compensation from T for the use of its seal on the Tint label, the seal both encouraged (and possibly obligated) T to advertise in M's magazine and functioned as advertising for the magazine itself.

Liability for negligent misrepresentation is usually limited to persons whom the defendant intends to reach or whom he knows the recipient intends to reach. Here, M obviously intended its seal to reach the customers of its advertisers and therefore G should be included in the group that M intends to reach.

Recovery for intangible economic interests is permitted to a successful negligent misrepresentation plaintiff. The requirements are the same as for an action in deceit. M should be liable to G for reliance damages and for her consequential damages (i.e., her physical injury and lost profits).

Answer to Question 17

Black (B) v. Alan (A) (Conversion):

B would sue A for conversion (the intentional exercise of substantial dominion and control over a chattel belonging to another). The control must be sufficient to constitute sufficient interference with the plaintiff's possession so that it becomes fair to require the defendant to pay full value for the plaintiff's property. A fine line is drawn between conversion and trespass to chattels. In the latter case, there is no forced sale of the property from plaintiff to defendant—the defendant only pays actual damages. B would contend that a conversion occurred when A removed the flashlight from his store and then eluded B when B demanded return of the item. B would contend that A is liable to him for the reasonable (forced sale) value of the flashlight. It's not clear, however, whether A had the intent necessary to constitute conversion. Because we know that A tried to return the flashlight when he learned that the sign referred to brochures and not to flashlights, we have to assume that he made an innocent mistake. However, an innocent mistake does not normally negate the intent to commit conversion, but it is a factor in considering the severity of the interference with the plaintiff's property.

A would assert the ***defense of consent***, arguing that B consented to his removing the flashlight by means of the wall sign just above the box of flashlights. If it was reasonable for A to conclude that B had consented to A's removal of the flashlight, consent will be established regardless of B's intent in placing the sign where he did. Assuming it was not clear to A that B was the owner of the store, A could explain that he ran away from B because he assumed that the person shouting at him was either a passerby who mistakenly thought A had stolen the flashlight or a store employee who did not know that the flashlights were being given away as a promotional offer. A would argue that B's behavior made him apprehensive and embarrassed, and that he wanted to avoid becoming involved in an altercation with B. However, the flashlights were not in fact free, and B did not in fact consent to A's conversion. Mistake as to ownership is not a defense to conversion. Moreover, it's not reasonable to conclude that a merchant would give away modern LED flashlights. A would be expected to have inquired of B whether the flashlights were in fact giveaways. Also, it was not reasonable for A to run away from B. On all the facts, it seems unlikely that a court would allow the defense of consent.

A would next argue that since he offered to return the flashlight (which was still presumably in good condition) he did not have the intent necessary for conversion and should be liable only for the tort of ***trespass to chattels***.

Under this tort, the owner of the item is only entitled to recover his actual damages (i.e., in this instance, probably at most the reasonable rental value of the flashlight). An important question is whether the flashlight was in the same condition when A offered to return it as when he took it from the store. If it was, then B's damages will be measured at that time. Because title to the article never leaves the owner in a trespass to chattels, B should have accepted the return of the flashlight. A's right to tender the flashlight will continue until the trial.

A v. B (Assault, Defamation):

Assault: An assault occurs when the defendant intentionally causes the plaintiff to be in reasonable apprehension of an imminent, offensive touching. A would contend that the assault occurred when B rushed after him in his attempt to repossess the flashlight. B would argue that (1) he was never able to get close enough to A to touch him, and, therefore, A was never reasonably apprehensive of an imminent contact, and (2) under both (i) the storekeeper's privilege (a store owner ordinarily has the right to detain a customer if he reasonably believes that the customer has unlawfully taken an item, provided the restraint is conducted in a reasonable manner and for no longer than is necessary to determine if the storekeeper's suspicions are correct) and (ii) the right to recapture one's chattels (when the defendant is in hot pursuit of an item which was unlawfully taken from him, the defendant may use reasonable force to reclaim the items), his actions were privileged. Since B had a reasonable basis for believing that A had stolen a flashlight, both defenses would be successful, unless the court holds that the privilege to detain does not extend to the premises surrounding the store.

Defamation: The torts of libel and slander are called the torts of defamation. A must show that B made a **defamatory statement** (a statement that was false and tended to harm A's reputation) about him, that he communicated that statement to others, and, in some circumstances, that B was at least negligent in making the statement. Libel is a defamatory statement reduced to written or printed form. Because this case involves an oral rather than a written statement, A will sue for slander rather than libel. A will argue that B's statement was false—he had not stolen the flashlight (i.e., he believed the flashlight was free and thus did not have the **mens rea** required to commit a theft) and therefore he was not a thief. A will also argue that accusations of criminal behavior clearly tend to lower one's reputation. Although B did not specifically refer to A by name, it was apparent from the context that the people present (the street was crowded) would recognize that B's statements were directed to A.

Were B's statements slanderous per se? In a slander action, the plaintiff must ordinarily show some special harm, usually monetary loss, as a direct consequence of the defendant's statements. However, when the words suggest the commission of a crime of moral turpitude, they are ***slanderous per se*** and special harm is presumed. Calling one a "thief" would satisfy the ***per se*** standard, and therefore it will not be necessary for A to prove special harm to recover for the humiliation and embarrassment he may have suffered as a consequence of B's remarks.

Defenses: Depending on the jurisdiction, B may be able to argue that he did not act with the state of mind necessary for slander. In general, in the case of private citizens like A, the plaintiff has to show either that the defendant knew the statement was false or that he acted negligently in not determining that it was false. A will not be able to satisfy these obstacles: B could not have known that his accusation was false, and he had every reason to believe that it was true. A person who observed A's actions would reasonably have concluded that A had stolen the flashlight.

B will also assert that his statement was covered by the qualified privilege extended to property owners to protect their property from theft. If a property owner reasonably suspects that someone has stolen his property, he has the qualified privilege (he may not act maliciously) to report his suspicions to the police and identify the suspect. B will argue that this privilege entitled him to try to stop A by calling out to the crowd that A was a thief.

A will argue that B lost this privilege by acting recklessly and spreading the defamation more widely than necessary. A will argue that B could have protected his interests by calling out to him and asking him some simple questions without accusing him of theft.

Damages: A would seek to recover for the humiliation and embarrassment caused him by B's accusation. (The damages would appear to be nominal because there is no indication that anyone in the crowd knew A.) Punitive damages are unlikely because B responded spontaneously and reasonably to what appeared to him to be the theft of a flashlight.

Carl (C) v. B (False Imprisonment, Defamation):

False imprisonment: C would assert a claim for false imprisonment against B. False imprisonment occurs when the defendant intentionally confines the plaintiff to a definable area from which there is no reasonably apparent means of escape. In this case, this tort occurred when B locked Carl in the restroom. Because an intentional tortfeasor is liable for all of the consequences of his actions, B would also be liable for the broken leg which C suffered in attempting to escape from the restroom.

B would initially assert the shopkeeper's privilege to protect his property (described above). However, the incident involving C occurred later that day and there was no reason to suspect that C had the flashlight in his possession. Further, the restraint imposed upon C was not reasonable under the circumstances, even if we assume that he did bear a sufficiently close resemblance to A to create a reasonable belief that he was A. B would not have been justified to restrain A in a locked restroom after the initial incident involving A. When exercising the shopkeeper's privilege, a defendant is liable for any physical harm sustained by the plaintiff. B would be liable for C's injuries.

B will argue that C caused or contributed to his injury by attempting to climb out of the bathroom window when he could see that the window was out of reach. In effect, B would be arguing that C was contributorily negligent. The plaintiff's negligence is no defense to an intentional tort in traditional contributory negligence jurisdictions. Under comparative fault principles in most jurisdictions, a plaintiff's negligence may bar or reduce recovery even against an intentional tortfeasor, depending on the form of comparative negligence adopted in the jurisdiction.

Defamation: It's not clear from the facts whether B made a statement to the police accusing C of theft. If B did make this statement, then C could try to sue B for defamation, as in the case of A above (*A v. B*).

Answer to Question 18

Peter (P) v. Jim (J) (Trespass to Chattels, Negligence):

Trespass to chattels: P will try to recover from J on a trespass to chattels claim, asserting that J intentionally interfered with his use of his wallet by failing to tell him that he had left the wallet on the counter. However, the facts do not suggest that J intended to interfere with P's use of his wallet. On the contrary, they speak only of J's "neglect." P will be limited to an action in negligence, if any.

Negligence:

Did J have a duty to advise P that he had left his wallet? In general, anyone who maintains business premises must furnish warnings and assistance to his business visitors, whatever the source of danger or harm. Here, P will argue that J had a duty to warn P that he had forgotten his wallet and to return it to him. A customer might reasonably expect that the owner of a business would return a wallet to him if he saw it lying on the cashier's counter. Whether J breached his duty will depend on additional facts: how busy the restaurant was; whether J was on the phone or in the middle of talking to a customer; whether J knew whose wallet it was; whether J was acting as cashier; whether P was headed out the door or was still in the restaurant; and so on.

Assuming J had a duty, was his inaction the actual cause of P's injuries and losses? In general, a person is not liable for harm to another for a failure to act. J is potentially liable here only because he maintained business premises and P was his business visitor. But even under these circumstances, J's conduct is required to be the "but for" cause of the plaintiff's harm. J can be expected to argue that David's conduct and Busco's negligence were the actual causes of P's harm. P should be successful in his argument that the entire incident would have been avoided had J not neglected to advise P that he had forgotten his wallet.

Was J's conduct the proximate cause of P's injuries and loss? When an unforeseeable intervening cause contributes to the plaintiff's harm, some jurisdictions hold that the defendant's conduct is not the proximate cause of the plaintiff's injuries. J will contend that while it may be foreseeable that someone would steal P's wallet from the counter, it was not foreseeable that the loss of the wallet would result in the events which followed (that P would run after D, that P would skin his knee, that D would throw the wallet at P, that the wallet would fall out of the bus, and that it would ultimately disappear). However, P would probably argue successfully that these events were indeed foreseeable. One hundred dollars may have represented a large sum to P—large enough to force him to take every reasonable measure to recover the wallet.

Defenses: J would argue that P was negligent in forgetting to take his wallet as he left the cash register. J would assert that P did not exercise due care and that this failure to act reasonably under the circumstances was the proximate cause of the harm P suffered. A court would probably find that P was contributorily negligent and that his negligence was the proximate cause of his loss. In a comparative negligence jurisdiction, P's negligence would reduce or bar recovery depending on the form of comparative negligence adopted in the jurisdiction.

P v. David (D) (Conversion, Trespass to Chattels, Assault, Battery):

Conversion and trespass to chattels: Conversion and trespass to chattels are both torts based on one person's intentional interference with another's property interest. The difference between the two relates to the degree of interference. In conversion, the interference must be sufficiently great as to make it fair for the defendant to pay for the full value of the property (resulting, in effect, in a forced sale). Here, although D acted in good faith when he took the wallet thinking it was his own, and though he attempted to return the wallet to P within a matter of minutes and as soon as he realized it was not his own, a court could still find that this was a conversion rather than a trespass. Because D threw the wallet at P instead of handing it to him and caused the wallet to fly out of the bus, D's conduct can be considered so substantial an interference with P's property interest as to impose liability for conversion on D and require him to reimburse P for the full value of the wallet and its contents.

Assault and battery: P will argue that by throwing the wallet at him, D committed an assault by intentionally causing him to be in apprehension of an imminent offensive contact. P will also argue that D committed a battery (the intentional infliction of offensive bodily contact) when the wallet actually hit him. While D may contend that he was acting in self-defense (i.e., he reasonably believed that P was about to cause an offensive contact upon him, and exercised reasonable force to prevent the contact), the facts do not indicate that P was in close physical proximity to D when the wallet was thrown, or that D had reasonable grounds to believe that P would actually strike him. On the contrary, P was "working his way" around other passengers and D probably had plenty of time to talk to P and offer him the wallet without throwing it. This defense should be unsuccessful.

P will recover nominal damages, damages for mental distress caused by the assault and battery, damages for any physical injury resulting from being hit in the face by the wallet, and possibly punitive damages, but only if a court finds that D's actions were particularly outrageous.

P v. Busco (B) (Negligence):

P will sue B for negligence for the injuries he suffered in his altercation with D. (It does not appear from the facts that the bus driver failed to exercise due care when P attempted to board the bus. On the contrary, it would appear that P boarded the bus only as it started to move. P probably cannot recover from B for his skinned knee.) P will argue that as a common carrier, B has a special relationship with its passengers and must take affirmative actions to protect them. Courts have held that bus companies have a ***duty*** to use the utmost care to protect passengers from assaults. Passengers have no control over who is on the bus and depend upon the driver to either get help or provide an escape. This duty means that a bus driver cannot simply stand by when passengers are in danger; instead, he must either warn a violent passenger to stop his behavior, stop the bus, or contact the police. P would assert that B breached this special duty by failing to assist P in any way. The driver should have stopped the bus when D began shouting "Stop, thief!" D's shouting—which we assume the driver heard—should have warned the driver that a fight between accuser and accused was imminent. If he had stopped, the altercation between P and D might never have occurred and the wallet might not have been lost. Because the driver's negligence is imputed to B under the doctrine of ***respondeat superior***, B will be liable to P for P's injuries to his face, his mental distress, and, probably, for the lost wallet.

D v. P (Defamation):

D would bring a defamation action against P for slander based on P's shouting "Stop, thief!" at D on a crowded bus. D has to show that P made a false ***defamatory statement*** (i.e., a statement tending to lessen his reputation) about him and that P communicated the statement to others. These elements appear to be satisfied. In some jurisdictions, D would also have to show that P acted at least negligently in making the statement. Here, D would argue that because P knew that he had originally made the mistake of leaving the wallet on the counter, he should have realized that another customer might make the innocent mistake of picking the wallet up thinking it was his own. He was at fault in jumping to the conclusion that D had stolen it. D would argue P was at least negligent, if not reckless, in assuming the wallet was stolen and in shouting out accusations of theft before giving D a chance to explain his actions or return the wallet. Although the plaintiff must ordinarily prove that he suffered some special harm (usually pecuniary) in a slander action, that requirement is deemed met where the defamatory statement is an accusation of criminal behavior.

P could assert the *qualified privilege of protection of property*. Under this doctrine, when one believes that another person has stolen his property and makes a statement identifying that person in order to obtain the return of his property, the statement is privileged. Since P reasonably believed that D had deliberately taken his wallet, P's statement was part of his effort to reclaim his property and was thus privileged.

D will argue, however, that P's statement was excessive (i.e., it resulted in advising more persons than reasonably necessary under the circumstances to protect P's interests). P did not have to yell across the bus (he could have made his way to D and confronted him face-to-face). Assuming D was not about to leave the bus, it may have been unnecessary to shout out that D was a thief.

D's recovery in defamation, if any, would appear to be nominal. Punitive damages would not be assessed under these circumstances because D has not sustained the requisite special harm.

Answer to Question 19

Zoe (Z) v. Resco (R) (Abnormally Dangerous Activity (ADA), Private Nuisance, Defamation, Fraud, Negligent Misrepresentation):

Abnormally dangerous activity: A defendant who has engaged in an ADA is liable for all personal injury and property damage resulting to the plaintiff from the activity. In determining if the conduct should be characterized as ADA, the courts will ordinarily weigh (1) whether there is a high degree of risk of some harm to others, (2) whether it is likely the harm will be great, (3) whether the risk can be eliminated by the exercise of due care, (4) whether the activity is a matter of common usage in the locale, (5) whether the value of the activity to the community is outweighed by its danger, and (6) whether the activity is appropriate in the place in which it is conducted. Z would argue that the risk involved here was very high (loss of all infected or exposed cattle in an area devoted to dairy farming), that the risk obviously could not be eliminated through the exercise of due care, that R's virus experimentation was highly inappropriate to the area because the cattle and dairy industries were its principal economic activities, and that the value of the activity to the community, although potentially great, was outweighed by the risk it posed and the losses it threatened.

R will contend that (1) experimentation on cattle diseases is vital to an area which has a thriving cattle and dairy industry, and (2) the activity was not dangerous to cattle or anything else when it was started 20 years before in a building in what was then an unsettled area. For these reasons, its experimentation should *not* be characterized as ADA. But Z will argue that R was indeed involved in ADA: (1) the risk to cattle is obviously one that could not be eliminated with due care, as shown by the fact that the virus escaped without negligence by R; and (2) the experimentation entailed a great risk to surrounding livestock, as evidenced by the fact that it was necessary to slaughter all cattle infected by or exposed to the virus. In light of the serious losses involved to an industry so vital to the community, and because R's experimentation could easily have been moved somewhere else, R will probably be liable for ADA.

R will argue that Z was negligent by establishing a cattle auction in proximity to R's plant. But even if Z was negligent (discussed below), the effect of his negligence will depend on whether the jurisdiction is a traditional contributory negligence jurisdiction or has adopted a form of comparative negligence. Under traditional contributory negligence, a plaintiff's negligence would not bar strict liability recovery. Under comparative negligence, it may reduce or bar recovery depending on the form of comparative negligence adopted in the jurisdiction.

Whether R will be liable for the harm that Z suffered will depend on whether the harm resulted from the kind of risk that made R's activity abnormally dangerous. The risk was that the virus would escape and infect cattle in the surrounding area. Z owned no cattle so it may be argued that the harm to him was not the kind of risk within R's ADA. But Z will argue that all injury to persons dependent on the cattle for their livelihood should be included within the scope of the risk even though they owned no cattle. R will respond that its liability should extend only to the owners of the infected cattle, not to persons with remote and intangible economic harm such as Z. Whether R or Z will prevail on this point will depend on how narrowly the court construes the scope of ADA liability.

Conclusion: R's experiments probably constitute ADA under all these circumstances. Whether Z can recover will depend on whether a court interprets the harm he suffered as within the scope of the risk posed by the ADA.

Nuisance: A private nuisance occurs when the defendant causes a nontrespassory substantial and unreasonable interference with the plaintiff's use and enjoyment of his land. It is different from trespass in that it depends not on possession of land but on its use and enjoyment. Whether Z can recover on this claim will therefore depend on whether he has an interest in land. All we know is that he "established a market." If, for example, he merely rented a lot for a few hours one day a week on which to hold his auctions, he probably does not have an interest in land and he will not recover, because courts do not allow private nuisance recovery for mere harm to a plaintiff's livelihood. If, however, Z had bought his own land or had leased a parcel of land for a term, he would have the requisite interest and he may be able to recover. Z will argue that the virus experiments were ADA and that the escape of the virus to the cattle on the nearby farms caused his market to become worthless, thereby causing an unreasonable interference with his use and enjoyment of his land. R will argue that only Z's business was interfered with, not his interest in the land—he could easily create another use for his land. Additionally, R would contend (1) that the escape of the virus was a one-time event and not a "substantial" interference with R's use of the land; and (2) that Z assumed the risk that the virus might escape by moving into an area in proximity to R's building. But Z will argue that he located the market near R precisely in reliance on P's statement that there was no risk at all that the virus would escape. Z's argument will be especially persuasive if he already owned the land before R began its experiments. Also, it would be reasonable and economically productive to conduct cattle auctions in an area devoted to cattle farming.

If Z does not succeed on his private nuisance claim, he can try to recover on a public nuisance theory, which relies on interference with a right common to the general public. He will argue that the escape of the virus and infection of the cattle was such an interference because the local community was dependent upon cattle ranching for its economic survival. He will argue that all the factors that determine whether R's activity was a public nuisance are present: (1) the neighborhood, a cattle and dairy district, made R's activities inappropriate; (2) the activity itself was ADA (as discussed above); (3) R's experiments were conducted in close proximity to those most likely to be affected by it; (4) the activity was ongoing and constant; and (5) the damage that resulted from it was substantial.

For Z to be able to recover damages, he will have to show that the damage he sustained is different in kind, not just degree, from that suffered by the public generally. Z will describe the harm to the general public as the general loss of revenue and the resulting economic hardship imposed on the community by the slaughter of its cattle. He will define his own unique harm as the direct interference with his right to buy and sell cattle. He can argue that he was a vital part of local commerce—without him the local dairy farmers would not be able to sell their cattle with maximum efficiency and at the lowest cost.

If the court finds that Z has not suffered a unique harm or that his damages do not fall within the ambit of the public nuisance caused by R, he may be able to get an injunction to stop R from conducting any further experiments. In applying for an injunction, he does not have to show that his harm was unique. He can sue for injunction as a member of the general public.

Conclusion: Whether Z can recover from R on a private nuisance theory will depend on whether he has an interest in land and whether he is deemed to have assumed the risk by submitting to the nuisance. Z can probably get an injunction against R on a public nuisance theory. Whether he can recover damages for a public nuisance will depend on whether he can show that he suffered a kind of harm different from that suffered by the public generally.

Fraud: Z can sue R in vicarious liability for fraud based on P's statement in *News* to the effect that there was "no danger at all" that the virus would escape. A fraud occurs when the defendant has intentionally or recklessly made a material misrepresentation of fact for the purpose of causing the plaintiff to rely on the statement, and the plaintiff has justifiably relied on the statement to his detriment. Because Prex (P) had made no investigation of the matter, his statement that there was "no danger at all" that the virus would escape would almost certainly be deemed reckless. R would respond that P's statement was not addressed specifically to Z and that there is no showing that P intended to mislead Z. However, because P made his statement in direct response to a request by the ranchers that he dispel Z's fears about opening his market, it's clear that he knew or should have known that the farmers would communicate his statement to Z with intent to induce Z to open the market. Z can show that he was a member of a class of persons who (as P would have reason to expect) would learn of and rely on P's misrepresentation, and that the transaction which resulted was one that P had reason to expect such a class to engage in because of such reliance. Z will argue that P had reason to know that a cattle auctioneer based in the area would learn of the statement (since it was published in the area paper) and rely on it. As a matter of fact, P knew that the statement was meant to dispel Z's fears. Furthermore, the transaction was clearly one that P would expect cattle auctioneers to engage in: the establishment of a market in local cattle. Z's reliance was clearly justifiable, since the statement was made by the person in the best position to know of the risks posed by R's activities.

R may try to argue that Z was negligent by establishing a market so close to R's activities. Under contributory negligence, a plaintiff's negligence is not a defense to a fraud action, unless the defendant's statement was obviously false and the plaintiff relied on it nonetheless. Under comparative negligence principles, it may reduce or bar recovery, depending on the form of comparative negligence adopted in the jurisdiction. R would likely be liable for fraud.

Damages: Z can recover damages for any harm proximately caused by R's misrepresentation. The loss of his cattle market seems clearly to have been proximately caused by R's misrepresentation—he would not have suffered the loss if P's statement had been true. The measure of damages will either be reliance (which would put Z in the same position he was in before the misrepresentation) or benefit of the bargain (which would put Z where he would have been if the misrepresentation had been true).

Negligent misrepresentation: If Z cannot establish that P was reckless in making his misrepresentation, he can try to sue R for vicarious liability for negligent misrepresentation based on P's statement. The elements of this action are essentially the same as for a deceit action. Z will have to show that P had a duty to exercise due care in making the statement because the statement was made in the course of R's business and R had a pecuniary interest in the transaction in which the statement was made. Z will argue that P's statement met those requirements—the statement was intended to enhance the public perceptions of the company and the safety of its activities. This would in turn affect the company's ability to conduct its research in the area, as well as the business and good will of the company. Z will show that R breached its duty of due care by not conducting any investigation into the safety of its experiments. To recover, Z will have to show that he belonged to a limited group of persons whom R intended to reach with P's statement, or whom R knew the recipient of the statement intended to reach. If Z cannot prove that R intended to reach him (as the facts indicate), he will argue that R intended to reach a class of persons that included all persons in the cattle and livestock business in the surrounding area in order to dispel their fears concerning the safety of the experiments.

Traditional contributory negligence jurisdictions recognize the defense of *contributory negligence* in a negligent misrepresentation action. This defense will probably fail, however—the court would find that Z acted reasonably under the circumstances by waiting to establish his market until P, who should have had the best access to the relevant safety information, publicly stated that R's experiments posed no risk. In any event, it ill becomes R to argue that conduct taken by Z in reliance on P's own false statement constitutes contributory negligence. Under comparative negligence, treatment of a plaintiff's negligence in a negligent misrepresentation action would be the same as in a fraud action.

Z will be able to recover reliance damages and consequential damages.

Defamation: Z will sue R for defamation under the doctrine of vicarious liability for P's statement at the press conference. Z would sue for slander because the statement was originally oral, not written. However, a spoken statement that is intended to be written down may constitute a libel. Here, P called a conference which the press was likely to attend, as he well knew. He should have known that his remarks would be reduced to print.

Z must show that P's statement (1) concerned Z; (2) was false; (3) tended to lower his reputation, or subjected him to hatred, contempt, or ridicule; and (4) was communicated to others. He will also have to show, depending on the jurisdiction, that P was at least negligent in making the statement.

In light of R's history of conducting no investigations, Z can show that P's statement was false. Further, the characterization "idiot" would almost certainly tend to lower a person's reputation and subject him to ridicule and, possibly, contempt. R will argue that P's statement was clearly a statement of his own opinion and not one implying a fact. He was merely comparing his own intelligence as it related to the experiments with the intelligence of people (like Z) who disagreed with him. However, a statement of opinion that implies assertion of an underlying fact can trigger defamation liability. Here, P's "opinion" certainly implied the underlying fact that he knew for certain that R's experiments were safe.

Although P will contend that his comment was not "*of and concerning*" Z (Z was not specifically named in the statement), Z will show that it was well known in the community that Z was the individual at whom the comment was aimed.

P clearly communicated the statement to others by making it at a press conference, and Z can show that P was at least negligent, if not reckless, in making so extreme and derogatory a remark when it would inevitably be construed as referring to him.

The plaintiff in a slander action must show that he suffered some special harm (usually a pecuniary loss) as a result of the defamatory statement, unless the statement falls into the category of *slander per se*, in which case, special harm is presumed. One of the elements of *slander per se* is an allegation that the plaintiff is unfit to conduct his business or trade. P's statement is probably not such an allegation. His remark was only generally disparaging and not specifically relevant to Z's fitness to conduct his auction business. But Z will argue that he established his cattle market in part out of the desire to dispel the public perception of him as an "idiot" and that he suffered pecuniary harm as a result when the virus escaped. This argument may not succeed, however, because the court may find that Z's loss was not the direct result of the defamatory statement but of P's misrepresentation and Z's decision to rely on it.

Z v. P (Fraud, Negligent Misrepresentation, Defamation):

The result would be the same as in the *Z v. R* case.

Z v. News (N) (Defamation, Negligence):

Z's suit against N would be essentially the same as in these claims against R and P, except that the basis for Z's suit against N will be its publication of P's slander. As above, Z would therefore have to show that he suffered special harm, which he may not be able to do.

N is a newspaper protected by the First Amendment. Because Z's claim involves a *media defendant* which printed a statement possibly referring to a private individual in an article on a public matter, Z will have to show that N was at least negligent (i.e., that it failed to act reasonably in publishing P's statement about an "idiot" without ascertaining whether it was true). This will be hard for Z to prove. As discussed above under *Z v. R* (Defamation), P's statement seems to be a mere *opinion* about the relative levels of knowledge by him and the person(s) referred to. It seems hardly reasonable to require N to attempt an investigation into whether anyone who would disbelieve P would be an idiot. Of course, the constitutional protections extended to media defendants do not extend in the same way to private defendants such as R and P.

Negligence: Z may try to sue N for negligence, arguing that N failed to exercise due care in publishing P's statement that there was "no danger at all" that the virus would escape from its facilities without investigating to see if the statement were true. The suit would probably fail, however. N probably acted reasonably under the circumstances by publishing the statement by P, because the president of a company would be presumed to have the best available information about the company. Because the statement was attributed to P, the newspaper was not itself asserting the truth of the statement; rather, it was merely reporting an event in which P made his own remarks. It would be an excessive burden to the press to require it to ascertain the truth of every statement attributed directly to individuals in the news.

Answer to Question 20

Polly (P) v. Norm (N) (Defamation, Intentional Infliction of Emotional Distress):

Defamation: P will sue N for slander (not libel, because his statement was oral, not written) on the basis of his statement that "one of the top leaders at this college is a high school dropout who was once arrested for peddling dope."

Were N's statements defamatory? A defamatory statement is one which is made at least negligently, which is false, and which exposes the subject to hatred, contempt, or ridicule by a considerable and respectable class of the community or which tends to lower the subject's reputation. Generally, the plaintiff has the burden of proving that the statement is false. P will have to show that it is not true either that she dropped out of high school or that she peddled drugs. Assuming that she makes this showing, she will then argue that an allegation that a college student is a high school dropout would tend to lower her reputation, because it might suggest that she used false information on her college application or that she was not academically or intellectually qualified to attend college. The allegation about a drug-related arrest—an allegation of criminal activity—would certainly lower her reputation.

Were N's statements "of and concerning" P? To qualify as defamation, a statement must clearly pertain to (i.e., be "of and concerning") the plaintiff. N's last two statements, however, refer to "one" of the "top leaders" at the college. The facts are not clear. Would the term "top leaders" be understood as referring to the officers of the Social Justice club? How large (or small) was that group of "top leaders" (5, 10)? N would argue that his statement did not refer to the Social Justice club and did not refer to P because she was not named. However, P only has to show that his statement was reasonably interpreted by at least one recipient as referring to her. Assuming that there are only a few officers, P could probably prevail on this issue, especially because we know the entire club was small and obscure and P was one of its officers. It should be noted that P's violent response to N's statements would not be admitted to show that N's statement was applicable to her (the defendant's statement must be analyzed on the basis of its own words).

Ordinarily, the plaintiff in a slander action must show that she has suffered some special harm, usually defined as *pecuniary*. Here, however, N's statement included an allegation of criminal behavior, and this constitutes *slander per se*. P does not have to make a showing of special harm and may recover presumed damages (i.e., a sum representing the harm that ordinarily stems from a similar defamatory statement).

Intentional infliction of emotional distress: The tort of intentional infliction of mental distress occurs when the defendant engages, either intentionally or recklessly, in outrageous conduct which has the purpose of causing (or which is substantially certain to cause) the plaintiff severe emotional distress, and the plaintiff actually suffers such distress, even in the absence of physical harm. On these facts, P may or may not succeed in this claim. N's conduct does not appear to rise to the necessary level of recklessness and outrageousness. First, there is no evidence that N even knew P or that she was in the audience, although it is clear that he knew enough about the school and the club to make some very specific charges. Further, N did not name P in his statement, address it directly to her, or describe the person he was referring to so specifically that anyone would necessarily know he was referring to P. The tort of intentional infliction of mental distress requires a clear showing of harm to a specific person—the doctrine of transferred intent is not generally applicable in this tort. Unless other facts which we do not have would show that people in the audience understood clearly that N was referring to P, the court will probably find for N.

P v. the Spector (S) (Defamation, Invasion of Privacy, Intentional Infliction of Emotional Distress):

Defamation: P would sue S for libel, because it would appear to have published N's defamatory statement in print (it "reported the episode"). But S went even further. It printed statements about P which were untrue. P would allege that S's statement that she struck N and made him bleed was false (which it was) and that it clearly tended to lower her reputation—it depicted her as a very violent individual who was capable of committing a criminal battery.

P will also allege that S accused her of having been convicted of selling drugs and that the statement was not true. First of all, N had not specifically named P, but S had. Second, N had stated only that someone had been arrested for peddling dope, not that she had been convicted. These statements were clearly damaging to P's reputation, because they caused people in the community to think of her as a criminal.

A **media defendant** cannot constitutionally be liable for defamation against a public figure unless the plaintiff shows it acted with actual malice—knowledge that the statement is false or recklessness as to its publication. P is likely a public figure because she is an officer of an organization that seeks to effect social change. Here, whether S acted with actual malice may depend on additional facts. The facts state that S interviewed several persons who were present at the event, but it is not clear what they told the reporter. Perhaps the reporter distorted or exaggerated what she was told, either out of some personal grudge against P or to make the story "juicier" and thereby draw more attention to herself. Furthermore, the facts do not make it clear who the people interviewed were; perhaps they were individuals who were politically opposed to members of the Social Justice club and thus had a reason to give false information. If the reporter knew that, she should have sought out other sources of information that would be more objective. Similarly, if these individuals were standing at the back of the room and could not see or hear events occurring near the stage, the reporter should have sought out people who were better positioned to hear the talk and observe the fracas. Thus, it is not clear from the facts whether S acted recklessly under the circumstances or whether it should have had serious doubts about the truth or accuracy of the facts in the article.

Damages: Although ordinarily P would not have to prove actual damages for S's libelous statement(s) (the defamatory nature of the statements is clear from the statements themselves) or special damages for S's republication of N's slanderous statement (this was slander *per se* because it involved an accusation of criminal behavior), presumed damages cannot constitutionally be awarded against a media defendant without a showing of actual malice, at least where the statement concerns a public figure or a private individual in a matter of public concern. P would argue that she was not a public figure and that the defamatory statement was not about a matter of public concern. As a college student and secretary of an obscure campus club, she probably is not a public figure. However, we know that N was a well-known author and presumably a public figure, and we may surmise that a fight on a college campus would probably constitute a matter of public concern. Therefore, P will probably have to show actual malice. Whether she will succeed will depend on additional facts, as we have shown. If P cannot get presumed damages because she can show only that S was negligent, P can recover actual damages (her postponed graduation and consequent lost income, her psychiatric treatment expenses, her mental distress, etc.).

Invasion of privacy: P will try to sue S for invasion of privacy on the grounds that S placed her in the public eye in an offensive false light. While S clearly placed her in the public eye by naming her, and clearly portrayed her in a false light (certainly by stating falsely that she had hit N, and perhaps by the statement about her conviction for dope peddling), P may not prevail if she cannot show that S acted with actual malice. This constitutional requirement may be relaxed, however, when the plaintiff is a private individual. Therefore, P may be able to convince the court that she need only show negligence to recover. Whether she can prove either negligence or actual malice will depend on the facts as they are developed at trial.

Intentional infliction of emotional distress: P will contend that S intentionally or recklessly inflicted severe mental distress on her by its publication of false statements about her. To prevail, however, P would probably have to show that S acted deliberately and with knowledge that the statements were false. This tort requires that the defendant's conduct be so extreme and outrageous as to be beyond the bounds of decency. From the facts provided, it is unlikely that P would be able to make this showing.

Answer to Question 21

Theories upon Which White (W) Would Base a Cause of Action Against News (N):

Defamation: W would not be successful in a suit against N for defamation. The facts show that the story N proposes to print is true; and **truth is an absolute defense** to a claim of defamation.

Invasion of privacy (publicity of private life): W can try to bring an action for invasion of privacy for N's publication of the details of his private life.

W would have to show that the publication of these details would be highly offensive to a reasonable person. He will argue that his conviction for murder and subsequent imprisonment were very painful events for him, that he has spent the last 30 years trying to put these events behind him, and that a reasonable person would find it offensive to be forced to recall these events in such a highly public way (i.e., the inevitable attention of the public and the media, whose reporters will surely try to contact him once the story comes out).

To establish this tort, W will also have to show that the details of his life are truly private—that is, that they are not contained in any public record. The Supreme Court has held that the First Amendment requires that matters of public record be freely disseminated. It is unlikely on these facts that there is no public record of the events.

W will also try to argue that his private life is not of legitimate public concern. He will argue that he has returned to a reclusive private life and that these events happened many years before and can be of no legitimate public interest at this time. He may or may not succeed in this argument (see below).

Intentional infliction of emotional distress: The tort of intentional infliction of mental distress occurs when the defendant has engaged in outrageous conduct which is substantially certain to cause (and does in fact cause) the plaintiff severe emotional distress. W will argue that N's conduct in raking up an old story at a time when he is in the hospital with a serious illness is indeed outrageous. He will point out that his vow of silence will be sorely tested when he is confronted with the almost certain pressure to respond to N's story. He will also argue that N has been warned by his doctor that his recovery will be impeded by the story. Under all these circumstances, W will make a strong argument that N is acting with outrageous disregard for his emotional and physical well-being. This argument will be especially persuasive in those jurisdictions which do not require a showing of physical harm, but it implicates the defendant's First Amendment rights, so its ultimate success is questionable.

Defenses Available to News (N) Against a Suit for an Injunction:

Invasion of privacy: N will argue that the details it intends to publish about W's private life would not be offensive to a reasonable person. N will argue that a reasonable person would be glad to have a public account of his exoneration for a crime he did not commit and that W is simply overly sensitive, possibly as a result of his membership in a religious order that values silence and privacy. N will also argue that the public has an interest in knowing a story like W's—it will serve as a lesson in human adversity and strength. On these issues, the court should rule in W's favor (see W's arguments above).

N will argue that all the material about W that it wishes to publish is available in the public record and that therefore there is no invasion of privacy. The court should rule in N's favor. There is no action for invasion of privacy when the events in a plaintiff's life that are the subject of the publication are already in the public record.

N will argue that the material it seeks to publish is of legitimate public concern (1) because W is a public figure and (2) because the public has an interest in having information about the workings of the judicial system, particularly when the justice system fails (even if only temporarily), and when it rectifies a miscarriage of justice. N should prevail on this point, because W was undoubtedly in the public eye in what must have been a highly publicized series of events. His notoriety made him a public figure, even if it was against his will and even if he has since fled from public attention. Furthermore, criminal cases and legal proceedings generally are matters of legitimate public concern.

Intentional infliction of emotional distress: While the facts indicate that W will, in fact, suffer emotional distress if the article is published, a court is probably unlikely to consider N's conduct outrageous enough to warrant liability. Generally, conduct that gives rise to liability is outrageous in the extreme. Examples would be a practical joke in which the prankster tells someone that his spouse has died, or a threat of serious physical injury, or conduct that causes someone to be humiliated in front of a large number of people, especially if the group includes his friends or family. If the publication by a daily newspaper of a possibly embarrassing but true story about a matter of public concern were considered outrageous conduct, the mass media would be severely limited in the choice of subjects they could present to the public.

Answer to Question 22

The facts are silent as to why the Masons' (Ms) mobile home was mistakenly repossessed. Did Finance Company make a mistake in naming its debtor or in giving Repo the wrong address, or did Repo's employees take the wrong mobile home despite an accurate description from Finance Company? If the former, then Finance Company (F) was almost certainly negligent, and would be directly liable to the Ms for the foreseeable consequences of its error. If, however, the mistake was made by Repo's employees, then a question arises whether F is responsible for their conduct. For purposes of our analysis, we'll assume that Repo's employees were furnished accurate information by F but took the wrong trailer.

Is F liable for the conduct of Repo's agents? There are two bases upon which F could be *vicariously liable* for the acts of Repo's employees.

An employer is liable for those acts of its employees which occur within the scope of their employment. Whether a person is an employee or not depends upon whether he is under the employer's "control." We don't know the relationship between F and Repo. We know only that Repo was "an entity specializing in repossession." Was it independent of F? Was it a division of F? A subsidiary of F? For this analysis, we will assume that Repo was an independent firm which did repossession work for many firms, including F.

F will therefore contend that Repo was an independent contractor and not under its control because (1) Repo, not F, had control over the physical details of the work; (2) Repo used its own equipment and hired and instructed its own employees; and (3) repossession of large equipment such as trailers is the work of highly trained and specialized crews requiring extensive control. The Ms will argue in turn that F controlled Repo by specifying (1) what to do (repossess a mobile home); (2) where the trailer could be found; and (3) where to take the trailer after it was confiscated. But the court would probably find that this amounted merely to control over the general nature and manner of the work, rather than the physical details of the work (what papers to serve; how to approach the debtor; what tools to use to attach the trailer to another vehicle; how to handle the personal property of the debtors; etc.). Repo will probably be found to be an independent contractor, and its employees will not be considered employees of F.

But F could be liable to the plaintiff for the acts of the contractor if F was negligent in hiring Repo—we don't know, for example, whether Repo had made a similar mistake in other assignments from F. Also, repossession may entail the kind of duty which the law considers nondelegatable. This would be true, for example, in the case of a municipality which hired an independent contractor to repair its streets or an overhead electric line. The Ms could make a strong argument that repossession of a trailer, a person's home, is such a responsibility. Also, some work is so inherently dangerous that the person who hires someone to perform the work remains liable unless special precautions are taken to avoid the risk of injury or damage. Repossession is that kind of work. It entails peculiar risks both to the repossessors and the debtors. Debtors do not take kindly to the removal of their homes, especially when there is no prior notice. Suddenly, a person is left homeless and without protection for his belongings. The plaintiffs will argue that neither F nor Repo took any of the precautions that would reasonably be required under the circumstances: Repo's employees either did not have or were unwilling to display any documents supporting their actions; these would have shown that they were attaching the wrong mobile home. Also, they refused to listen to the Ms' assurances that they had the wrong home, and they persisted in their actions even though it seemed reasonably clear that the Ms might be injured. The plaintiffs should prevail on the issue of F's responsibility for Repo's acts even if Repo was functioning as an independent contractor.

Ms v. F:

The Ms could sue F for the following torts.

Assault and battery: An assault occurs when the defendant intentionally causes the plaintiff to be in reasonable apprehension of an imminent, offensive touching. A battery occurs when the defendant intentionally causes an offensive contact upon the plaintiff. The intent required for these torts is the defendant's knowledge with substantial certainty that the result (i.e., the apprehension of contact or the contact itself) will occur from his action. Here, even though Repo's men may not have intended to harm Bill, they (and thus F) will still be liable to him for assault and battery, because they saw him standing on the trailer steps after refusing to step down and knew or should have known that pulling the trailer away would cause him to fall. Bill was thus in apprehension of an offensive bodily contact before he fell when he saw the trailer being pulled away, and he suffered an unwanted and offensive bodily contact when he hit the ground. Even though Repo's men never actually touched Bill, he can recover for the contact that they caused through their actions.

Bill can recover damages for his mental suffering and for his broken leg (his medical bills, pain and suffering, hedonic damages, etc.). He may be able to recover punitive damages if a court finds that the conduct of Repo's men was extreme and outrageous. Given (1) that the men apparently made no effort to confirm that they had the proper trailer; (2) that they ignored and brushed aside Bill's objections; and (3) that they acted with willful disregard for Bill's safety in driving away with the trailer; and in light of the distress, inconvenience, and loss that would inevitably result from their mistake, the court could easily find that their conduct was extreme and outrageous. Even though the scope of liability for intentional torts is very broad, Jane will not be able to recover for her mental distress on the basis of assault or battery, because she was not in apprehension of an offensive bodily contact and did not suffer an offensive contact. She may, however, be able to recover for loss of consortium.

Trespass: A trespass occurs when the defendant intentionally intrudes upon the plaintiff's land. Since Repo's employees must have entered upon the land the Ms were leasing for their mobile home, a trespass occurred. A possessor of land (e.g., a tenant) may sue in trespass. The mistaken belief by Repo's men that they had a right to enter upon the land does not relieve them of liability; as long as they intended to enter the land and were not privileged to do so, they have committed a trespass.

As trespassers, Repo's men (and thus F) will be liable for virtually all consequences of their trespass, no matter how they occurred. Bill can thus recover $5,500 in property damage (to repair the dent on the trailer and to replace the Ms' personal possessions) and damages for his personal injuries (medical expenses, pain and suffering, hedonic damages). Some courts even allow recovery for mental distress suffered by family members as a result of trespass; thus, Jane could recover for her mental suffering and her medical expenses.

Trespass to chattels/conversion: A trespass to chattels occurs when the defendant has intentionally caused interference with the plaintiff's ownership or control of a chattel. A conversion occurs where the defendant causes so substantial an interference with the plaintiff's right to possession or control of an item as to render it fair that the defendant be deemed to have purchased the item. The difference between the two torts is measured by the degree of interference with the property. The factors a court will consider in determining which of the two torts has occurred are as follows: the extent and duration of the defendant's dominion over the goods, the defendant's good faith, the harm done to the property, if any, and the inconvenience and expense to the plaintiff. Here, the defendant's dominion over the trailer was complete and was intended by Repo and F to be complete. Because both torts require proof that the interference was intentional, it's relevant to consider what the Repo men really intended. Obviously, their intent was to exercise complete dominion and control over the trailer. Apparently, the trailer was returned after the mistake was discovered, but the conversion had already occurred and mistake is not a defense to conversion. The harm done to the trailer was significant monetarily (to repair it would cost $1,500). The inconvenience and expense to the Ms was undoubtedly substantial (they had to find new accommodations while the trailer was out of their possession). If the court agrees that a conversion has occurred, the defendants will be liable for the market value of the trailer ($95,000). Because the trailer was returned, F may be able to mitigate its damages (the plaintiffs would recover only for their actual damages). But many jurisdictions would permit the plaintiffs to refuse the return of the trailer and to recover its value instead. Defendants are clearly liable in conversion for the personal property that was missing when the trailer was returned ($5,000) because the property is now lost to the Ms forever.

Invasion of privacy (intrusion on solitude): The tort of invasion of privacy has several branches. One of these branches enables a plaintiff to sue when the defendant has intruded into an area in which the plaintiff reasonably believed that he would have solitude. The place that is invaded must be private, and the intrusion must be one that would be highly offensive to a reasonable person. The Ms' trailer was clearly their private home, and it would be highly offensive to any reasonable person to have one's home towed away illegally. When Repo's employees abruptly towed away the Ms' home, they intruded upon their privacy. The Ms would thus be entitled to recover any reasonably foreseeable damages arising from the repossession.

Intentional infliction of emotional distress: The tort of intentional infliction of emotional distress occurs when the defendant intentionally or recklessly inflicts severe mental or emotional distress upon another by his extreme and outrageous conduct. The Ms will contend that removing someone's home without notice, especially, perhaps, as the result of a terrible mistake as to the debtor's identity, is reckless conduct which would cause anyone severe emotional distress. Whether Bill can recover on this basis will depend on whether a court finds that the Repo men's conduct was extreme and outrageous. A court might consider the fact that their actions were the usual actions of a repossessor of personal property and that they intended no greater distress that is usually caused by such work. They did not know that Bill was the wrong debtor, or that he would refuse to leave the trailer. However, on these facts a court is apt to find that their conduct was extreme and outrageous: They did not stop to confirm that they had the right trailer even though Bill protested, and they ignored the risk of harm to Bill when they pulled away while he was standing on the steps of the trailer.

Even if a court finds that the conduct of Repo's men was extreme and outrageous as to Bill, Jane will probably not be able to recover damages for her mental suffering because she was not present to witness the men's conduct. The men could not have had the requisite intent with respect to Jane; they did not know she existed, and thus could not have reasonably anticipated that she would suffer emotional distress. The doctrine of transferred intent would encompass Jane as a member of Bill's immediate family, but only if she witnessed the incident.

Negligent infliction of emotional distress: Jane (J) might consider asserting a cause of action for negligent infliction of severe emotional suffering, contending that she suffered emotional distress as a consequence of Repo's unreasonable conduct. The majority view is that the plaintiff can only recover for mental suffering which results from witnessing physical injury to family members, and some jurisdictions still require that the plaintiff must have been in the zone of danger. Since J did not see Bill being injured or the mobile home being towed away, it is unlikely that she can recover for the emotional distress resulting from these incidents.

Answer to Question 23

Ellen (E) would assert the following causes of action against Disco (D): intentional infliction of severe emotional distress; invasion of privacy (appropriation of name or likeness; false public light); and fraud or misrepresentation.

Intentional infliction of severe emotional distress: This tort occurs when the defendant has intentionally engaged in outrageous conduct that causes severe emotional distress to the plaintiff. The plaintiff must show that the defendant acted with the purpose of causing the distress, or that the distress was substantially certain to ensue, or that the defendant acted recklessly. E would contend that the elements of this tort are satisfied by D's conduct in deliberately misleading E as to the existence of a door prize and publicizing E as the award's winner for the selfish purpose of promoting D's new store. D deliberately set out to deceive a local resident into serving as its bait for new customers to the new store. It went so far as to procure the use of E's photo without her permission in a newspaper story. Many people would agree that this conduct was outrageous, especially because it involved a minor who was too unsophisticated to sense that she was being misused. However, some would consider it "mere" consumer fraud, albeit of an extreme variety. D would argue that humiliation and embarrassment alone are not generally enough to constitute "severe" emotional distress (i.e., there must be proof that the plaintiff also suffered physical harm). E would respond: (1) D should have realized that a 15-year-old would be especially sensitive to derision by her friends and classmates, and (2) a defendant who committed so unjust a misuse of another's emotional health should be held accountable. However, many jurisdictions would find for D in the absence of physical harm to E.

Misrepresentation (fraud): A *fraud* occurs when the defendant intentionally or recklessly misrepresents a material fact with the intent to induce the plaintiff's reliance, and when the plaintiff has justifiably relied on the misrepresentation to her detriment. Here, Disco's advertisement and Mana's statements clearly establish that D misrepresented material facts by declaring its intention to award a door prize, by falsely announcing that E had won the prize, and by inducing the local paper to print a photo of E with a report of the prize. Mana clearly intended E to rely on his oral statements to her, because he needed to induce E to allow him to take her publicity photos. Even if E cannot show that D specifically intended to induce her to rely on its advertisement, D will be liable for those statements because they were incorporated in a commercial document (i.e., a public advertisement). E's reliance was clearly justifiable, since she had no reason to doubt the truth of the ad or of Mana's statements. However, E may have trouble showing that she relied to her detriment. Although she suffered emotional detriment, most courts require that the detriment sustained by the plaintiff result in some type of pecuniary loss. D would argue that E has not suffered any pecuniary loss (i.e., she has only failed to receive a *gift*). A court might, however, decide to award her damages on the theory that no merchant should be allowed to abuse the rights of the public in this way. If the court awards her reliance damages, she can recover for her expenses in traveling to D's store on two occasions. If the court awards her expectation damages, she may recover for the value of the promised trip to Paris. If she recovers either reliance or expectation damages, she may be able to tack on consequential damages for the embarrassment she suffered as a result of the fraud and the publicity about it. She may also be able to recover punitive damages, if a court finds that D's conduct was malicious.

Invasion of privacy (appropriation of likeness, false light): An invasion of privacy occurs when the defendant has appropriated the plaintiff's name or likeness for the defendant's financial benefit. Because D utilized E's picture to promote the opening of its new store, E would assert that the elements of this tort are satisfied. D would probably argue that (1) E consented to being photographed, and consent is a defense to this tort; and (2) the local newspaper, not D, published E's picture and the picture was published not as D's ad but as a news story. But E would argue that (1) her consent was obtained by D fraudulently, and (2) D arranged to have the pictures taken expressly for publicity purposes (see Mana's statements to E), and arranged for newspaper coverage so that the photo would be published and thus attract customers to the new store. E should prevail and recover from D for invasion of privacy. E can recover damages for her embarrassment and mental suffering, damages for the economic value to D of the unauthorized use of her photograph, and possibly punitive damages.

E may consider asserting an invasion of privacy action against D for causing her to be placed in a false public light by inducing her to be portrayed in the newspaper as a winner of the trip, when in fact she was not. This tort requires that the defendant's conduct be objectionable to a person of ordinary sensibilities. E would probably not be able to establish that a reasonable person would object to the publication of her photo as the winner of a door prize. Because E is a private person, however, and especially in the light of D's deliberate misuse of her photo for its own commercial purposes, the court may wish to impose liability on D.

Answer to Question 24

Bank v. Ben (B) (Disparagement, Defamation):

Disparagement: The tort of disparagement (sometimes known as "injurious falsehood") occurs when the defendant has intentionally (or with reckless disregard for the truth) made a false statement about the plaintiff's business, with the result of (and in some jurisdictions, for the specific purpose of) causing the plaintiff economic loss. It is related to the tort of defamation, except that it is not an essential element of disparagement that the plaintiff show resulting humiliation or disgrace. Bank could assert that this tort occurred when B suggested in a loud voice in the presence of 14 customers that he'd heard that one of Bank's trust department employees was misusing trust funds. B would argue that his statement included his own belief that the report was not true, and that therefore the statement could not be construed as a falsehood. Further, as a beneficiary of a trust administered by Bank, he clearly had no interest in disparaging Bank and causing it economic injury. However, Bank can argue that B's statement showed reckless disregard for the truth. A more reasonable person would have been careful to inquire further into the facts, at least, by talking privately with a high-ranking officer of Bank. However, there is no indication from the facts that Bank has suffered any economic loss as a result of B's comment (i.e., loss of customers). To recover for the tort of disparagement, the plaintiff must prove special damages (i.e., a pecuniary loss).

In actions for defamation or disparagement, the defendant can assert the conditional privilege known as common interest. B can try to assert that privilege here. Under this theory, when the party making a statement has a common interest with the party to whom the statement is made (e.g., they are both members of the same club or owners of property in the same condominium), the statement is *not* actionable if it is made in good faith and without malice. B will contend that as a trust fund beneficiary he had a common interest with Bank, as the administrator of that trust, in making certain that funds were not misused. Also, he had a common interest with the other customers in Bank to state his concerns for the integrity of the trust funds. However, (1) it is unclear whether B had a "good faith" basis for his assertion that funds were being misused (i.e., had someone associated with Bank advised B that funds were being misused; was B simply restating a rumor; or did he have sound independent knowledge?), and (2) the manner and circumstances of B's statement showed a reckless disregard for the truth (i.e., it was communicated to more people than was reasonably necessary to protect the interest involved). It should have been made to a high-ranking officer of Bank in the privacy of his office. The common interest privilege would *not* appear to be available in this instance.

Defamation: Bank will contend that B slandered it by suggesting that one of its trust officers was misusing funds so loudly that 14 customers heard him. A statement like this would tend to impugn Bank's reputation in the community. The fact that B stated that he did not personally believe the allegation would not preclude liability because the people who heard him would probably not construe his personal belief as meaningful; whatever B's own belief, Bank's integrity was now at issue. Although the facts do not indicate that Bank suffered special damages (i.e., economic loss resulting from its injured reputation), B's statement is probably **slanderous per se** both because it imputes criminal behavior to Bank and because it implies that Bank is not fit to **conduct** the business most closely associated with banks—the management of customers' money. Bank can recover presumed damages, which are damages for the harm that would ordinarily result from a similar defamatory statement.

The discussion of the common interest privilege (above) would be applicable on the issue of defamation also.

Arthur (A) v. B (Defamation):

A's suit against B for defamation would be essentially the same as the *Bank v. B* case discussed above. A cannot avail himself of the tort of disparagement, which is confined to false statements about a plaintiff's business. The business affected by B's statement was not A's business, but the business of Bank.

On the issue of defamation, B would contend that his statement was **not of and concerning** A, because A was never mentioned by name. A will argue, however, that the group B referred to was so small (i.e., four people in the trust department) that B's statement would reasonably be construed as applying to everyone in the group. B would reply that his comment referred only to "one of" Bank's trust employees, not to all of them. It's not clear from the facts whether any of the trust officers was present when B made his statement, but certainly his statement might cause the customers present to question the integrity of each of the four. A should prevail on these facts.

As above, the fact that B indicated that he did not believe the statement about the trust officer to be true would ordinarily be no defense to A's action.

Finally, the discussion of the common interest privilege above would be equally applicable in this instance also.

Bill v. Jane (J) (Negligent Misrepresentation):

An individual is liable for negligent misrepresentation when she negligently misrepresents a material fact upon which the plaintiff justifiably relies to his detriment. The defendant must be under a duty to exercise due care with respect to the plaintiff. Under the usual circumstances, the defendant has furnished misinformation to the plaintiff in a business transaction in which the defendant had a pecuniary interest. Also, the plaintiff must belong to a limited group of persons whom the defendant intended to reach with the information, or whom he knew the recipient intended to reach. The group is construed more narrowly than when the misstatement is made fraudulently.

Bill would argue that J, as a representative of the bank, made the misrepresentation in a business context, and that J had a pecuniary interest in the transaction in that she had an interest, as employee of Bank, in serving Ed as a potential customer of Bank and as the friend of an existing customer. Bill will argue that J breached this duty when she repeated technical professional information which she had obtained in a casual, social context and which she was neither trained nor competent to provide. Bill will argue that it was justifiable of Ed to rely on J's advice, since she was a representative of the bank's trust department, which routinely handles questions involving trusts and wills. Bill will also argue that as an intended beneficiary of Ed's will, he clearly belongs to the limited group of people whom Ed would intend to reach with the information J gave him.

J will argue that the misrepresentation was not given in a business context, because Ed was not a customer of the bank (he was merely accompanying Ben). She will also argue that she had no pecuniary interest in the transaction personally. Her advice to Ed was merely a gratuitous remark which had no implications for business transactions between Ed and Bank. J will also argue that Ed's reliance on her statement was not justifiable. She had not represented herself to be an attorney, and her statement could not reasonably be relied on because she obviously did not have that status. Finally, she would contend that Ed was negligent in relying on her advice.

Bill will probably not prevail against J because the advice was given at no charge and outside a business relationship. Additionally, it was not reasonable for Ed to rely on the advice of a secretary, especially since he had had no previous relationship with her and had no reason to believe that she was either knowledgeable or competent on issues relating to wills. A reasonable person contemplating the execution of a will does not rely on the gratuitous advice of a secretary. Of course, there may be additional facts which would bear on Ed's reliance. Did the bank offer advice on the execution of wills?

Were the bank's trust officers trained to give advice about wills? Did J in the conversation with Ed pretend to have knowledge she didn't have? However, even if Ed's reliance was justifiable, he was probably negligent by failing to consult a lawyer; this negligence would be a full defense in a traditional contributory negligence jurisdiction and would bar or reduce recovery in a comparative negligence jurisdiction depending on the form of comparative negligence the jurisdiction had adopted.

Bill v. Bank (Negligent Misrepresentation):

Bill would also sue Bank for J's negligent misrepresentation on a ***respondeat superior*** theory. Bill would contend that Bank was vicariously liable for J's statements to him because an employer is ordinarily liable for the torts of its employees committed in the scope of their employment. If J's statement did constitute a negligent misrepresentation, then Bank will be liable as well, since the statement was clearly made in the scope of J's employment at the bank (i.e., while she was at work and to someone seeking advice from Bank). However, as discussed above, it is unlikely that Bill could succeed in his negligent misrepresentation action against J (and therefore his lawsuit against Bank would also fail).

Bill or Jane v. Larry (Negligent Misrepresentation):

Although it's doubtful that any lawyer would misstate the formalities for execution of a valid will or would discuss the instructions at a cocktail party, we have to assume that Larry gave the instruction to Jane that she quoted to Ed and that he did so not in jest. Nevertheless, it is unlikely that either Bill or Jane (Jane may elect to sue, for example, if she loses her job as a result of this incident) can recover from Larry for negligent misrepresentation. His statement was an opinion casually given to a social acquaintance in an informal setting, not the formal opinion of a lawyer who is talking to a client who will rely on the advice. Here, Larry gave the opinion to J outside the course of his usual professional work, and so he should not be liable for it.

Furthermore, Larry had no reason to expect that Jane would repeat the information to customers at the bank who would then use that information in preparing their wills. Larry would not be liable to Bill even if he did make a negligent misrepresentation to Jane. A lawyer cannot reasonably be held responsible for casual comments made to a layperson at a party.

Answer to Question 25

Mrs. Bird (B) v. Able (A) (Intentional Infliction of Mental Distress, Invasion of Privacy):

B will assert that A should be liable vicariously for the torts committed by the private detectives whom he hired to pursue her (see below). A will argue that the detectives were not his employees because they were not under his control; rather, they were independent contractors responsible for their own actions. A probably has the better of this argument. Detective work is so specialized and requires such particularized training that we generally assume a detective to be his own boss. But a person who hires an independent contractor can, under some circumstances, be responsible for the contractor's acts even when he does not control them. B will therefore argue that even if the detectives were not A's employees, he should be liable for their torts because the work he hired them to do posed a high degree of danger to others, especially to B. This basis for vicarious liability by an employer was first utilized in cases of inherently dangerous activities such as blasting. It has been extended to situations in which the work of the independent contractor poses a high degree of danger to others and the contractor fails to take adequate precautions. There is no indication that the detectives hired by A failed to take adequate precautions to avoid the risk of danger to others.

Intentional infliction of emotional distress: The tort of intentional infliction of emotional distress occurs when the plaintiff has intentionally or recklessly engaged in outrageous conduct which is intended to cause, or which is substantially certain to cause, the plaintiff severe emotional distress. B will contend that A's conduct in having her shadowed, tape-recorded, and spied on (via binoculars) in her own home satisfied the standard needed for this tort. A will argue that his conduct was not "outrageous": (1) people who make speeches in public on controversial subjects can expect to be recorded; (2) on a bitterly contested public issue such as a zoning amendment, it is not unusual for one side to try to investigate the opposition; and (3) B could easily have avoided being spied on by drawing her window shades. A court will probably find that it was foreseeable that a reasonable person would suffer severe emotional distress as a result of being spied on. For that reason, B could likely recover for her mental distress and for her psychotherapy treatment.

Invasion of privacy (intrusion on solitude): The tort generally described as invasion of privacy is actually four reasonably distinct torts. One of these is called *intrusion*. This tort occurs when the defendant intrudes into an area which the plaintiff would reasonably believe to be private under circumstances which would be "highly offensive to a reasonable person." B would argue that surveillance of her in her own home from adjoining buildings by use of binoculars constituted such an intrusion. It would certainly be offensive to a reasonable person to know that she could not walk freely around her own home without being watched. B might also argue that her privacy was invaded when the detectives followed her through the streets and, again, when her speeches were recorded, but a person's conduct in public is not "private" and therefore cannot be a basis for an intrusion claim.

A v. Cross (C) (Defamation):

A will contend that C's remark that A's proposal (and therefore A himself) was "idiotic" and "stupid" was defamatory (i.e., impugned A's reputation). A will also argue that C's statement that A must have been "flying on something" is also defamatory, because it suggests either that A was intoxicated or that he was under the influence of drugs. C will contend that his statements were in the nature of *opinion* and were directed not at A but at A's proposal to amend the City's zoning ordinance. The more extravagant or hyperbolic a statement is, the more likely it is to be treated by the audience as opinion rather than provable fact. It is doubtful whether anyone who heard C's interview would have seriously considered it an attack on A personally. When an allegedly defamatory remark is made in the context of a public controversy, courts ordinarily allow for some degree of exaggeration. C's statements would probably *not* be considered defamatory.

A v. XYTV (Defamation):

Even if C's comments were found to be defamatory, XYTV would *not be liable* for broadcasting them. Because XYTV is a *media* defendant, A must prove that XYTV either knew that C's statements were false or allowed them to be broadcast with reckless disregard for their truthfulness. The interview was broadcast live, so XYTV did not have an opportunity to verify C's statements. Imposing liability in these circumstances would be tantamount to imposing a rule of *strict liability on broadcasters* for statements made by people not subject to their control (i.e., not an employee) in live broadcasts. Such a result would be unconstitutional.

C v. A (Interference with Advantageous Relations):

A's actions in interfering with C's relationship with his tenants gives rise to two separate complaints by C. C can sue A (1) for intentional interference with existing contractual relationships, or (2) for intentional interference with C's prospective advantage. ***Interference with existing contracts*** occurs when the defendant, knowingly and for an improper purpose, induces another to breach an existing contract with the plaintiff. Interference with prospective advantage occurs when the defendant, knowingly and for an improper purpose, has intentionally interfered with a prospective contract or financial relationship which the plaintiff had a substantial likelihood of obtaining.

C may lose in the case of the tenants who terminated their tenancies at will. Most courts will not hold a defendant liable for inducing one party to terminate a contract which is terminable at will. With respect to the tenants whose leases will expire soon, A may be liable to C for ***interfering with prospective business relationships***, at least to the extent that C can show that these entities would have renewed the leases in the absence of A's threats. While a privilege is extended to competitors who are merely attempting to induce a customer to deal with them instead of with the plaintiff, in this instance A was motivated not by an effort to compete in business with C, but to undermine C's efforts to alter the existing zoning ordinance. C should be able to recover for the loss of tenants influenced by A's threats.

Answer to Question 26

Young (Y) v. Forger (F) (Negligence):

The statute is unlikely to have any effect in Y's effort to establish negligent conduct by F. An actor's violation of a statute will have a role in a tort case only if the statute was intended to protect individuals like the plaintiff from harms like the one the plaintiff suffered. These conditions apply because the reason for considering statutory violations in tort suits is to bring the wisdom of the legislature into the tort process; that goal can be served only if there is a reasonable assurance that a statute does in fact reflect a legislative judgment about the type of activity involved in the tort case. Since it is highly unlikely that this statute was intended to avert fire-related injuries, the statute is unlikely to affect Y's case.

This statute's purposes might have been to protect against identity theft, to avert bad driving by individuals not eligible for driver's licenses, or to protect individuals younger than 21 from injuries related to alcohol abuse. None of the likely purposes involves injuries from fire.

The individuals intended to be protected from that range of harms would be potential victims of identity theft, potential victims of bad driving, underage drinkers, and potential victims of underage drinkers. Y is included in a number of the categories of individuals the statute might have been intended to protect, such as underage drinker and potential victim of bad driving.

Because the problems the legislature was treating in this legislation are different from the risks and type of injury Y suffered, the statute should not be used to establish the unreasonableness of F's conduct with respect to Y's injury. That would contradict the reasons why tort law sometimes does treat violation of statute as relevant to establishing negligence, since it would be an attempt to import legislative wisdom on a problem to which the legislature had not paid attention.

Y v. F (Causation):

Y must establish cause in fact and proximate cause. He is likely to establish cause in fact and is unlikely to establish proximate cause.

Cause in fact is usually determined by applying the "but for" test. An action is a cause in fact of some other event if that other event would not have occurred in the absence of the first action. Here, if F had not given Y the license, it is likely that Y would not, in the words of the question, have "gained admission to the bar by using the counterfeit license."

Proximate cause is usually determined with a variety of approaches in various jurisdictions. Under the direct cause approach, F's conduct would be a proximate cause of Y's injury if the injury followed F's conduct in a continuous sequence unbroken by intervening events. A number of events intervened between F's conduct and Y's injury, such as Y's decision to go to a bar and the manager's unreasonable placement of candles. For this reason, establishing proximate cause under the directness test would fail.

The foreseeability approach to proximate cause asks whether an injury was within the scope of the risk set in motion by the defendant's conduct. Here, a straightforward description of those risks would involve alcohol abuse or identity theft. Understood that way, the consequences to Y are outside the scope of the risk and there would be no proximate cause connection. Describing the risk and the injury more generally might change the result, but that would require a level of generality that is almost meaningless, such as characterizing the risk as "some kind of bodily injury" and the occurrence as a "bodily injury." The manager's conduct could be a superseding cause if it was found that it is an unforeseeable consequence of providing a counterfeit license.

Under the substantial factor test, F's role in the injury would be put in context of other causes, such as the manager's conduct, and evaluated as to its overall significance. This analysis would treat the passage of time between the sale of the license and Y's injury as a factor that negates a finding of proximate cause. On the other hand, the original wrong (furnishing the license) might be treated as having continued on any occasion on which Y used the license, which would point the other way on proximate cause. The highly unusual nature of the whole sequence of events could protect F from responsibility. The substantial factor test does not require a showing of foreseeability, but if non-foreseeability seems clear in retrospect, that factor may block assignment of liability.

Answer to Question 27

Parker (P) v. Often (O) (Negligence, Res Ipsa Loquitur*):*

The *res ipsa loquitur* doctrine will not be helpful to P. It was developed to protect plaintiffs from having their negligence cases dismissed when there was strong circumstantial evidence suggesting that the defendant from whom the plaintiff sought damages had actually acted unreasonably. To identify cases that meet this description, the common law statement of the doctrine required the plaintiff to show that the injury is usually associated with unreasonable handling of something, that the thing probably involved in the negligence was under the exclusive control of the defendant, that the plaintiff did not cause his or her own harm, and that the defendant had greater knowledge than the plaintiff with regard to the cause of the event. The last two of these factors are often disregarded at present because of the advent of comparative negligence and the application of modern discovery rules.

Assuming that P's car was hit by another car, is it likely that the driver of that car acted negligently? A person can drive a car into a parked vehicle as a result of inattentiveness or bad judgment about speed and braking. These would likely be unreasonable acts. Nonnegligent explanations for driving a car into another car would include sudden, unanticipated mechanical failure, or a need to move a car quickly out of the way of emergency vehicles. Based on common experience, the negligence-related explanations are far more common than the others.

The exclusive control element eliminates P's chance to use the *res ipsa* doctrine. No one can know what car hit P's, so there is no way of asserting that O was in control of the instrumentality that was likely operated negligently. A statistics-based approach would fail. The data show that O was responsible for the majority of entries and exits from the lot during the critical time period, but they do not indicate how much driving or maneuvering any particular driver did on any particular entry or exit from the lot. Even if it were known that O did most of the driving in the lot, typical *res ipsa* treatment tolerates a probability-based inference of negligent conduct, but does not add to that a probability-based inference of identity of the negligent actor.

P v. O (Negligence, Market Share Liability):

The market share liability doctrine was developed to treat a specific and unusual type of tort case. In that situation, many defendants all acted in the same tortious way, many plaintiffs were injured, and circumstances precluded linking any particular defendant to any particular plaintiff. Imposing liability on defendants in proportion to their shares of the relevant market could direct the appropriate amount of compensation to each plaintiff and would extract from each defendant the appropriate amount of damages, even though cause-in-fact relationships could not be established between any particular plaintiffs and defendants.

P's case against O is different from those circumstances and for that reason the market share theory should not apply. There is no basis for believing that all users of the lot acted badly or acted in the same way, and there is no reason to anticipate a large number of cases. This means that cause-in-fact discrepancies could not be expected to "even out" in the long run.

Answer to Question 28

Carter (C) v. Baker (B) (Negligence, Comparative Negligence):

The child's standard of care is used for evaluating the conduct of children. It generally requires that a child act as reasonably as a typical child of similar age, experience, and intelligence. The standard is meant to facilitate children's participation in typical youthful activities, to help them learn and mature. Courts withdraw the standard in some cases because the child's activity is particularly dangerous, because it is an "adults-only" activity, or because it presents hazards to the public.

The activity in this case could be described in a variety of ways. It was a child's participation in a school play, a child doing gymnastics-like activity, or a child placing a dangerous and heavy thing (himself) over vulnerable people. Because there are a number of plausible ways to describe the conduct, a court would likely select a characterization that is consistent with or reinforces the reasons that led to creation of the child's standard. For example, characterizing the conduct as a "school play" would mean that the "adults-only" rationale for withdrawing the child's standard would not apply. Calling it a "heavy thing over people" would have the opposite result.

The court should reject C's claim that the nature of the activity precludes use of the child's standard. Using that standard would be consistent with the goal of facilitating children's development. B's activity was similar to lots of activities children typically do, like climbing, swinging, and jumping. It presented only small risks to people other than B himself. Finally, it was done by a school pupil in a school. Deciding this issue in a way that facilitates students' participation in school activities would be better than discouraging such participation. By contrast, courts will definitely withdraw the standard where a child uses a motor vehicle. Motor vehicle use is clearly unchildlike, and is clearly an activity that can cause serious harm to the actor and to others. The activity in this case primarily created a harm to B, and was not likely to impose a risk on others.

The policy goal of protecting third parties from injury might be harmed by using the child's standard here, but in the context of school pupils' participation in school activities, the fact that the operator of the school can be sued provides another way in which society can offer incentives for safety even while offering children some protection from liability.

Does the adoption of comparative negligence make the child's standard of care obsolete? As a matter of logic, the child's standard of care can continue to apply after the adoption of comparative negligence. In order to decide what percentage of responsibility to assign to any party, the jury must know what standard of care that party was supposed to meet. When the jury knows how careful the law requires a person to be, it can compare that person's conduct to the way the person should have acted and then can decide what percentage of responsibility it should assign to that person.

As a matter of policy, continuing to use the child's standard of care depends on understanding why it was adopted. The main reason it was adopted was to encourage children to act in society and develop. Another reason may have been that the contributory negligence doctrine was making too many children lose too many cases: adjusting the standard of care for children changed that pattern. If this second reason was the main reason for the doctrine, then the adoption of comparative negligence would eliminate the need for it.

B v. C (Causation):

The causation issues in a case of this type are cause-in-fact and proximate cause. The "but for" test would establish cause-in-fact. If an injury would not have occurred in the absence of an actor's conduct, that conduct is a cause-in-fact of the injury, under this test. If B had designed or operated his harness better, C's injury would not have occurred because B would not have fallen on him.

Proximate cause can be determined with any of three tests. The directness test treats a defendant's conduct as a cause of a plaintiff's harm if there were no intervening causes between the defendant's conduct and the harm. In this case, B fell directly onto C. No other actors or other forces were involved, so the directness test would be satisfied. The foreseeability test is based on analyzing the reasons why the defendant's conduct was characterized as negligent. If the risks that led to that characterization are the risks that harmed the plaintiff, the test is satisfied even if the facts of the occurrence are unusual. In this case, the risks related to B's conduct were bodily injury through falling; the most likely victim would have been B, but the injury to C is similar to the kind of injury B risked, and there were no unforeseeable intervening causes. The substantial factor test asks whether the defendant's conduct, considered among all the other causes of the plaintiff's harm, seemed significant. In this case, the only cause of the plaintiff's harm other than the conduct of B would have been poor supervision by school employees. A jury would probably be within its discretion to consider B's conduct significant in that context, particularly since there were no gaps of time or space between his conduct and C's injury.

Answer to Question 29

Thirsty (T) v. Vending Company (V) (Strict Liability, Causation):

To recover on a strict liability design defect theory, T must show that V's design was unreasonably dangerous. Jurisdictions differ on the tests used to establish this finding. One approach is the consumer expectation test. Under this test, T must persuade the jury that consumers who encounter vending machines expect them to be safer than V's machine was designed to be. V would likely prevail in application of this test, since consumers typically anticipate that vending machines can be touched without danger. In particular, the idea that a vending machine might give an electric shock to a person who touches it (even to a person who happens to touch it with both hands) would be rejected by almost everyone.

Another test for design defect is the risk-utility test. Applying this test, a jury will consider the trade-offs among many factors that influence the design of a product. The primary factors are the costs and benefits associated with greater safety. In this case, the cost of greater safety would have been the increased cost of a thicker cord (probably not much in the context of a large machine) and the impairment in usefulness caused by decreased opportunities to place the machine in cramped locations. It is likely a jury would find that these costs are far lower than the benefit of reducing the risk of electric shock.

V might argue that it should be protected from liability because Grabber (G) misused the product. Undoubtedly G's conduct is a wrongful use of the machine, since users of vending machines are supposed to only put money in and take products out. On the other hand, shaking machines of this type is fairly common. Therefore, G's conduct would be considered a foreseeable misuse. A design is required to be reasonably safe in the context of intended uses and foreseeable misuses.

G's conduct could make G partly responsible for damages to T, if T is successful in this suit. A jury would have to consider whether G had acted negligently and would then evaluate G's conduct, under the majority rule of comparative negligence, in the context of other causal factors.

V might also argue that it should be protected from liability because the operator of the swimming and tennis club was negligent in its use of the machine. V would suggest that careless moving of the machine, or failure to inspect the machine, had led to the circumstance in which a damaged cord came into contact with metal parts of the machine. While a jury finding of negligent conduct by the club would be appropriate on these facts, the consequence of that finding would likely be a reduction in V's liability, not a full defense for V.

With regard to causation, T will easily establish cause-in-fact. If the machine had been designed with greater safety, T would not have been harmed because G would not have received a shock and therefore would not have come into contact with T. Proximate causation will be slightly more difficult for T to establish. Under a foreseeability approach, T would argue that bodily harm is a likely consequence of a design defect that can give a product's user an electric shock. T was close to the machine when she was hurt, so she was a foreseeable plaintiff. The injury she suffered was bodily harm. The fact that she suffered the injury through the medium of G's bodily reaction to a shock would likely be treated as a variation in the mode of occurrence, but not a significant enough variation to take T's injury outside the range of type of harm likely to be imposed by V's tortious conduct. A substantial factor test would be similarly easy for T to satisfy, since only two factors were involved in her injury: G's grabbing and V's bad designing. A directness test would possibly be more difficult for T to satisfy, but it is a small minority view, and could ultimately be decided in T's favor since a reflexive movement by G would likely be treated as part of the original harm and not conduct that breaks a chain of causation.

Answer to Question 30

Estate v. KFC (Duty, Negligence, Causation, Contributory Negligence, Express Assumption of Risk):

This answer assumes that a wrongful death statute controls this action, and that the estate is permitted to vindicate a claim Able would have been able to make had he survived. KFC owed Able (A) a duty of care for a variety of reasons. He was a public invitee on KFC's premises since he was there for a purpose for which the enterprise held its facilities open to the public. Also, there was a special relationship between A and KFC created by KFC's invitation and A's acceptance of the free visit.

In evaluating KFC's conduct, a court would require a jury to apply a standard of care. The professional standard would likely be rejected, since it is usually used for learned fields or fields of work in which there are self-disciplinary bodies, where there is a personal connection between potential defendants and their clients or patients, and where the calling has a reputation for placing safety concerns above a profit motive. These factors would not likely apply to health clubs, so a typical reasonable person standard would govern the case.

A's negligence claim would be based on a cost-benefit analysis, showing that the extra costs that would have been incurred by KFC if it had operated a typically spacious facility would likely have been less than the costs of serious injuries or deaths, such as the death suffered by A. Violation of industry custom would also be relevant here. While proof of this aspect of KFC's conduct does not require a finding that KFC was negligent, it would support such a finding. Proof of custom shows that safer techniques were feasible, and that knowledge of those techniques was available to entities such as KFC.

A's estate would have to establish cause-in-fact. That is, the estate would have to show that the poor spacing of the treadmills, by a preponderance of the evidence, caused the fatal injury. Since there were no eyewitnesses, the jury would be required to reach a conclusion on circumstantial evidence. This is permissible. In this case, the jury would consider all of the possible explanations for the injury and would decide which one or more of them was the most likely. On these facts, the chances that the injury came from a fall are small, since falls do not usually happen with significant force. The risk that some other patron committed a crime against A is not infinitesimal, but it is certainly not large. Therefore, the likeliest explanation is that A was propelled from the treadmill into the wall.

The proximate cause inquiry requires the estate to prove that KFC's negligence in spacing the treadmills as it did was a substantial factor or a foreseeable cause of the injury. These two tests are the most common tests. A third test, directness, is less commonly used. The substantial factor test is easy for the estate to satisfy. The only cause of the injury was the negligent conduct, so it is clearly a substantial factor. The foreseeability test is also favorable to the estate. KFC's conduct created a risk that a patron would be thrown off the treadmill into a wall. This is exactly what the cause-in-fact analysis suggests did occur. The directness test would also be satisfied, since no intervening conduct occurred between KFC's choice of treadmill placement and A's injury.

KFC might seek to avoid liability on the theory that A was unusually susceptible to injury. This argument would fail because of the "eggshell plaintiff" rule—a tortfeasor whose conduct could have harmed someone with standard attributes is responsible for extra harm suffered by a victim with unusual weakness.

KFC will also claim that A was negligent, and that this should reduce or bar recovery if comparative fault is applied, or bar recovery if traditional contributory negligence is applied. A's conduct would be evaluated under a reasonable person test. A jury could well find that he had been negligent in choosing to exercise despite his history of dizziness and head injuries.

Finally, KFC will seek to avoid liability by relying on the release form, signed by A. In general, health or exercise facilities may be protected by such waivers, in contrast to the typical position that rejects enforcement of such waivers if they are obtained by operators of enterprises that are essential to safety or welfare, such as a hospital emergency room. However, to be enforced a waiver must be clear and free from ambiguity. This document was not titled "waiver" or "assumption of risk," but instead was called "Member Sign-in." Also, the provision about waiver was in upper- and lowercase letters while other provisions had greater emphasis. A court might hold that these factors preclude application of the release.

Conclusion: The estate will likely be successful in this suit, provided a jury chooses to conclude that cause-in-fact was established by these facts. With regard to the amount of recovery, a finding that A was negligent could reduce or bar recovery depending on the applicable doctrines governing plaintiffs' fault. Also, enforcement of the waiver could be decided either in favor of or against KFC, based on a court's analysis of the clarity with which the form's provisions were presented.

Multiple-Choice Questions

Questions 1-4 are based on the following fact situation:

Motorco is a manufacturer of motor vehicles. A federal regulation requires that all motor vehicles manufactured for sale in the United States be equipped with a seat belt for each passenger and prescribes specifications for the belts. Motorco equipped all its cars with seat belts. It purchased all the bolts used in its seat belt assembly from Boltco and it tested samples from each shipment received.

Dunn purchased a motor vehicle manufactured by Motorco. While operating the car, with Price as a passenger in the front seat, Dunn collided with another vehicle. The collision was caused solely by Dunn's negligence. Price had his seat belt fastened slightly loosely, but one of the bolts that anchored the belt to the frame broke. Price was thrown through the windshield, sustaining injuries. Dunn, whose belt was not fastened, was killed when, following the collision, the car went off the road, slid down an embankment, and overturned.

Subsequent to the accident, tests of the bolt that broke showed stress in the metal itself. Motorco's records showed that tests of samples taken from the shipment in which the defective bolt was contained had revealed no defective bolts.

1. If there is a comparative negligence statute in the state where the accident happened, what effect will the statute have in an action by Price against Motorco?

    A. It will bar recovery by Price against Motorco if the jury finds that Price was negligent in any degree.

    B. It will permit recovery by Price if his negligence is less than that of Motorco.

    C. It will bar recovery by Price unless he can prove that Motorco was culpable of more than ordinary negligence.

    D. It will require a comparison of Price's, Dunn's, and Motorco's shares of negligence.

2. In a negligence action by Price against Motorco, the proof needed to establish a prima facie case is

    A. Only that the bolt was defective.

    B. That the bolt was defective and had not been inspected by Motorco.

    C. That the bolt was defective and was inspected by Motorco.

    D. That the bolt was defective, that it should have been inspected, and that the defect would have been discovered if Motorco had exercised reasonable care in the inspection of component parts.

3. In a negligence action by Price against Motorco, the negligence of Dunn will be deemed

    A. Within the risk created by the action of Motorco.

B. The sole proximate cause of Price's injuries.

C. The sole legal cause of Price's injuries.

D. An independent, superseding cause of Price's injuries.

4. In a negligence action by Price against Motorco, a defense that is likely to prevail is that

A. Motorco exercised due care in testing the bolts.

B. Dunn's negligence was the legal cause of Price's injuries.

C. Price was a passenger in Dunn's car.

D. Boltco, as the manufacturer of the bolts, has the sole responsibility for any defects therein.

5. One night Paul and David were having a heated argument in Paul's office on the 40th floor of an office building. David became angry and left, slamming the office door violently behind him. The force of David's action caused the lock to jam and Paul was unable to open the door to leave his office until a locksmith was able to come the next day.

If Paul asserts a false imprisonment claim against David, will Paul prevail?

A. Yes, because David's act caused Paul to be confined.

B. Yes, if David was negligent in slamming the door.

C. No, because Paul was in his own office.

D. No, if David did not intend to jam the lock.

6. Daniel owned a restored "classic" automobile made in 1922. To discourage tampering with the car, Daniel installed an electrical device designed to give a mild shock, enough to warn but not to harm a person who touched the car. Paul, a heart patient with a pacemaker, saw Daniel's car and attempted to open the door so that he could sit in it and inspect it. Paul received a mild shock which would not have harmed an ordinary individual but which caused his pacemaker to malfunction, resulting in a fatal heart attack.

If Paul's estate asserts a claim against Daniel for the wrongful death of Paul, will the estate prevail?

A. No, because Daniel was not using excessive force to protect his car.

B. No, because Paul was a trespasser.

C. Yes, because Daniel's act was a substantial factor in causing Paul's death.

D. Yes, because Paul had no reason to suspect the presence of the electrical device.

Questions 7-8 are based on the following fact situation:

Paul was nine years old and a third-grade student at Lincoln School. While playing in the schoolyard during the recess period, Paul started a fight with David, ten years old and a student in the fourth grade. David kicked Paul in the leg to drive him away. As a result of the kick, Paul suffered a broken leg.

Through an appropriate legal representative, Paul has asserted claims for damages against David and against the school.

7. Will Paul prevail on his claim against David?

   A. Yes, because David kicked Paul.

   B. Yes, if David outweighed Paul.

   C. No, unless David used excessive force.

   D. No, if Paul's bones were unusually brittle.

8. Will Paul prevail on his claim against the school?

   A. Yes, because the fight took place on school premises.

   B. Yes, because the fight took place during the recess period.

   C. Yes, if David used excessive force.

   D. Yes, if the school district acted without reasonable care in supervising the school premises.

9. Boater owned a powerboat which he was operating on a large lake on a clear, calm day. He approached Sailor, whose sailboat was disabled by a broken rudder. Sailor asked Boater to tow his sailboat to shore but Boater refused because he feared the tow might damage the paint on his powerboat.

   Sailor was unable to bring his sailboat in and became severely ill from exposure before he was rescued. Sailor now asserts a claim against Boater for damages based on Boater's refusal to provide assistance. Will Sailor prevail?

   A. Yes, because Boater's failure to rescue Sailor worsened the situation.

   B. Yes, if the probability of harm to Sailor outweighed the probability of damage to Boater's property.

   C. No, unless there was some special relationship between Sailor and Boater.

   D. No, if Boater reasonably believed that towing Sailor's sailboat might damage the paint on Boater's powerboat.

10. Owner took his television set to Repairer for repair. Repairer sold the set to Buyer. Buyer believed that Repairer owned the set.

If Owner asserts a claim based on conversion against Repairer and Buyer, Owner will prevail against

A. Repairer but not Buyer, because Buyer was a good-faith purchaser.

B. Both Repairer and Buyer, because each exercised dominion over the television set.

C. Buyer but not Repairer because Repairer no longer has possession of the television set.

D. Buyer but not Repairer because Repairer had lawful possession of the television set.

Questions 11-12 are based on the following fact situation:

Al lived in a home adjacent to a large, open field. One afternoon Al took his dog, on a leash, for a walk across the field. Unknown to Al, Burt was also in the field, engaging in target practice with his revolver.

Burt was hidden from Al's view by a small clump of trees. As Al walked with his dog past the clump of trees, Burt fired at a target that he had pinned up to one of the trees. The sound of the explosion frightened Al's dog. The dog broke the leash and ran. The dog ran toward Charles, who was walking in the field about 100 feet from Al, and bit Charles.

11. If Charles asserts a claim for damages against Al, will Charles prevail?

A. Yes, because Al owned the dog.

B. Yes, because the dog escaped from Al's control.

C. No, unless the dog had previously bitten some other person.

D. Yes, because failing to restrain a dog is negligent.

12. If Charles asserts a claim against Burt for damages for the dog bite, will Charles prevail?

A. Yes, because Burt's firing the gun caused the dog to run away.

B. Yes, because firing a gun is an abnormally dangerous activity.

C. No, because injury to Charles from a dog bite was not a foreseeable consequence of Burt's act.

D. Yes, because the breaking of the leash was an intervening but not a superseding force.

13. Joe and Tom saw Bill's new automobile parked on a street. They decided to take the automobile for a joyride. Joe drove the automobile a few blocks before he turned the wheel over to Tom, who drove the car into a truck. The collision totally destroyed Bill's car.

If Bill obtains a judgment against Joe based on conversion and Joe pays the judgment, may Joe compel Tom to reimburse him for any part of the amount paid to Bill?

A. Yes, on a theory of implied indemnity.

B. Yes, because Tom was a joint tortfeasor.

C. No, unless Bill had joined Tom as a party defendant in the action.

D. No, because Bill's judgment was based on conversion.

Questions 14-17 are based on the following fact situation:

Driver drove his car negligently, at excessive speed. As a result, he lost control and hit Walker, a pedestrian on the sidewalk along the road. Pat, age ten, arrived at the scene several minutes later. Pat saw that Walker was in obvious need of medical attention, so she ran into the ground-floor lobby of Highrise, a nearby apartment building owned by Realty, to ask someone to phone for help. There was nobody in the lobby, so Pat dashed through a door marked "Stairs" and up a concrete stairway leading to the second-floor landing, hoping to find someone. She tripped over a skateboard which was lying on the second-floor landing, fell, and fractured an ankle. Prior to the accident, neither Realty's resident manager nor the maintenance staff at Highrise had known that the skateboard was on the landing.

14. If Pat asserts a claim against Driver based on negligence and Driver does not raise the issue of contributory negligence, will Pat prevail?

    A. Yes, because Pat's attempt to get help was foreseeable.

    B. No, because Driver could not have foreseen the skateboard.

    C. No, because Pat was not in the zone of danger.

    D. Yes, if the skateboard had been placed on the stairs by someone who had the intent to injure someone using the stairs.

15. Assume Pat lived in Highrise. If Pat asserts a claim against Driver based on negligence, and Driver claims Pat was contributorily negligent, which of the following facts could the trier of fact consider in assessing whether Pat had acted negligently?

    I. Pat was ten years of age.

    II. Walker was in obvious need of medical attention.

    III. Pat lived in Highrise and knew that items were sometimes left in the hallways and stairwells of the apartment house.

    A. I, II, and III.

    B. I and II but not III.

    C. II and III but not I.

16. Assume Pat did not live in Highrise. If Pat asserts a claim against Realty based on negligence and Realty does not raise the issue of assumption of risk, the likely result is that Pat will

    A. Prevail, because Realty's employees had a duty to discover and remove the skateboard.

    B. Prevail, because Realty's failure to have a doorman or other employee in the lobby created an unreasonable risk to its tenants.

    C. Not prevail, if a tenant of Highrise had left the skateboard on the landing just prior to Pat's fall.

    D. Not prevail, because Pat was a trespasser on Realty's property and therefore was owed no duty of care.

17. If Pat asserts a claim against Realty based on negligence for failing to remove the skateboard and if Realty claims that Pat assumed the risk, will Realty prevail on that issue?

    A. Yes, because Pat dashed recklessly onto the second-floor landing.

    B. Yes, if Pat should have seen the skateboard.

    C. No, because Pat was ten years of age.

    D. No, because Pat did not see the skateboard.

18. Jeff, who was 17 years old, was given a new speedboat by his parents. The internal controls of the boat had been defectively manufactured. They caused the boat to go backward when the direction lever was moved toward the "Forward" position, and forward when it was moved toward the "Reverse" position. Jeff and his parents knew this and learned to use the boat despite the defect. A state law prohibited minors (anyone under the age of 18) from operating a speedboat without the presence and supervision of an adult. But Jeff decided anyway to make a short trip to a nearby island by himself. He placed the key in the ignition, and then decided to purchase a sandwich and soda at a diner one block from the dock. Unfortunately, Jeff neglected to remove the ignition key before leaving the boat.

Mark, a 16-year-old who had been watching Jeff, decided it would be fun to take the boat for a brief jaunt. He turned the ignition key to start the vessel and moved the lever to the "Forward" position. The boat lurched backward, causing a huge dent in a boat owned by Jill. If Jill sues Jeff for the damage to her craft, the fact that Jeff violated the statute

    A. Will be one factor in determining Jeff's liability.

    B. Establishes Jeff's liability as a matter of law.

C. Establishes Jeff's liability as a matter of law, unless his conduct was excusable.

D. Is irrelevant in determining Jeff's liability.

19. Paul suffered an injury during abdominal surgery, and seeks damages from his surgeon, Dr. Alan Alpha. Paul claims that Alpha's technique for closing the incision was inadequate, and that a different technique would have prevented the injury. To support a verdict in favor of Paul, most jurisdictions would require Paul to introduce evidence of

A. Risks and benefits related to the technique Dr. Alpha used and the risks and benefits related to the technique Paul claims Alpha should have used.

B. Dr. Alpha's deviation from customary practices.

C. The increased risk of injury associated with the technique Dr. Alpha used.

D. Paul's freedom from contributory or comparative negligence.

20. Phyllis consulted Dr. Bob Bravo, a surgeon, to find out if a tattoo could be removed or changed in appearance. Dr. Bravo gave Phyllis certain information about a proposed procedure but did not tell her that there was a 5 percent chance of permanent discoloration in a large area surrounding the site of the tattoo. Phyllis agreed to have the procedure performed. The discoloration occurred, and Phyllis sued Bravo for damages, claiming that he had failed to obtain her informed consent to the surgery. Which of the following statements is true?

A. To win, Phyllis must prove that Dr. Bravo performed the procedure less well than a typical physician in Dr. Bravo's specialty would have performed it.

B. To win, Phyllis must prove that Dr. Bravo performed the procedure less well than a reasonable person, with the training and skill of Dr. Bravo, would have performed it.

C. Dr. Bravo will win if the jury believes Dr. Bravo made no errors in the procedure and that Phyllis would have undergone the procedure even if Dr. Bravo had disclosed the risk of discoloration.

D. Dr. Bravo will win if the jury believes Dr. Bravo made no errors in the procedure and that Dr. Bravo said nothing about the discoloration risk because having the tattoo removed would be beneficial to Phyllis.

21. John bought a package of bologna from Don's Supermarket. It was packaged by Packo, which delivered the sealed packages in airtight plastic. John made a sandwich with the bologna for his wife Nancy.

When Nancy bit into the sandwich, she was seriously injured by a small nail embedded in the bologna.

If Nancy sues Don on a *negligence* theory, she will most likely

A. Recover, on the theory of *res ipsa loquitur.*

B. Recover, on the theory that Packo was negligent and Don is liable for the negligence.

C. Not recover, because Packo actually sealed the bologna.

D. Not recover, because John (not Nancy) purchased the bologna.

Questions 22-23 are based on the following fact situation:

John was driving through a rural area on his way to a job interview. Suddenly, a moose started to run across the road. John quickly applied his brakes, but struck the animal anyway. He had been driving within the speed limit. Ellwood, a local resident who saw the accident, walked over to look at the moose. He told John, who had stopped his vehicle and gotten out, that it was already dead. John said, "Well, there's nothing we can do," and drove away. Ellwood walked away. Ten minutes later, Phil drove along the road, also within the speed limit. Phil struck the slain moose, causing damage to his car and injury to himself.

22. If Phil sues John, who will prevail?

A. John, because he was driving within the speed limit when he hit the moose.

B. John, because he was under no legal duty to remove the moose from the road.

C. Phil, because John failed to act reasonably with respect to the risk his driving created.

D. Phil, because he was free from contributory negligence.

23. If Phil sues Ellwood, who will prevail?

A. Ellwood, because it was John who hit the moose.

B. Ellwood, because John never specifically asked Ellwood for assistance in removing the moose.

C. Phil, because Ellwood's having witnessed the accident obligated Ellwood to remove the moose from the road.

D. Phil, because he was driving within the speed limit when the accident occurred.

Questions 24-26 are based on the following fact situation:

For Son's seventh birthday, Father bought Son a small bicycle at Hardware. The bicycle was manufactured by Bikeco.

A week later, Son asked Sis, his 11-year-old sister, to get out his new bicycle so he could show her how well he could ride it. Sis went to the garage, sat on the bicycle seat and began to "walk" the bicycle between the two family cars and out of the garage.

As Sis neared the doorway of the garage, the rod on which the seat was mounted snapped, causing Sis to fall backward over the bicycle and to suffer severe head injuries. Friend, standing about ten feet from Sis, was horrified to see what happened to Sis, but she suffered no other harm.

Most bicycle manufacturers make the supporting rods for seats from a metal which is much stronger than the metal used by Bikeco. The use of the stronger metal increases the cost of manufacture by about $1.50 a bicycle.

24. If Sis asserts a claim against Bikeco based on strict liability, the likely result is that Sis will

   A. Recover, if use such as hers was foreseeable.

   B. Recover, because Bikeco can spread the risk of loss.

   C. Not recover, if the bicycle was intended for use by very small children.

   D. Not recover, because the bicycle was purchased for Son.

25. If Sis asserts a claim against Hardware based on strict liability in tort, is it likely that Sis will prevail?

   A. Yes, if the bicycle was defective.

   B. Yes, but only if Hardware could have discovered the defect by a reasonable inspection.

   C. No, because Hardware sold the bicycle in exactly the same condition as that in which it was received.

   D. No, because Sis was not in privity with Hardware.

26. If Friend asserts a claim against Bikeco based on emotional distress, is it likely that Friend will prevail?

   A. Yes, if the bicycle was inherently dangerous.

   B. Yes, because Friend was within a few feet of Sis when she was injured.

   C. No, because Friend was not using the product when the accident occurred.

   D. No, because although Friend was horrified, she suffered no other harm.

27. Cattle Company paid $30,000 for a tract of land ideally suited for a cattle feedlot. The tract was ten miles from Metropolis, then a community of 50,000 people, and five miles from the nearest home. Six years later, the city limits have extended to Cattle Company's feedlot and the population has grown to 350,000. About 10,000 people live within three miles of the cattle feeding operation.

Cattle Company uses the best and most sanitary feedlot procedures to keep down flies and odors. Despite these measures, an action has been filed by five individual homeowners who live within half a mile of the Cattle Company feedlot. The plaintiffs' homes are currently valued at $25,000 each. Recently, flies in the plaintiffs' area have become ten times more numerous than in other parts of Metropolis. The flies and odors are identified as a substantial health hazard.

If the plaintiffs assert a claim based on private nuisance, the plaintiffs will

A. Prevail, because Cattle Company's activity unreasonably interferes with the plaintiffs' use and enjoyment of their property.

B. Prevail, because Cattle Company's activity is being carried on in a negligent manner.

C. Not prevail, because Cattle Company has operated the feedlot for more than five years.

D. Not prevail, because Cattle Company uses the most reasonable procedures to keep down flies and odors.

28. Susie Blake went to Roger's Market, a local self-service grocery, and bought a can of corned beef. The can had printed on its label "A Product of West Beef Company." The company was a reputable supplier of beef products. Susie prepared a sandwich for lunch the next day, using the corned beef. When Susie bit into her sandwich, a large sliver of bone concealed in the corned beef pierced her gum, broke off one of her teeth, and lodged deep in the roof of her mouth. This accident caused her severe pain and medical expenses of $2,000.

Susie brought two claims for damage: one against Roger's Market and the other against West Beef Company. The claims were tried together. At the trial, Susie proved all of the above facts leading up to her injury, as well as the elements of her damage. West Beef Company, one of the defendants, proved that it had not processed and packed the meat, but that an independent supplier, Meat Packers, Inc., had. West Beef Company further proved that it had never previously obtained defective meat products from Meat Packers, Inc., and that it had no way of knowing that the can contained any dangerous material. Roger's

Market, the other defendant, proved that it had no way of knowing the contents of the can were likely to cause harm, and that it had sold the products of West Beef Company for a number of years without ever having been told by a customer that the products were defective. Both defendants agreed by stipulation that Meat Packers, Inc., had been negligent in packing the corned beef containing the sliver of bone.

If Susie's claim against West Beef Company is based on the theory of strict liability in tort, Susie will

A. Recover, because the can contained a sliver of bone when the defendant sold it.

B. Recover, because any breach of warranty chargeable to Roger's Market would be imputed to the defendant.

C. Not recover, because there was not privity of contract between her and the defendant.

D. Not recover, because any breach of warranty was that of Meat Packers, Inc., and not that of the defendant.

29. Householder resented the fact that joggers and walkers would some-times come onto his property along the sidewalk and just outside his fence, in order to enjoy the feel of walking or running on grass. He put up a sign, "No Trespassing," but it did not stop the practice. He then put up a sign, "Beware of Skunk," and bought a young skunk which he intended to tie to the fence. He took the skunk to Dr. Vet to have its scent gland removed. Unfortunately, Dr. Vet did not perform the operation properly, and the scent gland was not removed. Householder was unaware that it had not been removed.

One day Walker was out for a stroll. When she came to Householder's property, she walked on the grass alongside the sidewalk onto House-holder's property. The skunk came up behind Walker and sprayed her with its scent.

The smell was overpowering, and she fainted. She struck her head on the sidewalk and suffered serious injuries.

The probable result of a claim by Walker against Householder is that she will

A. Recover, because the skunk was a private nuisance.

B. Recover, because the skunk was not a domesticated animal.

C. Not recover, because Walker was a trespasser.

D. Not recover, because Dr. Vet's negligence was the cause of her injury.

Questions 30-31 are based on the following fact situation:

Actor, a well-known film star, was photographed by a freelance photographer, while sitting at a sidewalk café, drinking beer, with a bottle of Foamus Beer on the table in front of him. The picture was reproduced in *Magazine*, a publication containing stories and articles about the film industry, in connection with a story about the eating and drinking tastes of film stars. The label on the beer bottle was clearly visible in the picture.

The following month, advertisements for Foamus Beer appeared in other publications and carried a reproduction of the page from *Magazine* on which Actor's picture appeared, with the heading, "Drink the beer that movie stars drink."

30. If Actor asserts an invasion of privacy claim against *Magazine*, will Actor prevail?

  A. Yes, if Actor had not authorized any use of the picture.

  B. Yes, because *Magazine* was using Actor's picture for its commercial purposes.

  C. No, because Actor's picture was taken in a public place.

  D. No, if Actor's career was advanced by the publicity.

31. If Actor asserts a claim against Foamus Beer based on the advertisements in the other publications, will Actor prevail?

  A. Yes, if Actor had not consented to having his picture taken.

  B. Yes, if Actor had not consented to the use by Foamus Beer of Actor's picture for commercial purposes.

  C. No, because Actor's picture had already appeared in *Magazine*.

  D. No, if Actor was already a public figure.

32. Alma, a well-known literary critic, wrote a review of the latest book written by Bessy, a well-known author. In the review, Alma said that Bessy did not use the English language effectively and that the political and social views expressed in the book were "inane." Bessy has not suffered any pecuniary loss.

  If Bessy asserts a claim against Alma based on defamation, Bessy will *not* recover

  A. Because Bessy is a well-known author.

  B. Because Alma's literary criticism is an expression of opinion.

  C. Because Alma's remarks could be regarded as implied assertions of fact.

  D. Because Bessy did not suffer any out-of-pocket loss.

33. Caster, who conducted an evening news broadcast on television, reported on one of his evening broadcasts that Teacher, an instructor in a private school in the community, was being discharged for incompetence. In fact, Teacher was not being discharged for incompetence but was leaving to accept a better position at another school.

    If Teacher asserts a claim against Caster based on defamation, Teacher will not prevail if Caster

    A. Used reasonable care to investigate the statement prior to his broadcast.

    B. Honestly believed the statement to be true at the time of the broadcast.

    C. Promptly retracted the statement upon learning of its falsity.

    D. Had no ill will toward Teacher.

34. Purchaser paid Vendor $50,000 for a deed to a parcel of land in reliance on Vendor's statement that the land was free from encumbrances. Vendor knew that the land was subject to a recorded and unsatisfied mortgage of $15,000. Immediately after the closing, Purchaser was offered $60,000 for the land.

    If Purchaser asserts a claim for damages against Vendor, will Purchaser prevail?

    A. Yes, because Purchaser has been damaged.

    B. Yes, unless a reasonable person in Purchaser's position would have discovered the mortgage before purchase.

    C. No, because the land was worth more than the purchaser paid for it.

    D. No, if Vendor is willing to return Purchaser's money and cancel the transaction.

Questions 35-36 are based on the following fact situation:

Mrs. Ritter, a widow, recently purchased a new, uncrated electric range for her kitchen from Local Retailer. The range has a wide oven with a large oven door. The crate in which Stove Company, the manufacturer, shipped the range carried a warning label on the oven door that the stove would tip over if a weight of 25 pounds or more were placed on the door. Mrs. Ritter has one child, Brenda, age three. Brenda was playing on the floor of the kitchen while Mrs. Ritter was heating water in a pan on top of the stove. The telephone rang and Mrs. Ritter went into the living room to answer it. While she was gone Brenda decided to see what was cooking in the pan. She opened the oven door and leaned on it with all her weight (28 pounds) to see what was in the pan. Brenda's weight on the door caused the stove to tip over and fall forward. Brenda fell to the floor and the hot water in the pan spilled over her, burning her. Brenda screamed. Mrs. Ritter ran to the kitchen and immediately gave her first-aid treatment for burns. Brenda thereafter received medical treatment.

Brenda's burns were painful. They have now healed and do not hurt, but she has ugly scars on her legs and back. Brenda's claim is asserted on her behalf by the proper party.

35. If Brenda asserts a claim based on **strict liability** against Stove Company, she must establish that

   A. The defendant negligently designed the stove.

   B. Stoves made by other manufacturers do not turn over with a 25-pound weight on the oven door.

   C. The defendant failed to warn the Ritters that the stove would turn over easily.

   D. The stove was defective and unreasonably dangerous to her.

36. If Brenda asserts a claim based on **strict liability** against Local Retailer, she must establish that

   A. Local Retailer did not inform Mrs. Ritter of the warning on the crate.

   B. The stove was defective and was substantially in the same condition at the time it tipped over as when it was purchased from Local Retailer.

   C. Local Retailer made some changes in the stove design or had improperly assembled it so that it tipped over more easily.

   D. Local Retailer knew or should have known that the stove was dangerous because of the ease with which it was tipped over.

37. Bill liked to dance. One evening he went to his usual hangout—a local club. As he entered, he heard what sounded to him like a gunshot. Everyone stopped dancing for a moment and looked around. Someone yelled, "You got me, Bart. See you on the other side." As everyone else knew, the statement was made by someone in jest. But Bill believed that someone had fired a gun and panicked. He ran toward the exit as fast as he could, colliding with several people who were trying to get in. Joan, one of the persons whom he inadvertently knocked down, suffered a broken arm when she fell to the floor. The "shot" was actually caused by the backfire of a car outside the club.

   Based upon the foregoing, if Joan sues Bill for battery, it is most likely that

   A. Joan will prevail because the impact upon her was substantially certain to occur as Bill ran to the exit.

B. Bill will prevail because he did not desire to injure anyone as he fled.

C. Bill will prevail because he honestly believed that a gun had actually been fired.

D. Bill will prevail because an injury to Joan or anyone else was not reasonably foreseeable.

38. Joe lived in a home in Central City. While looking out his window one day, Joe saw Bart dealing in drugs to the local teenagers. Intending to frighten Bart away, Joe bought a toy gun. The gun looked real. When Joe saw Bart again in front of his home, he approached Bart and said, "Get away from my house. If you don't, you'll be sorry." As he made the statement, Joe opened his overcoat so that Bart could see the toy gun. Bart sensed that Joe was bluffing, but afraid that Joe might call the police, Bart walked away. As he left, Bart yelled to Joe, "Okay, I'm out of here."

Based upon the foregoing, if Bart sues Joe, it is most likely that

A. Bart will prevail because Joe has committed an assault.

B. Bart will prevail because Joe has committed an intentional infliction of emotional distress.

C. Joe will prevail because Bart was engaged in illegal conduct.

D. Joe will prevail because Bart was not afraid of him.

39. Alan is a student at law school. He often worked in a small reading room in the school library. One evening, about two hours before the library was to close, Alan felt unusually tired. Alone in the reading room, he lay down on the floor behind his desk and fell into a deep sleep. The janitor opened the door to the room and looked to see if anyone was left, but failed to see Alan lying on the floor. He locked the door behind him. Alan awoke suddenly about 2:00 A.M. and turned the lights on, only to find that the door was locked. Realizing that he would have to stay in the library all night, Alan fell asleep again. When he awoke the next morning, he found that he had several animal bites on his legs and arms. He believed he had been bitten by a rat.

Based upon the foregoing, if Alan sues the janitor for false imprisonment, it is most likely that

A. Alan will prevail because he was confined to the room against his will.

B. Alan will prevail because the janitor was negligent in failing to walk through the typing room to look for students.

C. The janitor will prevail because he never saw Alan.

D. Alan will prevail because he suffered physical injury as a consequence of the confinement.

40. Max took a bus to Crescent City to pick up a new car. Unknown to Max, the bus line had received several bomb threats the previous day. As Max attempted to board the bus, the driver announced that every passenger had to submit to a "pat down" search by security personnel. Anyone refusing to do so would not be permitted on the bus. Max had been abused as a child and was unusually sensitive to touching. However, he reluctantly submitted to the "pat down." Nothing was found on Max, and he was permitted to board the bus. Ten minutes later, he became ill and vomited.

If Max sues the bus line for battery, it is most likely that

A. Max will prevail because he was prevented from boarding the bus without submitting to the "pat down."

B. Max will prevail because he suffered physical harm as a consequence of the "pat down."

C. The bus line will prevail only if its judgment in requiring the "pat down" was reasonable.

D. The bus line will prevail because Max consented to the touching.

41. Bill and Joe were partners in a retail carpet business. One day, as Bill was parking his car about one block from their store, he saw two burly men beating Joe up. Because he was afraid of the attackers' violence, Bill did not interfere, but he was very upset by the incident and now becomes violently ill whenever he recalls the attack. Joe's attackers were recently identified. They are two customers who believe that Joe overcharged them for a rug.

Based upon the foregoing, if Bill sues Joe's attackers for intentional infliction of severe emotional distress, it is most likely that

A. Bill will prevail under the transferred intent doctrine.

B. Bill will prevail because he actually suffered physical harm as a consequence of the attack.

C. Bill will not prevail unless he and Joe were related.

D. Bill will not prevail because he was not a person upon whom the customers intended to inflict emotional distress.

42. Tim planned to shoot Frank from the fourth floor of an apartment building as Frank drove by the building. Tim shot his rifle at Frank but missed. The rifle had a very effective silencer and the shot was not heard by anyone. The bullet hit a grassy area behind Frank, and Frank drove

on, unaware that he had been shot at. Before Tim could shoot again, Frank had disappeared from sight. A week later, the police found the bullet and notified Frank of the attempt to kill him. Frank became hysterical and has suffered nagging stomach pains and crippling anxiety.

Based upon the foregoing, if Frank sues Tim, it is likely that

A. Frank will prevail if he alleges assault.

B. Frank will prevail if he alleges battery.

C. Frank will prevail if he alleges intentional infliction of severe emotional distress.

D. Frank will not prevail.

43. Frank, a ten-year-old child of typical intelligence, was a student at Learnwell, a private school located near a rock quarry. One day, while the school was staffed with a reasonable number of teachers and other supervisory personnel, and while those individuals were acting with reasonable care, Frank left the building and went to play at the quarry. He walked past a sign saying "Danger" in large letters and fell into a pit, suffering an injury. Assuming his jurisdiction applies pure comparative negligence, if Frank sues Learnwell for damages, what result is most likely?

A. Frank will win, because Learnwell owed him a duty of care.

B. Frank will win, because the child's standard of care prevents his conduct from being treated as a superseding cause of his injury.

C. Learnwell will win, because the quarry operator's liability will supersede any liability that otherwise would have been imposed on Learnwell.

D. Learnwell will win, because its operations were free from negligence.

44. Albert and Bill were neighbors. Albert installed a basketball hoop over the front door of his garage and would often shoot baskets, sometimes as late as 10:00 P.M. Bill complained to Albert several times about the noise and the late hours. One night, Bill decided to water his lawn and plants before going to bed. Angry with Albert, he deliberately directed his hose at Albert's driveway and hoop, hoping that the water would prevent Albert from shooting baskets. Albert saw the puddles of water on his driveway but decided to shoot baskets anyway. After a few minutes, he slipped and fell, suffering a broken leg.

If Albert sues Bill for his injury, it is likely that

A. Albert can recover for trespass.

B. Albert can recover for negligence.

C. Albert can recover under the nuisance doctrine.

D. Albert cannot recover, since Bill never actually entered upon Albert's land.

45. Howard stole a television set from Randy's home. He took the set to the local flea market, where he sold it to Jesse for $100. Jesse took it home, confident that the set was lawfully his. In carrying the set into his house, Jesse accidentally scraped it against the door. This damaged some of the input connections on the back of the set. As it happened, Jesse and Randy were good friends, and one evening Jesse invited Randy to his home. Jesse turned on the television set and Randy realized that this was the set that had been stolen from him. Randy picked the set up and told Jesse that he was going to take it home with him. Jesse responded, "No way," and stood in front of the set with his fists raised. Anxious to avoid a fight, Randy turned and left.

If Randy sues Jesse for conversion, it is likely that

A. Randy will prevail because Jesse damaged the television set.

B. Randy will prevail because Jesse bought the set intending to own it.

C. Jesse will prevail because he paid for the set in good faith without knowing that the set had been stolen.

D. Jesse will prevail if he can show that Randy failed to exercise reasonable care in protecting the set from being stolen.

46. Exco Company sent its employee, Joe, to repossess a motor home purchased by Owner. When Joe arrived, Owner objected and stated that he was current in his payments. Owner thought this was the case, although he had absentmindedly forgotten to pay the last two installments. As Joe was about to tow the motor home off, Owner defiantly mounted the steps to its doorway. Joe advised Owner, "You had better get off, or you might fall." Despite this warning, Owner remained on the steps. As Joe started to drive off, Owner slipped off and fell to the ground. Owner sustained a broken hip as a consequence of the fall.

If Owner sues, it is likely that

A. Exco will prevail because Owner owed two installments to the defendant.

B. Exco will prevail because Owner assumed the risk of falling off the steps.

C. Owner will prevail because Exco had no right to remove the motor home.

D. Owner will prevail because he believed in good faith that he was current in his payments.

47. Anthony was playing basketball at a public schoolyard. Leo, who was the same size as Anthony, ran up to Anthony and grabbed his basketball. When Anthony attempted to retrieve the basketball, Leo pulled a knife with a four-inch blade from his belt. Leo took a single step toward Anthony, but Anthony suddenly pulled a pistol from underneath his sweatshirt and shot Leo. Anthony had no license to carry a concealed weapon, or to own a gun. Leo suffered a serious injury.

Based on the foregoing, if Leo sues Anthony for battery, it is most likely that

A. Leo will prevail because Anthony had no right to use deadly force in defense of property.

B. Leo will prevail because Anthony never shouted, "Stop!"

C. Leo will prevail because Anthony's possession of the gun was illegal.

D. Anthony will prevail because he was entitled to utilize deadly force.

48. Xavier and Chuck were watching a football game broadcast in a bar. It soon became obvious that they were cheering for opposing teams and they began to taunt each other. Finally, their bickering became so intense that they decided to go outside and fight about it. They both intended a fistfight. Once outside the bar, Chuck formally challenged Xavier and raised his fists in a "boxing" pose. Xavier let loose with a left jab that struck Chuck in the chin. Chuck did not know—and Xavier did not tell him—that Xavier had boxed for his college boxing team. Chuck fell to the ground but was not significantly injured by Xavier's jab.

If Chuck sues Xavier for battery, it is most likely that

A. Chuck will prevail because he was unaware that Xavier was a boxer.

B. Chuck will prevail if fistfights in a public area were illegal in this jurisdiction.

C. Xavier will prevail because Chuck consented to being hit by Xavier.

D. Xavier will prevail because Chuck initiated the fight by raising his fists.

49. Aaron and Eddie hated and taunted each other. One day, Eddie accosted Aaron's girlfriend and made lewd remarks about Aaron. When

Aaron heard about this, he went after Eddie and lunged at him. Aaron was 4 inches taller and 22 pounds heavier than Eddie. Unknown to Aaron, Eddie was a prominent karate expert who taught advanced self-defense techniques at a local karate gym. Eddie was able to block all of Aaron's punches, and to kick Aaron in the right leg. Although Eddie only intended to disable Aaron, the blow caused Aaron a serious arterial injury. Eddie did not know that Aaron had previously had a major operation upon that leg.

If Aaron sues Eddie for battery, it is likely that

A. Aaron will prevail because his attack upon Eddie was justified by Aaron's comments.

B. Aaron will prevail because Eddie used unreasonable force in protecting himself.

C. Eddie will prevail because he was defending himself from serious bodily harm.

D. Eddie will prevail because, although his conduct imposed the risk of significant harm, he did not use a weapon.

50. Darren learned that Sam was secretly dating Darren's girlfriend. Darren was furious at the news and decided to attack Sam with a knife. He happened to see Sam the next day as Sam was leaving a supermarket. Sam is a karate expert, trained in aggressive self-defense techniques. Darren lunged at Sam with his knife, but Sam blocked Darren's move and simultaneously punched Darren in the stomach. Darren fell to the ground, but Sam stood his ground instead of running away. After a few seconds, Darren recovered his breath and lunged at Sam again. Sam again blocked Darren's blow. This time, he kicked Darren in the left knee, breaking it.

If Darren sues Sam for battery, the likely result is that

A. Darren will prevail because Sam could have escaped and avoided the second attack by Darren.

B. Darren will prevail if Sam could have seized Darren's knife without serious risk to himself.

C. Sam will prevail if Darren was illegally carrying the knife.

D. Sam will prevail because his conduct was privileged.

Questions 51-52 are based upon the following fact situation:

The state of Utopia has a law providing that hotels, motels, and other establishments that have accommodations for eight or more overnight guests must have at least two fire exits per floor. The Argyle Hotel has only one fire exit per floor. Recently, there was a fire at the Argyle. The fire was an accident for which the Hotel was not immediately responsible. When the firefighters arrived, they were informed that a 70-year-old invalid (Martha) lived on the second floor. Gordon, one of the firefighters, immediately ran up the steps to Martha's room, broke down the door, and found her weeping in a corner. She resisted Gordon's efforts to carry her away. After five minutes of assuring her that "everything would be all right," Gordon finally lifted Martha to his right shoulder and walked to the doorway. The entire hallway was now engulfed in flames. Unable to use the hallway, Gordon went to the nearest window, and jumped onto a first-floor awning. Martha suffered a broken leg.

51. If Martha sues the Argyle for her injuries, it is most likely that

    A. Martha will prevail because the Argyle was **negligent per se.**

    B. Martha will prevail because she was injured as a direct result of the Argyle's failure to construct the prescribed number of fire exits.

    C. The Argyle will prevail because the entire hallway was engulfed in flames.

    D. The Argyle will prevail because Martha failed to respond immediately to Gordon's rescue efforts.

52. If Gordon was also injured and sued the Argyle, it is most likely that

    A. Gordon will prevail because the Argyle was **negligent per se.**

    B. Gordon will prevail because the Argyle was liable for failing to have an adequate number of fire exits.

    C. The Argyle will prevail because Gordon was injured in the course of his duties.

    D. The Argyle will prevail because Gordon's conduct was a negligent and superseding cause of his injury.

53. Chef operates a restaurant. Chef buys all of the restaurant's vegetables from Restaurant Produce Corporation. One day, while making a delivery to Chef's restaurant, a Restaurant Produce Corporation employee named George Grant dropped a heavy box of artichokes on the foot of Plaintiff, a customer who was standing near an entrance to the restaurant kitchen. Plaintiff seeks damages from Chef for this injury, claiming that Grant acted unreasonably by walking too quickly and dropping the box in a part of the restaurant where customers are present. Chef moves for summary judgment. What result is likely?

    A. The court will grant the motion because Plaintiff's evidence of negligent conduct by Grant is too weak to support a judgment in Plaintiff's favor.

    B. The court will grant the motion because Grant was an employee of an independent contractor and not an employee of Chef.

C. The court will deny the motion because Chef may be liable under a respondeat superior theory.

D. The court will deny the motion because Chef, if liable, may seek contribution from Grant or Restaurant Produce Corporation.

54. Louis was a burly night watchman at a truck storage facility. The facility had been robbed in the previous week. As Louis sat in his guardhouse, the electronic system indicated that someone was scaling the wire fence surrounding the facility. Louis did not know that the person scaling the fence was someone named John, who lived near the facility. John had gone outside for his evening jog. He soon realized that he was being closely followed by two rough-looking men. When John increased his speed, the men began running after him. In an attempt to escape from the men, John scaled the wire fence at the northeast corner of the facility and dropped to the other side.

Alerted by the alarm, Louis went to see what was happening at the fence. When Louis arrived, John was running away from the two men, who stood on the other side of the fence. Louis did not see the men and ordered John, who was about 20 feet away, to stop. John hesitated, but then continued running away from the fence and from Louis. Louis drew his gun, and shot John in the leg.

If John sues Louis for battery, it is most likely that

A. John will prevail because Louis was not privileged to shoot him.

B. John will prevail if he could not reasonably see that Louis was a security guard.

C. Louis will prevail because he was privileged to use reasonable force under the circumstances.

D. Louis will prevail because the two men pursuing John were primarily responsible for the injuries to John.

55. Steven owned a luxurious mansion in the state of Utopia. While driving by the mansion one morning, George noticed that a fire had broken out in the woods and was moving toward Steven's large garage. George ran to the garage, hoping to save any cars inside. He found eight vintage Cadillacs in the garage. The keys for the cars were hanging near the door. Working at top speed, George was able to drive all the cars out before the garage was engulfed in flames. He did not—and could not—know that he had driven the cars not onto Steven's land, but onto Laura's carefully landscaped lawn. The lawn was served by an expensive sprinkler system installed just beneath the surface. In his effort to save the cars, George had caused over $8,000 in damage to Laura's lawn and sprinkler system.

If Laura sues George for her $8,000 loss, what is the likely outcome?

A. George will prevail because he had no way of knowing that he was on Laura's land.

B. George will prevail under the private necessity doctrine.

C. Laura will prevail because George failed to act reasonably under the circumstances.

D. Laura will prevail because George trespassed upon her land.

56. Plaintiff sues Defendant One, Defendant Two, and Defendant Three in a pure comparative negligence jurisdiction that applies traditional joint and several liability doctrines. The jury finds these shares of responsibility: 10 percent for Plaintiff, 30 percent for Defendant One, 20 percent for Defendant Two, and 40 percent for Defendant Three. Plaintiff's damages are $100,000. Defendant Three has no money. Which party or parties will likely bear the financial consequences of Defendant Three's inability to pay a judgment?

A. Plaintiff.

B. Defendant One.

C. Defendant Two.

D. Defendants One and Two.

57. For his son's twelfth birthday, Dad gave him a small, motor-powered "race car." By law, this vehicle could only be used in driving areas specifically designated by the city for that purpose. One day the boy came home from school to find no one at home. He went looking for the car and found it in the garage. With some difficulty, he was able to dislodge the race car from its container. He took it outside and began driving it on the sidewalk. Jane, an 80-year-old neighbor, was struck by the car, fell to the ground, and broke her leg.

If Jane sues Dad for her injuries, it is likely that

A. Jane will not prevail because the boy was engaged in an activity reserved for adults.

B. Jane will prevail because Dad should have been more careful in securing the "race car."

C. Dad will prevail because parents are not strictly liable for the torts of their children.

D. Dad will prevail if a normally agile adult would have been able to avoid contact with the car.

58. Bill purchased a chain saw from the Hardware Store, a local business. The saw was manufactured by the Roo Company. The store manager was careful to tell Bill to read the instruction booklet that came with the saw. But because Bill had often worked with chain tools before, and this particular saw seemed easy to operate, Bill did not read the instructions. The first time he used the chain saw, the blade flew off and severely injured Joe, Bill's neighbor.

The instruction booklet emphasized that the blade was very powerful, that it was essential to operate it with both hands, and that some things should not be cut with it. However, Bill was utilizing the chain saw in a proper manner when the blade flew off.

Neither Bill nor the store manager knew that while the saw was being put onto a Roo Company truck for delivery to the hardware store, it had fallen 15 feet to the ground. The blade was loosened in the fall and was delivered to the store in that condition.

If Joe sues the Roo Company for his injuries, it is most likely that

A. Joe will prevail because Bill was negligent in failing to read the instruction booklet.

B. Joe will prevail because the chain saw was in an unreasonably dangerous condition when it left Roo's possession.

C. Joe will not prevail because Bill was the purchaser and Joe was a mere bystander.

D. Joe will not prevail if the Hardware Store failed to make a reasonable inspection of the chain saw.

59. Dr. Blaine Baker treated Alan Able for an illness, but negligently failed to diagnose Able properly. With a proper diagnosis, Able would have had a 30 percent chance to survive the illness. Able died from the illness. To recover damages for Able's death from Dr. Baker under a loss of a chance theory, Able's estate must prove

A. Dr. Baker's conduct was a cause of Able's death, by a preponderance of evidence.

B. Dr. Baker's conduct was a cause of Able's death, by a 30 percent likelihood.

C. Dr. Baker's conduct was a cause of the loss of Able's survival chance, by a preponderance of evidence.

D. Dr. Baker's conduct was a cause of the loss of Able's survival chance, by a 30 percent likelihood.

60. John and Mary met at Sue's birthday party. John offered to drive Mary home and Mary accepted his invitation. John drove off with a flourish and within a few seconds was 20 mph over the speed limit. Mary told John that she did not believe in exceeding the speed limit. John responded, "Get out if you don't like it." Afraid to get out in the dark, Mary decided to remain in the vehicle. John stopped at the next stop light, but his car was struck from behind by Harvey. Harvey had been distracted and failed to notice that John had stopped for the light. Mary sustained serious injuries in the crash.

If Mary sues both John and Harvey for her injuries, contending that they each acted in a negligent manner, it is likely that

A. Mary will prevail against both.

B. Mary will prevail only against Harvey.

C. Both defendants will prevail because Mary had assumed the risk by remaining in the car after complaining of John's negligent driving.

D. The defendants will prevail if there is a typical "guest" statute in this jurisdiction.

61. The U.S. Postal Service placed a mail collection box in the parking lot of a large shopping center. The box was on a small paved area in the middle of the lot, elevated about five inches higher than the pavement of the lot. Plaintiff was injured when he mailed a letter in the box, stepped off the raised area, and was hit by a car. Plaintiff claims that because of the direction in which the deposit slot of the mailbox faced, it was difficult for someone who had used the mailbox to have a clear view of traffic in the lot. Plaintiff seeks damages from the United States, on the theory that a reasonable person would have oriented the mailbox in a different direction, because of the risks presented to individuals who might use the mailbox and then step away from it into the parts of the parking lot where vehicles might be in motion. If the United States seeks summary judgment, the most likely action by the trial court would be to

A. Grant the motion because the challenged conduct is discretionary within the meaning of the discretionary function exception in the Federal Tort Claims Act.

B. Grant the motion because no reasonable juror could conclude that the challenged conduct was negligent.

C. Deny the motion because all reasonable jurors would conclude that the challenged conduct was negligent.

D. Deny the motion because the challenged conduct might be negligent and it is outside the coverage of the discretionary function exception in the Federal Tort Claims Act.

62. Jane, who is 72 years old, went to see Dr. Smith for treatment of a skin infection. The doctor prescribed Donatol for Jane's condition and gave her a handwritten prescription for the drug. Jane took the prescription to Maxwell, her local druggist. Maxwell was busy trying to fill a number of orders for customers who were waiting in line. He asked Ann, his clerk, to read Jane's prescription to him. Ann did her best, but mistakenly read the drug as Ponatol. Ponatol is a drug typically prescribed for persons who have experienced excessive sunburn. It is never prescribed for elderly persons. Jane took the drug and promptly suffered nausea and severe stomach cramps.

If Jane sues Maxwell for her injuries,

A. Jane can recover under a negligence theory.

B. Jane can recover under a products liability theory.

C. Jane can recover under an abnormally dangerous activity theory, since the pharmacy industry is highly regulated.

D. Jane cannot recover against Maxwell.

63. Best-Buy Car Sales (Seller) is a car vendor that sells cars manufactured by CarCo, Inc. (CarCo). Seller sold Susie Flake (Buyer) a new CarCo vehicle which contained the appropriate number of seat belts. However, Buyer found that the driver's seat belt did not fit comfortably. Buyer was somewhat overweight, and the seat belt felt too tight. When Buyer took the car back and complained to Seller about this condition, Seller stated, "I'll fix it ASAP. I can make the belt a little looser." However, Seller loosened the strap too much, and Buyer was severely injured in a collision caused by Bob Olsen's negligent driving.

Based upon the foregoing, if Buyer sues CarCo for her injuries, it is most likely that

A. Buyer will prevail under a products liability theory.

B. Buyer will prevail under a negligence theory.

C. Buyer will not prevail because she acted negligently in having the seat belt adjusted.

D. Buyer will not prevail because Seller modified the car's seat belt.

64. Tess was a 38-year-old woman who weighed 100 pounds. She purchased a rocking chair from Romo Department Store (Romo). The chair was manufactured by Zero Manufacturing Company (Zero). Melba, a neighbor of Tess, was asked by Tess to come to her home.

Melba sat in the new rocking chair. Melba weighs 62 pounds more than Tess. After Melba had rocked back and forth for about six minutes, the chair suddenly collapsed, seriously injuring her. Tess immediately called paramedics. When they arrived, they helped Melba out of the chair, but in the process, they inadvertently worsened her injuries.

Based upon the foregoing, if Melba sues Romo, what outcome is likely?

A. Melba will prevail if Romo had failed to make a reasonable inspection of the chair before delivering it to Tess.

B. Melba will prevail because the rocking chair was defective.

C. Romo will prevail because Melba did not purchase the rocking chair.

D. Romo will prevail because Zero manufactured the rocking chair.

65. Defendant, who had a severe mental illness, drove his car into Plaintiff's house. Because of his illness, Defendant mistook the house for Defendant's garage. In a negligence action by Plaintiff against Defendant, seeking damages for the cost of repairing the house, what outcome is likely?

A. Defendant will win if the jury believes Defendant's mental illness prevented Defendant from acting reasonably.

B. Defendant will win if the jury believes that a typical person with the mental illness from which Defendant suffered would have acted the same way Defendant acted.

C. For Plaintiff to win, the jury must conclude that a reasonable person would have acted more carefully than Defendant acted.

D. For Plaintiff to win, the jury's members must conclude that they would have acted more carefully than Defendant did.

66. Plaintiff went to Defendant Hospital to have X-rays taken of his abdomen. A nurse employed by Defendant told Plaintiff to use a small stool to get up onto the X-ray table. Plaintiff was not tall enough to get onto the table without using something as a step. After the X-rays were taken, the nurse told Plaintiff to get off the table. While taking the X-rays, the nurse had moved the stool away from the table. The nurse did not replace the stool, and Plaintiff failed to notice that it was missing. Plaintiff fell while getting off the table because the stool was missing, and was injured. In a suit by Plaintiff against Defendant, which one of the following propositions would be *true*?

A. Defendant has no responsibility for the nurse's conduct because carelessness of this type is outside the scope of the nurse's duties.

B. The nurse's conduct and Plaintiff's conduct were both essential for the occurrence of the injury, so Plaintiff's conduct is not a "but for" cause of the injury.

C. Plaintiff must present expert testimony of the professional standard of care for enabling patients to move on and off X-ray tables.

D. The connection between the nurse's conduct and Plaintiff's injury is close enough to satisfy the substantial factor test for proximate cause.

67. John made his living growing prize-winning tulips. He often won prizes of $1,000 or more at flower shows throughout the state. John purchased a new lawn mower from the Hardware Store. The item was manufactured by Dynatron, Inc. The lawn mower worked well for two weeks. But after that time, John always had difficulty shutting the motor off. The mower would sputter and shake violently before shutting down.

One month after the purchase, John was mowing his lawn when he heard his telephone ring. He turned off the motor switch and began to walk toward his home to answer the phone. The lawn mower suddenly started to move across the lawn on its own. Before it stopped, it had chewed up all of John's tulips. John estimated his loss at $25,000.

If John sues Dynatron for his property damage, it is likely that

A. John will prevail because Dynatron manufactured the lawn mower.

B. John will prevail, if Dynatron should have discovered the problem prior to its sale of the mower to the Hardware Store.

C. Dynatron will prevail because John did not suffer physical injury.

D. Dynatron will prevail because John assumed the risk of damage to his property by using the lawn mower with knowledge of a defect.

68. Bill stopped at a local fast food restaurant. While he was inside eating, Joe, Bill's devil-may-care friend, happened by and saw Bill's car. As a practical joke, Joe tried the back door, found it open, and threw a foul-smelling pile of rags into the vehicle. Bill returned to the car, and started off down the road. Smelling the rags behind him, Bill turned to see what was producing the odor. As he did so, he lost control of the wheel and struck and damaged an expensive parked car owned by Oscar.

If Oscar sues Bill for the damage to his car, what outcome is likely?

A. Oscar will prevail because Bill was negligent in leaving the back door of his car unlocked, permitting Joe to get access.

B. Oscar will prevail because Bill acted unreasonably in turning around while driving.

C. Oscar will not prevail because Joe's conduct was an intentional, superseding cause.

D. Oscar will not prevail because Bill had acted reasonably.

69. In a failure-to-warn case, the "learned intermediary" doctrine is **most** likely to be applicable to the conduct of a defendant manufacturer of which of the following?

A. Vaccine administered in a mass-inoculation program.

B. Dangerous drug used in treating a rare disease.

C. Truck's tailgate mechanism.

D. Asbestos insulation materials.

70. Arnold, a prominent politician, gave a speech at a luncheon attended by approximately 30 people. Arnold railed against all attorneys, asserting that they were "a band of overcharging, unscrupulous rascals who do whatever it takes to win, regardless of ethics." Malcolm, a trial lawyer who advertised on television and who was sitting in the group, became increasingly uncomfortable. As Arnold's diatribe continued, several of the other attendees who knew Malcolm looked in his direction and smirked.

If Malcolm sues Arnold for defamation, what outcome is likely?

A. Malcolm will prevail because Arnold's statements clearly applied to Malcolm.

B. Malcolm will prevail because any reference to attorneys as a group constituted a defamation of every attorney individually.

C. Malcolm will not prevail because Arnold's remarks pertained to all attorneys, not to trial attorneys.

D. Malcolm will prevail only if he proves that he lost clients as a consequence of Arnold's statements.

71. While driving his car and talking with Rex, his passenger, Albert went through a red light. Eddy was approaching the same intersection from the right. Eddy increased his speed to "beat" the light. Although Eddy "hit" his brakes when he saw Albert, he was unable to avoid the collision. Eddy and Rex were not hurt at all, but Albert did sustain several painful bruises and significant damage to his car. Under traditional contributory negligence principles, what outcome is likely if Albert sues Eddy for his injuries and property damage?

A. Albert will prevail because Eddy had the last clear chance.

B. Albert will prevail because he was hurt and Eddy was not.

C. Albert will not prevail because he was contributorily negligent.

D. Albert will not prevail because Eddy acted reasonably under the circumstances.

72. At a high school reunion, Joseph saw Bill, a childhood friend, talking with Joseph's wife, Josephine. Bill was now the manager of a local department store. As Joseph and Josephine were driving home, Josephine casually mentioned that Bill had invited her to "stop by" if she ever passed the store. The more Joseph thought about Bill's invitation, the more enraged he became.

The next day, Joseph was talking with a group of people at a bar about a marital infidelity. He said, "There's a guy I know who works at a local department store. I thought he was my friend, but he's a rotten womanizer. He's after my wife, just the way he's been after every woman in town. He's a depraved person." That night, a friend who had heard Joseph's remarks and had seen both Joseph and Bill at the reunion called Bill to tell him about Joseph's diatribe.

If Bill commences an action against Joseph for defamation,

A. Bill will prevail because Joseph's statements subjected him to hatred, contempt, or ridicule.

B. Bill will prevail because Joseph's statements were factually inaccurate.

C. Bill will not prevail because a reasonable person would not have associated Joseph's statements with Bill.

D. Bill will not prevail because Joseph's remarks were merely verbal.

73. Harry was standing at the counter in the office of the FixWell car repair shop, asking about what the company would charge for a certain repair, when someone ran in and startled Harry. Harry lurched around suddenly and cut his arm on a sharp piece of metal beneath the edge of the counter. If Harry seeks damages from FixWell, it is likely that

A. Harry will win if Harry was an invitee at the time of the injury.

B. Harry will win if FixWell had failed to take reasonable precautions to protect against the kind of injury Harry suffered.

C. Harry will lose if the counter is typical of counters in common use at car repair shops and other similar businesses.

D. Harry will lose if Harry was not yet a customer of FixWell at the time Harry suffered the injury.

74. Bruce, David, and Mark were drag racing down a public street one evening, when one of them lost control of his car. Drag racing violates a local statute. The three cars collided in a burning mass. Carl, an off-duty police officer who happened to be walking by, suffered severe burns when he attempted to pull Mark from his vehicle. Carl sued all three for his personal injuries, pain, and suffering. He obtained a $120,000 judgment against them. The defendants were adjudged to be joint and severally liable. The jurisdiction applies comparative negligence. The jury found Carl free from responsibility and found Bruce, David, and Mark each one-third responsible for the injury.

Carl proceeded to recover the entire amount of the judgment from Mark. If Mark seeks to recover $80,000 from Bruce and David, what outcome is likely?

   A. Mark is entitled to contribution from Bruce and David, each in the amount of $40,000.

   B. Mark is entitled to indemnity from Bruce and David, each in the amount of $60,000.

   C. Mark is barred from seeking contribution from Bruce and David because he was at fault.

   D. Mark is not entitled to contribution from Bruce or David if he was the one who lost control of his car.

75. Gardener violated a water conservation statute by watering his lawn for more than 30 minutes on a day during a month when a water shortage notice was in effect. Some of the water caused a muddy puddle to form on Gardener's driveway, and caused Painter (an invitee) to slip and fall. In a suit by Painter against Gardener seeking damages for the fall, Painter's only evidence concerning the quality of Gardener's conduct is proof that Gardener violated the statute. How should the court rule if Painter seeks a directed verdict on the issue of whether Gardener failed to act reasonably?

   A. Grant the motion, since the statutory violation is negligence per se.

   B. Grant the motion, since Painter's injury was a foreseeable consequence of Gardener's statutory violation.

   C. Deny the motion, since Gardener's statutory violation is relevant but not conclusive on the issue of Gardener's reasonableness.

   D. Deny the motion, because Painter has not offered sufficient evidence of unreasonable conduct by Gardener.

76. Compco manufactured a computer which was distributed by Middle-ManCo. The computer was defective when it left Compco's plant. It was eventually sold to Barney by ComputerStore, a large retail store. In setting up his computer, Barney followed all of the instructions exactly as written. When Barney used the computer for the first time, it blew up in his face, causing him serious injury. He decided to sue Computer-Store only. He obtained a $400,000 judgment against the retailer.

If ComputerStore sues Compco and MiddleManCo for indemnity for the full amount of the judgment against it,

    A. ComputerStore will be entitled to indemnity from Compco or MiddleManCo for the full amount of Barney's judgment against it.

    B. ComputerStore will be entitled to indemnity from Compco, but not MiddleManCo.

    C. ComputerStore will be entitled to indemnity from MiddleManCo, but not Compco.

    D. ComputerStore will not prevail against either defendant under an indemnity theory.

77. Cooker was lighting a charcoal fire in a barbecue. He sprayed some gasoline on the coals to help them ignite, but that caused a sudden explosion. Passerby, who had been nearby, saw the explosion and ran to help Cooker. Passerby was burned while trying to help Cooker. Passerby sues Cooker, seeking damages for his injury. In evaluating the quality of Passerby's conduct,

    A. The sudden emergency doctrine would preclude a jury finding that Passerby was negligent.

    B. The rescue doctrine would preclude a jury finding of negligence.

    C. Both A and B are correct.

    D. Both A and B are wrong.

78. Pete was fumigating Bill's house against termite infestation. He was proceeding in a reasonable manner. Despite his care, fumes leaked out of Bill's home into the yard of Bill's neighbor, Bob. Bob was planting flowers at the time. He inhaled the fumes and became slightly ill. Later that day, Kevin, Bob's son, came home from college. Bob told Kevin that Pete's house was being fumigated. Kevin could smell the fumes, but nevertheless, Kevin lit a match to start a cigarette. This resulted in a mighty explosion that caused substantial damage to the house of another neighbor, Carol.

If Carol sues Pete for the damage to her home,

A. Carol will prevail because a peculiar risk associated with fumigation is the inflammability of the gas utilized.

B. Carol will prevail because the fumes which escaped were a contributing cause in her damage.

C. Carol will not prevail because she incurred only property damage.

D. Carol will not prevail because Pete's liability was superseded by Kevin's intervening recklessness.

79. Dr. Carol Clark treated Ed Edgar for a serious illness. Her treatment satisfied the professional standard of care in every way but one: Edgar asked her to estimate how long he would probably be sick and she negligently said "about a month." She should have known that the illness would likely last about a year. Edgar relied on Dr. Clark's estimate and invested money in a business that required his personal attention for about a year in order to be successful. Because he was too ill to supervise the business after he made the investment, the business failed and he lost the investment. Edgar has sued Dr. Clark for the lost investment. What outcome is likely?

A. Edgar will likely win because his loss was a foreseeable consequence of Dr. Clark's conduct.

B. Edgar will likely win because he and Dr. Clark had a special relationship.

C. Edgar will probably lose because he is seeking recovery for a "mere economic loss" and was outside a zone of danger in connection with this loss.

D. Edgar will probably lose because recovery for economic losses is permitted only when a defendant has inflicted some physical harm on the plaintiff in addition to causing an economic loss.

80. Danco Incorporated, a multistate construction company, undertook some blasting along a country highway. Danco's workers posted a large, conspicuous sign, advising motorists to utilize another roadway because of the danger of flying rocks. Carl, who was driving along the highway, failed to notice the sign when he passed it. He was looking down at the dashboard, trying to change radio stations. Carl was struck by debris from the next blast. He sustained serious injuries and sued. This jurisdiction adheres to contributory negligence principles. In Carl's suit against Danco to recover for his injuries and lost income, what outcome is likely?

A. Carl will prevail because Danco failed to undertake adequate safety measures.

B. Carl will prevail because Danco was engaged in an abnormally dangerous activity.

C. Danco will prevail because Carl assumed the risk of injury from the blast.

D. Danco will prevail because Carl was contributorily negligent in failing to see the warning sign.

81. Susan, a famous TV soap opera actress, takes her docile poodle Doggy with her wherever she goes. Doggy has never bitten anyone. Susan has never obtained a license for Doggy (although she was required to do so under applicable state law). One day, while Susan was at a manicure salon, Doggy was sitting meekly at Susan's feet, next to Susan's large satchel bag. Cindy (another patron) decided to peek into Susan's bag to see what Susan was carrying. As Cindy reached into the bag, Doggy bit her on the hand. It took almost three minutes before Susan could get Doggy to release her grip on Cindy's hand. Cindy's hand was permanently paralyzed.

If Cindy sues Susan for the injuries she sustained, it is likely that

A. Cindy will not prevail because Doggy had not previously exhibited a propensity to bite human beings.

B. Cindy will not prevail because she was injured while engaging in an improper act.

C. Cindy will prevail because Doggy was an abnormally dangerous animal.

D. Cindy will prevail because Susan's failure to obtain a license for Doggy constituted negligence *per se.*

82. Wecut Company manufactures a line of power saws. One of the saws was sold to the Max Brothers, a distributor of power tools. The Max Brothers resold it to Tom's Hardware Store, which sold it three months later to the Blue Company, a builder of commercial buildings. Steve, one of Blue's employees, was using the saw on a Blue Company construction site when it malfunctioned, causing him serious injury. Steve was using the saw carefully and properly. There is no evidence that the power saw was negligently manufactured. In fact, Wecut has an excellent reputation for careful craftsmanship.

If Steve joins Wecut Company, the Max Brothers, and Tom's Hardware in a lawsuit, which will be found to be liable?

A. Only Tom's Hardware Store is liable to Steve under a products liability theory.

B. Only Wecut Company is liable to Steve under a products liability theory.

C. Wecut Company, the Max Brothers, and Tom's Hardware Store are all liable to Steve under a products liability theory.

D. Wecut Company is liable to Steve under a negligence theory.

83. Andrew purchased a new car from Just Cars For You, a local retailer of unusual sports cars. The vehicle was manufactured by the MotorCo Company. After driving the car for one week without problems, Andrew sold it to his neighbor, Charles. Charles was so anxious to buy the car that he paid Andrew $3,000 more than Andrew had paid. Unfortunately, two days later, the car abruptly malfunctioned, causing a collision, which caused Charles to suffer personal injuries and loss of income.

If Charles sues Andrew,

A. Charles will recover for a breach of implied warranty of merchantability.

B. Charles will recover under a strict liability theory.

C. Charles will recover under a negligence theory.

D. Charles will not recover under any theory.

84. Alex began to experience constant and severe pain in his lower back. He visited Dr. Miriam Frank, a highly recommended physician; Dr. Frank gave Alex a packet of pills manufactured by Drugco. Although Dr. Frank usually sent her patients to a pharmacy for the drugs she prescribed, the packet she gave to Alex had been given to her by a contact person for Drugco as part of its nationwide effort to promote the drug. Soon after he took the pills, Alex's eyesight failed, and he became partially blind. Alex's attorney can introduce proof sufficient to support a finding that there was a causal connection between the pills and Alex's partial blindness.

If Alex sues Dr. Frank and/or Drugco, what is the likely outcome?

A. Alex can recover against Dr. Frank on a products liability theory.

B. Alex can recover against Drugco on a products liability theory.

C. Alex cannot recover against Dr. Frank on a breach of implied warranty of merchantability theory.

D. Alex cannot recover against Drugco on a breach of implied warranty of merchantability theory.

85. Brett bought a toy rocket at Jolson's Toy Store for his seven-year-old son, James. The rocket contained methane cylinders that caused it to fire and lift several feet off the ground. The rocket became James's favorite toy, and he played with it constantly. One month after the purchase, James invited Margaret, a neighborhood playmate, to join him in playing with the rocket. Margaret was using the toy in the way it was intended when it suddenly exploded and caused serious injury to her hands and arms.

It is most likely that

A. Margaret's guardian can recover against James's parents for negligence.

B. Margaret's guardian can recover against Jolson's Toy Store under a products liability theory.

C. Margaret's guardian cannot recover against Jolson's Toy Store under a breach of implied warranty of merchantability theory.

D. Margaret's guardian cannot recover against either Jolson's Toy Store or James's parents.

86. To impress his many rich and famous friends, John purchased an eight-seat airplane. He also hired a professional pilot to fly it. John then invited some friends to go with him to the Super Bowl. On the way to the game, the plane's engine malfunctioned and it crashed. John and all his friends were killed instantly. John had purchased the plane from Equinox Leasing, a company that ordinarily leased, but sometimes sold, small airplanes.

If the executors of the estates of John's friends sue Equinox Leasing on a products liability theory, it is likely that

A. They will prevail even though the friends were merely passengers in the airplane.

B. They will prevail unless Equinox can prove by clear and convincing evidence that the pilot contributed to the accident by failing to maneuver the airplane correctly when the engine began to fail.

C. They will not prevail because Equinox did not ordinarily sell aircraft.

D. They will not prevail if Equinox can prove that it inspected and tested the plane before selling it to John.

87. Ralph Renter, a tenant who rented an apartment in a large apartment building, was injured in one of the building's elevators. If he sought damages against the owner of the building, how would Mr. Renter likely be characterized?

A. Trespasser.

B. Licensee.

C. Invitee.

D. None of the above.

88. Remodeler and Nextdoor are neighbors. Remodeler hired an experienced architect and an experienced builder to remodel and expand his garage. After the project was completed, Remodeler discovered that the expanded garage was built partly on Nextdoor's land. If Nextdoor brings a trespass action against Remodeler,

A. The reasonableness of Remodeler's conduct will be a defense.

B. The reasonableness of Remodeler's conduct will not be a defense.

C. Remodeler's belief that the construction was being done on Remodeler's land will be a defense only if that belief was objectively reasonable.

D. Remodeler's honest belief that the construction was being done on Remodeler's land will be a complete defense.

89. If a plaintiff was injured by a professional fireworks display and sought damages from the fireworks display company, which of the following statements best explains why it would be helpful to the plaintiff if the court classified the defendant's activity as abnormally dangerous?

A. The plaintiff would not be required to show unreasonable conduct in order to recover.

B. The plaintiff would not be required to show proximate cause in order to recover.

C. A standard of care that requires conduct that is more careful than only "reasonable" would apply.

D. This classification would support applying the *res ipsa loquitur* doctrine.

90. Defendant drove a car into Plaintiff while Plaintiff was crossing a street. A jury found that Plaintiff was 50 percent responsible for the event, and that Defendant was 50 percent responsible. The jury also found that Plaintiff's damages were $100,000. An applicable statute provides: "Contributory fault does not bar recovery in an action by any person or the person's legal representative to recover damages for fault resulting in death, in injury to person or property, or in economic loss, if the contributory fault was not greater than the fault of the person against whom recovery is sought, but any damages allowed must be diminished in proportion to the amount of fault attributable to the person

recovering." Which of the following amounts should Defendant be required to pay to Plaintiff?

A. Zero.

B. $25,000.

C. $50,000.

D. $100,000.

91. Xavier Company (Xavier) manufactures television sets. It sold 100 sets to Yattle, Inc., a major distributor of radios and television sets. Yattle subsequently sold 20 of these televisions to Zerio Stores, a major retailer. The televisions were sold to Zerio by Yattle in the identical and unopened cardboard boxes in which they had been received from Xavier.

Amy bought one of the sets from Zerio. Shortly thereafter, Amy invited her boyfriend, John, to her home to watch some of their favorite programs. While Amy was out of the living room preparing some lemonade, the set exploded. As a result of the explosion, several metal pieces were imbedded in John's face and neck, causing him significant personal injuries.

If John sues Yattle under a products liability theory,

A. John cannot recover from Yattle because Yattle was not at fault.

B. John cannot recover from Yattle because he was a mere bystander.

C. John can recover from Yattle, but Yattle can obtain indemnity from Zerio.

D. John can recover from Yattle, but Yattle can obtain indemnity from Xavier.

Multiple-Choice
Answers

1. **B** All comparative negligence statutes allow a negligent plaintiff to recover if the plaintiff's share of negligence is less than that of the defendant. Some comparative negligence statutes may allow recovery for a plaintiff whose share is equal to that of the defendant. "Pure" comparative negligence statutes allow a plaintiff to recover so long as the plaintiff's share of negligence is less than 100 percent. Choice **A** is wrong because no comparative negligence statutes bar recovery by a plaintiff who is negligent "in any degree." Choice **C** is wrong because comparative negligence statutes permit recovery when ordinary negligence by a plaintiff is less than ordinary negligence by a defendant. Choice **D** is wrong because Dunn's conduct has no relevance to the suit between Price and Motorco.

2. **D** A manufacturer acts negligently when it fails to act with due care—i.e., it fails to act reasonably under all the relevant circumstances. The question specifies that Price has brought a negligence, not a strict liability, action. Therefore, Price must prove more than that the bolt was defective. For this reason, choice **A** is wrong. Price *must show* not only that the bolt was in fact *defective, but also* that Motorco had *failed* to exercise reasonable care in inspecting the parts used to assemble the seat belt. Choice **B** is wrong because it understates the amount of proof required. It's not enough to show that the bolt was defective and was not inspected. Price must also show that the defect would have been discovered with a reasonable inspection. Choice **C** is wrong because, again, Price must also show that Motorco failed to exercise reasonable care in making its inspection of the bolt. Only choice **D** states correctly all the elements of proof required of Price.

3. **A** The terms "proximate cause" and "legal cause" are different names for the same basic legal concept—the liability of a person who is negligent extends to all the consequences of his conduct which are reasonably foreseeable. Proximate cause does *not* exist when an unforeseeable, intervening cause results in an injury which was not likely to occur as a consequence of the defendant's negligence. Dunn's negligence was an intervening cause of Price's injuries because it occurred subsequent to Motorco's actions, but it was *not unforeseeable* (negligent driving must always be anticipated). Furthermore, the type of harm (physical injury resulting from a collision) is exactly what is likely to occur as a *consequence* of a defective seat belt bolt. Choice **D** is wrong because even though Dunn's negligence was an independent cause of Price's injuries, it

was foreseeable and, therefore, not a ***superseding cause***. Choices **B** and **C** are wrong because, in a negligence action by Price against Motorco, the negligence of Dunn would ***not*** be looked upon as the "sole" proximate or legal cause of Price's injuries, since Dunn and Motorco's conduct both operated as proximate or "legal" causes of Price's injuries. Remember, events can have more than one "legal cause" or "proximate cause."

4. **A** If a jury is not persuaded that a defendant failed to exercise due care, or that it failed to act reasonably under the circumstances, the plaintiff must lose. On these facts, Motorco's best defense is that it exercised due care in testing the bolts. As an assembler of components manufactured by others, it will have done everything reasonable by testing the bolt before it integrated it into the seat belt. The correct answer is choice **A**. Choice **C** is wrong because guest statutes concern only the relationship between a driver and his own passengers, not third parties who may have contributed to the accident. Choice **B** is wrong because it's not enough for Motorco to show that Dunn was negligent. It must also show either that it itself was not negligent or that Dunn's negligence was an independent, supervening cause. Finally, choice **D** is wrong because Boltco does not have the sole responsibility for defects in the bolt. As the assembler of components including the bolt, Motorco has a responsibility to exercise reasonable care in checking every component that goes into its finished product.

5. **D** The tort of false imprisonment occurs when the defendant has ***intentionally caused*** the plaintiff to be confined to an area which has definite physical boundaries and from which there is no reasonable means of escape. There is ***no indication*** on the facts that David ***intended*** to lock Paul in his office, nor is it reasonable to anticipate that a lock will jam when a door is slammed shut. Therefore, the correct answer is choice **D**. Choice **C** is wrong because intentional confinement to any definable area will result in liability. It doesn't matter that Paul was in his own office. The tort of false imprisonment can be inflicted on a person when a defendant intentionally confines the person anywhere, including his office, his home, or his car. Choice **B** is wrong because false imprisonment is an intentional tort. It does not include negligence as one of its elements. Finally, choice **A** is wrong because, although David intended to slam the door, he did not intend to confine Paul. The intent to confine is an essential element of the tort of false imprisonment.

6. **D** To use force against another person in defense of property, the owner must use only as much force as is necessary to protect the property

and the owner must first make a verbal demand that the potential intruder stop his or her interference with the property (unless it appears that harm will occur immediately or that the demand will be ignored). When mechanical devices are used, only the same degree of force may be used as if the owner were present and acting himself. Daniel's device failed to provide a reasonable means of notifying trespassers of its existence. The correct answer is choice **D** because Daniel failed to provide any notice that would have caused Paul to suspect the presence of the device. Choice **A** is wrong because, although the force may not have been excessive if its use followed a warning, Paul was not furnished with the requisite notice. Choice **B** is wrong because a trespasser is entitled to notice before an owner uses force. Choice **C** is wrong. While Daniel's act was a substantial factor in Paul's death, that is not the reason he's liable. His liability is based on his failure to give Paul notice or warning about the device.

7. **C** A person is entitled to use reasonable force to prevent a threatened harmful or offensive contact with his person. This is true whether the threatened contact is intentional or the result of negligence. David had the *right to defend himself* against Paul's attack and will not be liable to Paul as long as he *did not use excessive force.* On these facts, which indicate that Paul began the fight, there is nothing to indicate that David used excessive force. Choice **D** is wrong because once Paul instigated the fight, the law treats him as having consented to the injuries which might occur if David defended himself. Choice **A** is wrong. David had the right to kick Paul if he reasonably believed his response was necessary to repel Paul's attack upon him. Finally, choice **B** is wrong because the fact that David outweighed Paul would not, in itself, establish that David's kick was not reasonably necessary to defend against Paul. So long as David reasonably believed the kick was necessary to beat off Paul's attack, the self-defense privilege would be sustained.

8. **D** In some situations involving a special relationship between the plaintiff and the defendant, the courts have imposed liability when the defendant fails to act to protect the plaintiff against injury from a third person. The school/student relationship is one of these special relationships. A school may be liable in negligence for injuries caused by the conduct of others when it fails to fulfill its duty to exercise reasonable care in the *supervision* of a third person or in the *protection of the plaintiff.* On these facts, the school district would *not* be liable unless it failed to exercise *reasonable* care with respect to the

supervision of the schoolyard, and there is nothing in these facts to indicate that failure. It does not appear that the fight between Paul and David could have been anticipated, nor that it could have been prevented or even stopped. A fight can be over in seconds, before anyone has a chance to intervene. Choice **A** is wrong because, although a fight on school grounds may impose a duty on the school to intervene, there is nothing on these facts to indicate that the school failed to observe that duty. Choice **B** is wrong because the facts do not show that the school could have prevented or anticipated an unprovoked attack by Paul. Choice **C** is wrong because the facts do not show any reason for the school to anticipate that David would use excessive force.

9. **C** A person ordinarily has no duty to come to the aid or rescue of another, unless a special relationship exists between them. Since there is nothing in the facts to indicate that Boater and Sailor had any type of special relationship between them, Boater was *not legally obligated to respond to* Sailor's requests for assistance. Choices **B** and **D** are wrong because Boater had no obligation to assist Sailor, even if the probability of harm to Sailor outweighed the probability of harm to Boater, and even if Boater's belief that rendering assistance to Sailor would damage his own boat was not reasonable. Choice **A** is wrong because Boater was not responsible for creating Sailor's predicament.

10. **B** A defendant is liable for a conversion when he exercises *unauthorized substantial dominion and control* over the owner's personal property. Both Repairer and Buyer exercised dominion and control over Owner's television set in an *unauthorized* manner. The fact that Buyer was unaware of the true ownership of the television would not preclude a suit for conversion by Owner. In most states, even a bona fide purchaser would be deemed a converter on these facts. Buyer would, however, have a right of indemnity against Repairer for any judgment against Buyer, because Buyer was entitled to rely on Repairer's apparent ownership of the television set. Choice **A** is wrong because even a good-faith purchaser of an item is subject to liability for conversion. Choice **C** is wrong because Repairer committed a conversion when he sold the television set to Buyer. Finally, choice **D** is wrong because, while Repairer initially had lawful possession of the television set, his sale to Buyer was a conversion.

11. **C** Injuries from a domestic animal do not give rise to strict liability unless the animal has shown signs of being dangerous and the

owner is aware of the animal's dangerous tendencies. These facts do not disclose that Al's dog had ever bitten anyone. Al was not guilty of ordinary negligence, because he had the dog on a leash, and the dog broke the leash in response to an unexpected explosion. Because Charles could not establish a negligence claim on these facts, Al's liability could be based only on strict liability. But strict liability will not permit recovery because Al had no notice that the dog was dangerous. Choice **A** is wrong because mere ownership of a domestic animal does not make one liable for all harm caused by the animal. Choice **B** is wrong. It would impose strict liability for any harm caused by one's pet while the pet was beyond its owner's immediate control, which is inconsistent with the rules respecting domestic animals. Choice **D** is wrong because Al was not negligent; he acted reasonably under the circumstances by walking his dog on a leash. In any event, any possible negligence by Al would be superseded by Burt's unforeseeable conduct. Al could not reasonably foresee that someone would discharge a gun in an open field on which people walked.

12. **C** On these facts, choice **C** is probably the best answer. We are not told whether the field was public land or private land. Under this circumstance, Burt could reasonably argue that there was no basis on which to foresee that a dog on a leash would escape and bite a stranger. Nor was there any reason for him to suspect that anyone else—let alone someone with a dog—was in the area. Choice **B** is wrong because, although firing a gun may be a dangerous activity under some circumstances, it can be carried out safely with reasonable care. It is not necessarily dangerous in an open field when no one else is visibly present, and there is nothing in the facts to indicate that Burt used the gun carelessly (he couldn't see Al or his dog). Choice **A** is wrong because Burt could not reasonably anticipate that the dog was in the area, or that he would break loose from a leash, or that he would bite a stranger who was not visible to Burt. Choice **D** is wrong because the breaking of the leash was an independent, intervening force that was not reasonably foreseeable by Burt. Because it was unforeseeable, it was not a superseding cause that would shield Burt from negligence liability.

13. **D** An intentional tortfeasor is ordinarily not entitled to indemnity or contribution from a fellow tortfeasor. Because *conversion is an intentional tort*, Joe may *not* obtain indemnity or contribution from Tom. The correct answer is choice **D**. Choice **C** is wrong

because the right to indemnity or contribution does not depend on the plaintiff's choice of defendants. In any case, even if Tom had been joined as a defendant, Joe would not be entitled to indemnity or contribution. Choice **A** is wrong because Joe cannot recover in indemnity, implied or otherwise. Choice **B** is wrong because Tom was a joint *intentional* tortfeasor.

14. **A** The law encourages rescuers by imposing liability upon negligent tortfeasors who create circumstances to which a rescuer is likely to respond. The intervention of the rescuer is ***deemed*** a foreseeable consequence of the negligence. Choice **A** is therefore the correct answer. Choice **B** is wrong. Cases involving rescuers are sometimes treated as exceptions to the general rule that a specific consequence must be foreseeable to impose liability for negligence, to further the public policy of encouraging rescuers. Also, the foreseeability of a rescuer's encountering a hazard is likely to be a question of fact for a jury. Choice **C** is wrong because the rescuer need not be in the zone of danger to recover. Choice **D** is wrong because an intentional tort would likely supersede the mere negligence of Driver and shield Driver from liability.

15. **A** The standards for determining a plaintiff's negligence are the same as for determining a defendant's negligence. A person is negligent if he or she fails to act with due care (i.e., reasonably under the circumstances). In determining if Pat failed to act in a reasonable manner, ***all three of the listed factors are pertinent.*** The fact that she was ten years old would be relevant in that she would be held only to the standard of a child of like age, experience, and intelligence. The fact that Walker was in obvious need of medical attention would justify her dashing with less care than normal through Highrise. Finally, her awareness that objects were often left in the hallways would be offered by Driver to support a contention that Pat failed to act reasonably under the circumstances.

16. **C** This question asks us to assume that Pat did not live in Highrise. This would make her either a trespasser or a licensee. The only duty Realty might have owed to Pat is a ***duty to warn*** Pat of known dangers but ***not to inspect.*** If the skateboard had been left just before Pat's fall, then Realty would not have breached its duty, since choice **C** suggests that Realty would not have known the skateboard was there. Choice **D** is wrong. Even if Pat was a trespasser, that would not necessarily relieve Realty of all responsibility to her. Because Pat was only ten, Realty had a duty to her greater than to adults. Choice **A** is wrong because Realty's employees probably did not have a duty to

Pat to discover the skateboard. Finally, choice **B** is wrong because Realty probably did not have a duty to have an employee in the lobby of the apartment building. Most apartment houses do not have workers posted in their lobbies.

17. **D** An assumption of risk defense to a negligence cause of action (which allows a jury to reduce a plaintiff's recovery in most jurisdictions and is a total bar to recovery in a minority of jurisdictions) is available if the plaintiff knew the risk and assumed it voluntarily. Because Pat was ***not aware*** of the skateboard until she tripped over it, she could not have possibly assumed the risk. The correct answer is choice **D**. Choice **C** is wrong because a minor can assume a risk. Choice **B** is wrong because, even if Pat should have seen the skateboard, that fact might establish negligence, but it would not support a finding of assumption of risk. Finally, choice **A** is wrong because a plaintiff who has no knowledge of risk—whatever the reason for the plaintiff's ignorance of the risk—cannot be treated as having assumed the risk.

18. **C** Breach of a "safety" statute ordinarily constitutes negligence ***per se*** when (1) the plaintiff was ***within*** the class of persons intended to be protected by the statute, (2) the statute ***sought to prevent*** the type of harm suffered by the plaintiff, (3) the defendant's ***violation*** of the statute is not excusable, and (4) there is a ***causal relationship*** between the statutory violation and the plaintiff's harm. Here, Jill was clearly within the class of persons the statute meant to protect (i.e., swimmers and boaters). The statute was designed to prevent physical injury and property damage from the operation of boats by youthful and inexperienced boaters. Leaving a key in the ignition is one of the very acts an inexperienced operator might do. Choice **A** is wrong because Jeff's violation is negligence ***per se***, not merely one factor evidencing negligence. Choice **B** is wrong because under some circumstances even a person who violates a safety statute may be able to show that his violation was excusable. Choice **D** is wrong because, as discussed above, the statutory violation is relevant to establishing negligence.

19. **B** The ***professional standard of care*** applies to a claim of a surgeon's negligent performance of surgery. In general, that standard requires a plaintiff to show that the defendant failed to follow the typical practice of other doctors in the relevant specialty. Choice **A** is wrong because it would allow the jury to use its own judgment about reasonableness and reject the professional consensus. Choice **C** is

wrong in the same way, since it suggests that in a case governed by the professional standard of care, a jury could use its own reasoning to decide whether the defendant's conduct was too risky. Choice **D** is wrong because in almost all jurisdictions a plaintiff whose own negligence contributed to his or her injury can still be entitled to recover some damages. Also, the burden of proof with regard to a plaintiff's negligence would be placed on the defendant, so it would be wrong to state that the plaintiff must introduce evidence of freedom from negligence.

20. **C** Physicians must obtain **_informed consent_** from their patients before performing procedures on them. Nonetheless, under the circumstances described in choice **C**, Dr. Bravo would prevail. The circumstances are that he performed the surgery without committing any errors, and unfortunately for Phyllis, she would have undergone the procedure even if Dr. Bravo had actually given her a full disclosure about the discoloration risk. Since shortcomings in disclosure, if there were any, would not have had a causal impact on Phyllis's conduct, there can be no liability for those shortcomings, if any. Choices **A** and **B** are wrong because the care with which a doctor performs a procedure has no bearing on liability for failure to obtain informed consent. Choice **D** is wrong because a doctor's view about benefits to a patient does not excuse a doctor from the typical requirements of obtaining informed consent.

21. **C** These facts raise the issue of whether a negligence theory can support recovery against a retailer for injury caused by something that had been sold to the retailer in a sealed package. The correct answer is choice **C** because a retailer is liable only if he had a duty to inspect the goods and had a reasonable chance of finding the defect. No court would expect a retailer to open prepackaged bologna to look for a nail. On the contrary, opening the package might itself constitute negligence because it would expose the bologna to contamination. Choice **A** is wrong because, while the doctrine of **_res ipsa loquitur_** might impose liability on Packo, it would not apply to Don because Don was not in exclusive control at the critical time—i.e., when the bologna was packaged. Choice **D** is wrong because horizontal privity is generally no longer required in suits involving defective products. Finally, choice **B** is wrong because nothing in these facts suggests that Don had any special relationship with Packo which would make Don liable for Packo's negligence.

22. **C** Negligence is unreasonable conduct in the face of a foreseeable risk to others by the person who creates the risk. Even though John **_did_**

not act negligently in hitting the moose *initially*, he *did act unreasonably by leaving it in the middle of the road where it would foreseeably pose a great risk of harm to others*. Because Phil was injured as a consequence of this risk, he can successfully sue John for damages. Choice **D** is wrong because freedom from contributory negligence does not entitle a person to recovery; the injured person must still establish that the defendant breached a duty of care. Choice **A** is wrong because, while John was not at fault in hitting the moose, he was nevertheless under a duty to remove it from the road. Finally, choice **B** is wrong because John did have a duty to remove the risk of harm to others which he had accidentally created by striking the moose.

23. **A** When one creates a risk to others (whether intentionally or accidentally), he has a *duty to make a reasonable effort to remove the risk before someone is foreseeably damaged by it*. The converse is also true. Because Ellwood was not responsible in any manner for the death of the moose or for its presence in the road, he was under no obligation to assist in its removal. Choice **B** is wrong because, even if John had asked Ellwood for assistance in removing the animal, Ellwood would have been under no obligation to cooperate. Choice **C** is wrong because Ellwood's duty was not increased either by his having witnessed the accident or by his knowledge that the moose had been left in the road. Finally, choice **D** is wrong because the fact that Phil may have acted reasonably under the circumstances does not affect or enlarge Ellwood's liability.

24. **A** The commercial manufacturer of a *defective item* (i.e., one which is unreasonably dangerous in light of its anticipated and normal use) is liable for *any* personal injuries or property damage suffered by a purchaser or user of the item as *a consequence of such defect*, under the doctrine of strict liability. Since Sis was using the bicycle in a *reasonably foreseeable manner* when she was injured by the defective product, she should be able to recover against Bikeco based on strict liability. Here, a court would probably find the bike was defectively designed and constructed because it was unreasonably flimsy, and because the cost of constructing it properly was small when compared to the resulting risk. Choice **B** is wrong because it merely restates one of the public policy rationales that support the strict liability doctrine. Choice **C** is wrong because a commercial supplier or merchant is liable for personal injuries to any user caused by a defective product purchased from him, so long as the

item was used in a reasonably foreseeable manner. It was certainly foreseeable that an 11-year-old child might temporarily ride a bicycle sold to a 7-year-old. Choice **D** is wrong because strict liability extends to any foreseeable user or consumer of the product, not only the purchaser or the intended user.

25. **A** The ***commercial supplier*** of a defective item (i.e., one which is unreasonably dangerous in light of its anticipated and normal use) is liable for any personal injuries or property damage suffered by a purchaser or user of the item as a consequence of such defect. Because Hardware is a commercial supplier, ***it will be liable in strict liability in tort*** to Sis if the bicycle was defective (i.e., in an unreasonably dangerous condition) at the time of sale. Choice **B** is wrong because recovery under strict liability does not require proof that a defendant acted unreasonably. Choice **C** is wrong because each commercial supplier in the chain of distribution may be liable to the injured user even though it merely resold the item in its original form. Finally, choice **D** is wrong because strict liability in tort does not require privity between the commercial supplier and the injured party.

26. **D** In most jurisdictions, a plaintiff may recover for ***emotional distress suffered*** as a consequence of ***observing an injury to another,*** only if the plaintiff was in a zone of danger. That is, the plaintiff must show that he or she might have suffered physical injury from the defendant's actions. Although Friend was horrified by the unpleasant sight of seeing Sis injured severely, she can ***not*** recover for her own mental distress as a consequence because she was outside the zone of danger. Choice **A** is wrong because the source of harm need not be inherently dangerous for the plaintiff to recover for mental distress. Choice **B** is wrong because Friend was not actually imperiled by the breaking of a part of the bicycle. Choice **C** is wrong because the fact that Friend was not using the item would not, by itself, preclude a recovery for mental distress.

27. **A** A ***private nuisance*** occurs when the defendant intentionally, negligently, or by conducting an ultrahazardous activity causes an unreasonable and substantial interference with the plaintiff's use and enjoyment of his land, especially if the activity is identified as a substantial health hazard. The flies and noxious odor around Plaintiffs' homes as a consequence of Cattle Company's activities probably constitute an ***unreasonable interference*** with Plaintiffs' use of their property. Choice **B** is wrong because the Cattle Company was not negligent (it was using the "best and most sanitary" equipment).

Choice **C** is wrong because the mere fact that the Cattle Company has been operating for more than five years would not, in itself, constitute a defense to Plaintiffs' private nuisance action, especially since the plaintiffs are not the only people whose interests are at stake. Approximately 10,000 others live nearby. Finally, choice **D** is wrong because the fact that Cattle Company uses reasonable procedures does not relieve it of liability. Cattle Company's continuation of its activities, especially once it became aware of the impact of its activities on the plaintiffs, makes its conduct intentional, and thus Cattle Company is liable for a private nuisance.

28. **A** A commercial supplier who sells a *defective* and unreasonably dangerous item in the ordinary course of its business is liable for any personal injury or property damage resulting from the defect, whether or not the commercial supplier was negligent in the design or production of the product. The corned beef was *defective and unreasonably dangerous* by reason of the fact that it contained the sliver of bone. The fact that West Beef Company may have exercised *reasonable care* in purchasing the product from Meat Packers is *irrelevant* in a products liability action based on a strict liability theory. Choice **B** is wrong because a vendor's breach of warranty is not imputed to a distributor or manufacturer. Choice **C** is wrong because privity of contract is not required in strict liability suits. Finally, choice **D** is wrong because Susie is suing in strict liability, not for breach of warranty.

29. **B** A person who keeps a wild animal is *strictly liable for all damage* done by it if the damage results from a dangerous propensity that is typical of it. A skunk is considered a wild animal because it is *not* one which is customarily used in the service of mankind.

Even though Householder *thought* the skunk's propensity to spray an offensive scent had been eliminated, Householder is still strictly liable for all damage resulting from the original propensity. Choice **A** is wrong because a private nuisance must interfere with another's property interest, and Walker's harm is based on personal injury, not damage to property. Choice **C** is wrong because there is an exception to the general freedom from liability to trespassers when the landowner knows that a portion of her land is frequently used by trespassers as a crossing or path. Although the landowner can usually satisfy this exception with a warning, the warning may not be enough when it is apparent that the trespassers will not respect the warning, as is the case here (trespassers ignored the first sign he erected, so he should have foreseen that the second would not be respected either). Choice **D** is wrong because Householder will be strictly liable, and thus antecedent conduct by Dr. Vet is not relevant.

30. **C** *Magazine* utilized Actor's picture within a general story about the eating and drinking tastes of film stars. Movie actors expect that newspapers and magazines will run stories of this kind. The use of Actor's photo was merely *incidental* to the overall subject matter of the article. Furthermore, Actor could not reasonably argue that his privacy or solitude had been invaded when he was drinking beer in a public place. Choice **A** is wrong because a person in a public place like a sidewalk café does not have an expectation of privacy. Choice **B** is wrong because Actor had no legitimate expectation of privacy and because the publication of Actor's photo by *Magazine* was only incidentally for commercial purposes. To hold otherwise would result in a ban on publication of the photo of any public figure in a newspaper or magazine of general circulation. Choice **D** is wrong because the impact of a publication upon the subject's career or profession is not pertinent to the issue of invasion of privacy.

31. **B** One who uses another's *name or likeness* for one's financial benefit or gain is liable for the tort of invasion of privacy. In this instance, Foamus is using Actor's likeness *for its commercial and financial benefit*. The use is not incidental to a proper purpose but clearly for the sole benefit of Foamus, without the authorization or consent of Actor. Choice **A** is wrong because the mere fact that Actor had not consented to having his picture taken is not enough to make Foamus liable: It is Foamus's use of the picture in selling beer without his consent that creates liability. Choice **C** is wrong because the fact that the photo had appeared in *Magazine* did not constitute permission to Foamus to use the photo for its own gain. Finally, choice **D** is wrong because Actor's status as a public figure does not entitle others to use his likeness to profit from his fame.

32. **B** *Pure expressions of opinion are not defamatory.* Alma's criticism of Bessy is an *opinion* about the quality of Bessy's work, *rather than a statement of fact* about Bessy herself or about facts contained in her work. Literary criticism is probably the best example of opinion which is not usually actionable. Choice **C** is wrong on the facts, which do not show any statements by Alma constituting assertions or implications based on fact. Implied assertions of false facts can be actionable, but that is not the case here. Choices **A** and **D** are wrong because the threshold elements of a cause of action for defamation are not met (since Alma's statement was one of

opinion, not fact), and therefore it is irrelevant that Bessy cannot show out-of-pocket loss and that she is a well-known author.

33. **A** To recover against a public medium for defamation, a public figure must show either knowledge of falsity or reckless disregard of the truth. A private citizen, on the other hand, need show only that the medium acted unreasonably in ascertaining the facts. But if the medium can establish that it acted reasonably, even a private person cannot recover for defamation. The correct answer is choice **A**. If Caster, a media defendant, exercised reasonable care in investigating the statement which he broadcast, a defamation action can *not* be successfully sustained against him (*even though* his statements were false). Choice **B** is wrong because the medium's belief with respect to the truth is not the measure of liability. It must make a reasonable investigation into the truth. Choice **C** is wrong because a retraction will bar Teacher's recovery only in some states where case law or a statute gives that force to retractions. Choice **D** is wrong because Caster's ill will toward Teacher, if it exists, will be relevant on the issue of damages, not liability, which will depend on the extent to which Caster investigated the truth of his statements.

34. **B** The elements of a cause of action for *misrepresentation* are (1) a misrepresentation of a material fact, (2) scienter, (3) intent to induce reliance, (4) justifiable reliance, and (5) damage to the plaintiff stemming from the reliance. Here, Vendor *intentionally made a misrepresentation* that the land was free from encumbrances in order to induce Purchaser to buy the land. However, despite Purchaser's damage, the correct answer is choice **B**. Purchaser's reliance on the misrepresentation would not have been justified if a reasonable person would have discovered the mortgage before the closing of the transaction (i.e., through a routine inspection of the title to the land). Choice **A** is wrong. Although Purchaser has been damaged, he cannot recover because he had constructive notice of the mortgage. Choice **C** is not correct. Though the value of the land itself may have increased, Purchaser's interest is worth $15,000 less than the price he paid. Choice **D** is wrong because the choice between equitable and legal remedies is up to the plaintiff, not the defendant. The plaintiff may choose whether to sue for rescission or for damages.

35. **D** The manufacturer of a product will be *strictly liable* if the product was defective *at the time of sale* and was unreasonably dangerous to a consumer or foreseeable user. The correct answer is choice **D**. It

states the rule of law applicable in strict liability cases. Choice **A** is wrong because proof of negligence is not required in strict liability cases. Choice **B** is wrong because, although the conduct of other manufacturers may be relevant to the "defect" issue, it is not dispositive. Choice **C** is wrong because a defective product cannot be made nondefective through use of a warning, nor will a warning relieve the manufacturer of liability for a defective product.

36. **B** A commercial supplier who sells a *defective* and unreasonably dangerous item in the ordinary course of its business is *strictly liable* for any personal injury or property damages resulting from consumption or use of the item. To support her claim, Brenda must show only that the stove was defective and in the same condition as when her mother purchased it. Local Retailer is therefore liable for any physical injuries arising from the product's use, *so long as the injury did not result from changes made to the product after it was purchased.* Therefore, the correct answer is choice **B**. Choice **A** is wrong because a warning about defects in the product will not relieve the retailer of liability if the product is defective. Choice **C** is wrong because a retailer can be strictly liable without being at fault in any way for the design or assembly of the product. Finally, choice **D** is wrong because strict liability does not require proof that the retailer know or have constructive knowledge that the product is dangerous.

37. **A** A person intends to commit an act either when he means to carry out the act or when he knows with substantial certainty that his movements or actions will result in the act. When Bill ran off a crowded dance floor and through the exit, it was substantially certain that he would collide with another patron. Joan can recover against Bill for battery. The correct answer is choice **A**. Choice **B** is wrong because Bill's lack of desire to injure anyone is not controlling. As long as his actions were substantially likely to result in contact with another patron, he is liable. Choice **C** is wrong because Bill's reason for his actions is irrelevant. What is relevant is that his conduct was substantially certain to result in contact with another patron. Finally, choice **D** is wrong because an injury to Joan or to someone else resulting from the contact with Bill was reasonably foreseeable under the circumstances of a crowded dance floor and Bill's actions.

38. **D** An assault occurs when the defendant intentionally causes the plaintiff to apprehend that he is in imminent danger of an offensive touching. The intent of the defendant and the apprehension of the plaintiff must coexist. If the plaintiff is not put in apprehension

of an imminent contact, there is no assault. On these facts, Bart believed Joe was bluffing and did not fear an offensive touching. Therefore the best answer is choice **D**. Choice **A** is wrong because Bart did not apprehend that Joe would actually make an offensive contact upon him, and a necessary element of assault was therefore lacking. Choice **B** is wrong because Bart will not be able to show that he suffered emotional distress; the facts tell us that he did not believe Joe would harm him. Choice **C** is wrong because it is immaterial to the issue of Joe's liability for assault that Bart may have engaged in illegal conduct.

39. **C** A false imprisonment occurs when the defendant has intentionally confined the plaintiff to an area with defined physical boundaries from which there is no reasonable means of escape. The intent to confine is an essential element of the tort. Because the janitor was unaware that Alan was in the reading room, he did not have the requisite intent and the janitor is not liable for false imprisonment. Therefore, the correct answer is choice **C**. Choice **A** is wrong. Even though Alan was indeed confined to the room against his will, the janitor did not intend the confinement. Choice **B** is wrong because negligence in causing confinement will not support an action for false imprisonment. Choice **D** is wrong. Physical injury is not an element of false imprisonment.

40. **D** Consent by the plaintiff is a valid defense to a claim based on an intentional tort. Because Max voluntarily consented to the "pat down" search, he cannot recover for battery. Faced with the demand that he submit to the search, Max could either accede to the demand or decline to board the bus. The choice was voluntary. The correct answer is choice **D**. Choice **A** is wrong because Max was not "compelled" to submit to the search. Although he had planned to board the bus, the decision to consent to the "pat down" was voluntary. Choice **B** is wrong. The fact that Max subsequently suffered physical harm by becoming ill is irrelevant to whether the defendant committed a battery and to whether Max consented to the battery. Choice **C** is wrong because the defendant does not have to prove that it was reasonable in requiring the "pat down." So long as Max submitted to the search voluntarily, the bus line has a valid defense.

41. **D** The tort of intentional infliction of emotional distress occurs when the defendant, through intentional or reckless outrageous conduct, causes the plaintiff severe emotional distress. The plaintiff may

recover if he can prove the defendant intended the distress, knew with a certainty that the distress would occur, or acted recklessly. The transferred intent doctrine does not ordinarily apply to this tort (to prevent litigation by people who happen to see an outrageous act and claim to be distressed by it). Therefore, the correct answer is choice **D** because the defendants did not intend their actions to have any effect on Bill. Choice **A** is wrong because it misstates the law of transferred intent as it applies to the tort of infliction of emotional distress. Choice **B** is wrong; it is not necessary that a plaintiff who is entitled to sue for infliction of mental distress prove physical harm; nor does physical harm entitle a plaintiff to sue for emotional distress. Choice **C** is wrong. Under the majority rule, only a member of the intended victim's *immediate family* may recover on the theory of transferred intent. (However, some jurisdictions extend the doctrine to anyone who is in the vicinity of the act and who suffers bodily harm.)

42. D Although Frank has suffered injury and distress, he will probably not be able to recover from Tim on any theory. Both assault and intentional infliction of mental distress require that the plaintiff be aware of the threat to him at the time of the action upon him. The impact upon him must be contemporaneous with the defendant's action. Choices **A** and **C** are therefore wrong. Choice **B** is wrong because the tort of battery requires some harmful or offensive contact with the body or personal effects of the plaintiff, and the bullet never touched Frank. The correct answer is choice **D**.

43. D Choice **D** is correct because the school was staffed with a reasonable number of teachers and other personnel, and because those employees acted with reasonable care. Choice **A** is wrong because showing that a defendant owes a plaintiff a duty of care is not enough to support liability. In addition, a plaintiff must show that the defendant breached a duty. Choice **B** is wrong because there is no basis for imposing liability on Learnwell, so consideration of causation has no relevance. Choice **C** is wrong because Learnwell is free from liability because it is free from negligence, not because of causation issues. The quarry's conduct, however, is not likely to be treated as superseding had Learnwell been negligent, since playing at a quarry is foreseeable conduct for a child who wanders away from a school.

44. A A trespass occurs when the defendant intentionally, negligently, or by engaging in an abnormally dangerous activity causes an encroachment upon the land of another. When Bill sprayed water on

Albert's driveway, he committed an intentional trespass. He caused a tangible object—water—to enter Albert's driveway. Because of the trespass, Bill is liable for any injuries resulting from his acts, including the injury to Albert. The correct answer is choice **A**. Choice **B** is wrong because Bill intentionally sprayed the water on Albert's land. Choice **C** is wrong. Although trespass and nuisance can sometimes coexist, that is probably not the case here. A nuisance occurs where the defendant substantially and unreasonably interferes with the plaintiff's use or enjoyment of his land. Here, we are dealing with a single trespassory act, not a continuing interference with use or enjoyment of Albert's land. Finally, choice **D** is wrong because it is not necessary for the defendant himself to enter on the plaintiff's land. He is liable if he causes an object to touch or encroach on the land.

45. B A conversion occurs when the defendant takes possession of the property of another with the intent to interfere with his use or possession of the property. A bona fide purchaser of stolen goods is considered by most courts to be a converter. (In some states, a bona fide purchaser is not a converter unless he refuses to give the goods back to the lawful owner.) The correct answer is choice **B**. Because Jesse purchased the television set from Howard intending to be the legal owner, a conversion occurred. Jesse is liable to Randy for the reasonable value of that item. Choice **A** is wrong. The tort of conversion is not triggered by causing damage to the property of another but by interfering with its use or possession. Choice **C** is wrong. In most states a bona fide purchaser for value would be liable for conversion even if he did not know the goods were stolen. Even in states where return of someone's property precludes liability for conversion, Jesse would be liable because he refused to return the set to Randy. Finally, choice **D** is wrong because it is not supported by the facts we are given, which show no negligence. Also, Randy's failure to exercise reasonable care in protecting the TV set from being stolen is irrelevant to the issue of conversion.

46. C A merchant who has parted willingly with possession of a product cannot use force to regain it. He must use judicial process instead. Although Exco may have been entitled to repossess the motor home, it could not do so by force. Exco's employee committed both assault and battery upon Owner, and the correct answer is choice **C**. Choice **A** is wrong because Owner's default did not entitle Exco to use force. Choice **B** is wrong because assumption of risk is not a defense to an intentional tort. Choice **D** is wrong because it does not state the reason that entitles Owner to recover. Whether or not Owner was in default, Exco had no right to attempt repossession by force.

47. D One is entitled to use deadly force when threatened with serious bodily harm or death by another person. Because Leo had taken a step toward Anthony with his knife drawn, Anthony was entitled to respond with deadly force. Choice **A** is wrong because Anthony, when he shot Leo, was defending himself (rather than attempting to reclaim the basketball). Choice **B** is wrong because the imminence of harm would authorize an immediate response. Choice **C** is wrong because the fact that Anthony was in illegal possession of a firearm does not affect the right to use it against Leo under these circumstances.

48. B In virtually all jurisdictions, there can be no valid consent to conduct that constitutes a crime or a breach of the peace. In a fistfight between two men, each will be allowed to sue the other because their consent to the fight is deemed ineffective. Xavier is liable to Chuck because he participated in the fight. Choice **A** is wrong since Xavier's boxing skill and Chuck's ignorance of it are immaterial. Choice **C** is wrong because Chuck could not validly consent to a public fistfight. Choice **D** is wrong because it's immaterial who struck the first blow. Each fighter is liable to the other because neither could legally consent to the fight.

49. C One who is attacked by another may use whatever force is reasonably necessary under the circumstances to prevent serious bodily harm or death to himself. Because Aaron initiated the attack by lunging at Eddie and was 4 inches taller and 22 pounds heavier than Eddie, Eddie was entitled to use reasonable force to repel him (Aaron's height and weight are relevant to the issue of whether Eddie's force was reasonable). Because Eddie was unaware of Aaron's previous operation and only intended to disable him, the force utilized was justified. Choice **B** is wrong because Eddie's force was reasonable under the circumstances. Choice **A** is wrong because insults do not justify a physical attack. Choice **D** is wrong. Eddie was entitled to use reasonable force to repel the attack, but there is no absolute rule that use or nonuse of a weapon controls the characterization of a self-defender's conduct as reasonable or unreasonable.

50. D One who is attacked may use whatever force is reasonably necessary under the circumstances to prevent serious bodily harm or death to himself. Because Darren was attempting to attack Sam with a knife, Sam was entitled to disable Darren. Choice **A** is wrong because, in most jurisdictions, one has no duty to retreat from an attacker. In this situation, Sam could justifiably assume that Darren might pursue him. Choice **B** is wrong because Sam was not obliged to choose the alternative of wresting the knife away from Darren instead of blocking it and punching Darren. Because Darren had attacked with deadly force, Sam was entitled to respond as he did. Choice **C** is wrong because the mere fact that Darren was illegally carrying a knife would not privilege Sam to injure him. The privilege arose when Darren threatened Sam with the knife.

51. **C** Violation of a statute constitutes *negligence per se* when (1) the conduct prescribed by the statute is clear, (2) the plaintiff is in the group sought to be protected by the statute, and (3) the plaintiff suffers an injury of the kind the statue was intended to avert. Even if these factors are present, a plaintiff must still establish a causal link between the defendant's negligence and the plaintiff's harm. Because the entire hallway was engulfed in flames, it cannot be said that the Argyle's failure to have at least two fire exits caused Martha's injuries. Choice **A** is wrong because, as explained above, there was no causal connection between the Argyle's failure to comply with the statute and Martha's injuries. Choice **B** is wrong for the same reason. Choice **D** is wrong because Martha's apprehension and concerns could reasonably be anticipated in light of her advanced age and disability.

52. **C** In most states, rescue personnel cannot recover in negligence for injuries incurred during the performance of their duties. Since Gordon, a firefighter, was injured in the course of his duties, he probably will be unable to prevail against the Argyle. The facts that the fire was an accident and that violation of the statute by the Argyle was not the cause of any injuries to Gordon would also shield the defendant from liability. Choice **A** is wrong because, as explained in the answer to the previous question, there would be no causal connection between the Argyle's failure to comply with the statute and Gordon's injury. Choice **B** is wrong because the lack of fire exits was not the cause of Gordon's injuries and the fire was not the fault of the Argyle. Also, in most jurisdictions, firefighters are precluded from recovering for injuries sustained in the performance of their duties. Choice **D** is wrong because Gordon probably did not act unreasonably in jumping onto the awning. This would appear to be the only option he had.

53. **B** A supplier like Restaurant Produce Corporation is an independent contractor, not an employee or agent of Chef, and therefore Chef will be free from responsibility for any negligent acts by Grant. Choice **A** is wrong because regardless of Grant's quality of conduct, Chef would have no responsibility for injuries he inflicts, for the reason stated above. Choice **C** is wrong because respondeat superior applies only when a defendant controls the conduct of an employee, not when a defendant hires someone else's workers. Choice **D** is wrong because availability of postjudgment recourse would have no effect on a defendant's initial liability.

54. **A** One has no privilege to use force capable of causing death or serious bodily injury in the defense of property. Although John was a trespasser, Louis had no right to shoot at him. There was nothing to indicate to Louis that John had committed a felony or that he was threatening Louis with injury. On the contrary, John was running away when Louis shot at him. Choice **B** is wrong because, even if John recognized that Louis was a security guard, Louis was not privileged to shoot at him. Choice **C** is wrong because the force used by Louis was not reasonable under the circumstances. Finally, choice **D** is wrong because, although the pursuit by the two men caused John to climb the fence, Louis will not prevail because he was not privileged to shoot at John.

55. **D** The private necessity doctrine confers a privilege even upon a volunteer to prevent injury to the person or property of another, even at the risk of damaging private property, if there is no other reasonable way of preventing the harm. Here, for example, the choice for George was between saving eight vintage Cadillacs and driving onto a lawn. However, if the person who attempts to prevent the injury causes damage to the property of another, he must reimburse him for it. Because George trespassed upon Laura's land, he is liable for the damage to her sprinkler equipment. Choice **A** is wrong. Laura was not required to prove that George knew he was on her land to support a trespass claim. Choice **B** is wrong because under the private necessity doctrine the actor is liable for any injury or damages he causes. Choice **C** is factually wrong. George did act reasonably under the circumstances, especially since he had no way of knowing he was on Laura's land.

56. **D** Under traditional joint and several liability doctrines, all defendants are potentially responsible for paying all of a plaintiff's judgment. In this case, Defendants One and Two would be responsible for the amount of damages that were uncollectable from Defendant Three.

Choice **A** is wrong because joint and several liability prevents a plaintiff from bearing the financial consequence of the insolvency of one of a group of multiple defendants. Choices **B** and **C** are wrong because both Defendant One and Defendant Two would be responsible for paying the judgment owed by insolvent Defendant Three. There is no reason to believe that either one of them would be more likely than the other to be called upon to satisfy that amount.

57. **B** One acts in a negligent manner when he fails to act reasonably under all the prevailing circumstances. Dad should have been more careful in securing the "race car." Because the boy was able to retrieve the vehicle, although with some difficulty, Dad is probably liable to Jane. Choice **A** is wrong because the fact that driving the "race car" was an adultlike activity increases the likelihood that Dad was negligent in failing to prevent his son from having unsupervised access to the car. Choice **C** is wrong because, although a valid statement of the law, the claim here is not based upon strict liability but upon Dad's negligent failure to secure the car to prevent its use by the boy. Finally, choice **D** is wrong because a negligent defendant ordinarily takes the plaintiff as he finds her, infirmities and all.

58. **B** Under the doctrine of strict products liability, a commercial supplier who, in the regular course of business, provides a defective product is liable to the purchaser or user for personal injury or property damage resulting from the defect, even when the defendant exercised due care in the item's production. We may conclude that, because the saw had fallen and the blade had become loose the first time it was utilized, it was in an unreasonably dangerous condition when it left Roo's possession. Thus, Joe can recover against Roo for his injuries under a products liability theory. Choice **A** is wrong because it is unclear that Bill was negligent in failing to read the instruction booklet. In any event, he was utilizing the power saw properly; nothing he might have read in the book would have prevented the accident; and the accident was caused entirely by a defect in the saw. Choice **C** is wrong because, in most jurisdictions, bystanders may recover under a strict products liability theory. Finally, choice **D** is wrong because the Hardware Store was probably under no duty to inspect the item or to test its use. In any event, its intervening negligence, if any, in failing to detect the loose blade would not relieve Roo of liability as the manufacturer.

59. **C** The loss of a chance doctrine allows wrongful death recovery in a medical malpractice case even if the patient's death would have

been more likely than not to occur regardless of the quality of medical care. If a patient had a quantifiable chance of survival, even if that chance was 50 percent or less, some recovery is allowed. Choice **C** describes the proper application of this doctrine, since it states that the necessary fact—the loss of a particular chance of survival—must be established by a preponderance of the evidence. Choice **A** is wrong because denying a 30 percent chance of survival does not "cause" death. Choice **B** is wrong because recovery cannot be based on proof of any required fact by less than a preponderance of evidence. Choice **D** is wrong for the same reason, since it fails to apply the preponderance standard of proof.

60. B A defendant is liable for negligence only if there is a causal connection between his conduct and the plaintiff's injury. Although John had been exceeding the speed limit, he was stopped at a light when his vehicle was struck from behind by Harvey. Mary could only prevail in a negligence action against Harvey. Choice **A** is wrong because John's prior negligence in speeding did not contribute to Mary's injuries. Choice **C** is wrong because Mary cannot be held to have assumed the risk of John's speeding. It would be unreasonable to require a woman to leave a car in the dark if she was afraid to do so. As to Harvey, she obviously did not assume any risk of his supervening negligence. Finally, choice **D** is wrong because a typical guest statute protects from liability only the driver of the vehicle in which the guest is riding.

61. D Under the Federal Tort Claims Act, the United States is liable for negligent conduct by its employees if state law would impose liability for such conduct on a nongovernmental employer. However, liability may not be imposed if the government employee's conduct involved "discretion." The conduct in this case, choosing where to place a mailbox, is different from the kind of conduct shielded by the discretionary function exception. That exception is intended to protect against liability for actions that involve public policy choices, typically connected with allocation of limited public resources or typically associated with broad policy choices. Choice **A** is wrong because this type of operational decision is unlikely to be characterized as discretionary. Choice **B** is wrong because the facts present a situation in which a juror could (but would not be required to) find the conduct negligent. Choice **C** is wrong because, as in most negligence cases, these facts present a circumstance in which jurors would have adequate support for *either* a finding of negligence or a finding that there was no negligence.

62. **A** A druggist must act reasonably, and relying on a clerk's interpretation of a prescription form is likely to be characterized as unreasonable. Many drug names are confusingly similar to the names of other drugs. Maxwell's failure to read the prescription himself constituted negligence. Choice **B** is wrong because there is no indication that either Donatol or Ponatol was defective as a product. Choice **C** is wrong. The rules that impose strict liability for accidents which occur as a result of abnormally dangerous activities were not meant to cover the pharmaceutical profession. Otherwise, all druggists would be strictly liable for their mistakes. Instead, they are held to the level of care that is normally practiced by druggists. Finally, choice **D** is wrong because, as discussed above, Jane could successfully sue Maxwell for his negligence.

63. **D** When a manufacturer's product is substantially changed by a subsequent seller and a subsequent buyer or user is injured, the manufacturer is relieved of culpability under a products liability theory. Because Buyer's injuries were attributable to Seller's loosening of the seat belt, Buyer will be unable to recover from Carco. Choice **A** is wrong because Carco ceased to be culpable under a products liability theory when Seller refitted the seat belt. Choice **B** is wrong because there is no indication that Carco failed to act reasonably in the manufacture of the seat belt or that the seat belt was defective. Finally, choice **C** is wrong because there is nothing to indicate that Buyer realized that the strap was too loose to prevent injury if a collision occurred; also, any negligence by Buyer would likely reduce but not bar recovery.

64. **B** A retailer who sells a product which is in an unreasonably dangerous condition is liable to the consumer or user for physical harm if the retailer was in the regular business of selling that product, and the product is expected to, and does, reach the buyer or user without substantial change from the condition in which it was sold. Because the rocking chair collapsed almost immediately after it was purchased, Romo (as a commercial supplier) would be liable under a products liability theory. There is no indication that the chair was intended to be used only by persons of a certain weight. Nor is it reasonable to expect that a chair would be sold to the general public if it was unsafe for a person weighing 162 pounds. Choice **A** is wrong because, even if Romo had made a careful inspection of the rocking chair, it would still be liable to Melba under a strict products liability theory. Choice **C** is wrong because foreseeable users (as well as

purchasers) can assert a products liability theory. Finally, choice **D** is wrong because Romo is a commercial supplier of chairs. (Romo would presumably have a right of indemnity against Zero.)

65. **C** A person with a mental disability is required, under the majority view, to act as reasonably as a person with typical mental abilities would act. Choice **A** is wrong because mental illness does not permit a defendant to act less reasonably than a mentally healthy person would act under the same circumstances. Choice **B** is wrong because it states a standard of care different from the one that applies to individuals with mental illness. Choice **D** is wrong because it misstates the test used for negligence: Jurors must compare an actor's conduct with what they think the hypothetical reasonable person would do, not with what they think they themselves would do under the circumstances.

66. **D** Under the substantial factor test for legal (or proximate) cause, the connection between the nurse's conduct and Plaintiff's injury is close enough in time and space and significant enough in terms of its contribution to the injury to satisfy a finding of proximate cause. Choice **A** is wrong because moving the stool is clearly within the nurse's scope of employment. Carrying out an act unreasonably does *not* take that action out of the scope of a worker's employment. Choice **B** is wrong because events can have multiple causes-in-fact, as is the case in this situation. Choice **C** is wrong because the professional standard of care is withdrawn for cases involving ministerial or nontechnical conduct, such as providing and moving a stool.

67. **A** A manufacturer is strictly liable for damage caused by a defective product distributed by it in commerce. Because the lawn mower was defective—no mower should move when the motor switch is turned off—John can successfully recover from Dynatron. Choice **B** is wrong. Although it is a general statement of a manufacturer's duty, it is not dispositive on these facts. The relevant facts are that the mower was sold by Dynatron's customer to John in a defective condition and that liability follows. The essence of strict liability is that the defendant is liable even if due care was exercised. Choice **C** is wrong. Liability by Dynatron is not limited to personal injury. Property damage resulting from the mower's malfunction is covered as well. Finally, choice **D** is wrong because John did not assume the risk of the lawn mower's moving on its own. Although it had apparently sputtered on other occasions before shutting down, the facts do not show that the mower had ever moved on its own when

it was shut off. John cannot be held to have assumed a risk he did not know existed.

68. B Negligence consists of a failure to act reasonably under the applicable circumstances which results in injury or damage to the person or property of another. Except under the most unusual and compelling circumstances, it is not reasonable for a person driving a motor vehicle in traffic to turn his head around. Confronted only by a bad odor, Bill should have pulled over to the curb before inspecting the rear of his car. Choice **A** is wrong because Bill was not negligent in leaving the back door of his car unlocked. A driver would ordinarily have no reason to foresee that another person would place foul-smelling rags in the back of his car. Choice **C** is wrong because Joe's conduct was not a superseding cause of the accident. Joe's actions preceded the collision. Finally, choice **D** is wrong because, as discussed above, Bill was unreasonable in allowing himself to become distracted under the circumstances and in not pulling over to a stop before turning his head.

69. B The learned intermediary doctrine excuses a product manufacturer from providing appropriate warnings to a foreseeable ultimate user of its product, if someone such as a doctor would necessarily have an opportunity to provide that information to the product's user. Typical prescription drugs are an example of frequent application of this doctrine. Choice **B** is one example of the doctrine in that context. Choice **A** is wrong because mass-inoculation programs often do not involve the kind of professional relationship that justifies application of the doctrine. Choices **C** and **D** are also wrong because the circumstances in which the products are used do not necessarily involve an opportunity for delivery of warnings or other information that the ultimate user of the product is entitled to have.

70. C The essence of a claim for defamation is that the defendant's statement had a tendency to harm the reputation of the plaintiff. If the plaintiff belongs to a large class of persons, it is difficult to argue that a remark about that entire class should be construed as a reflection on his own individual reputation. Because Arnold's comments pertained to lawyers in general, Malcolm will be unable to sustain an action for defamation. Choices **A** and **B** are wrong because general statements of the type Arnold made are highly unlikely to be construed as describing any particular individual. Choice **D** is wrong because it is not always necessary to show monetary damage to support an action for defamation.

71. **C** Contributory negligence, now applied in a small minority of states, is a complete defense to an action for negligence. Therefore, the correct answer is choice **C**. Arthur was clearly negligent in going through the red light and his negligence contributed to the accident. Choice **A** is wrong, because the last clear chance doctrine does not apply unless the defendant had an *actual* opportunity to avoid the accident at the last moment. On these facts, it cannot be said that Eddy had an opportunity to avoid the accident. He did apply his brakes, but it was too late. It is not even clear that the accident would have been avoided if he had not increased his speed. Choice **B** is wrong because it's immaterial to recovery by Albert that Eddy was not hurt. Choice **D** is wrong. Eddy did not act reasonably under the circumstances. No one is supposed to increase his speed at an intersection to "beat" a light.

72. **A** A defamatory statement must be reasonably susceptible of application to the plaintiff to be actionable. Because Joseph's statements were made indiscriminately to an indeterminate number of people at the bar and because his remarks were interpreted by the friend as applying to Bill, Bill probably does have a cause of action. The plaintiff in a defamatory action must show that the statement in question was reasonably interpreted by at least one listener as referring to him. Joseph's remarks are clearly defamatory. Choice **B** is not the best answer because a falsity alone does not make a statement defamatory. It's also necessary that the statement be published and the publication must be done either negligently or deliberately. Choice **C** is wrong on the facts because a reasonable person—the friend—did associate the statements with Bill. Choice **D** is wrong on the law. Defamation can be committed verbally.

73. **B** Harry was a public invitee when he was injured, because he was in a place held open by its owner to members of the public for a specific purpose (car repair transactions) and he was there for that purpose. An invitee who is injured by a condition on the defendant's land is entitled to recovery if the defendant failed to act reasonably. Reasonable care would require a warning or a repair of something dangerous like a sharp piece of metal under a counter. Choice **A** is wrong because status as an invitee does not guarantee recovery for an injury in the absence of proof that the defendant acted wrongly. Choice **C** is wrong because adherence to custom is relevant but not conclusive as a defense to a negligence claim. Choice **D** is wrong

because Harry attained invitee status when he entered the premises in connection with the purpose for which they were held open to the public.

74. **A** A joint and several tortfeasor who has paid more than his share of a judgment ordinarily has a right of contribution from the other tortfeasors who participated in the accident. Because Mark's proportionate share of the joint and several judgment is one-third of $120,000, or $40,000, and he paid the full $120,000, he will be entitled to recover $40,000 each from Bruce and David. Choice **B** is wrong because Mark cannot recover from Bruce or David under an indemnity theory. They were all equally culpable in causing the injury to Carl. Choice **C** is wrong because contribution is expressly intended to reimburse a defendant who was at fault when co-defendants have failed to pay their shares of a judgment. Finally, choice **D** is wrong on the facts, which tell us that the three defendants were adjudged jointly and severally liable.

75. **D** The best choice is **D**, because Painter has introduced no evidence that would support a finding of unreasonable conduct by Gardener. The statutory violation has no application in this case because the harm it was intended to avert, excessive use of water, is different from the kind of harm Painter suffered. Also, Painter is not in the class of individuals meant to be protected by the statute, since the statute meant to protect potential users of water, not visitors to someone's house. Choice **A** is wrong for the reasons stated above. Choice **B** is wrong because causation cannot support recovery when there is no proof of unreasonable conduct. Choice **C** is wrong because the statutory violation is *not* relevant at all, for the reasons stated above.

76. **B** Computers are almost always sold by retailers in their original cartons. There is no way for the retailer to determine whether or not the computer is defective or will cause injury. Under these circumstances, especially because the retailer is strictly liable to the consumer for injuries caused by the defective products, it is only logical and fair to permit the retailer to secure indemnity against the manufacturer. Because MiddleManCo also received the computer in its original carton from Compco and, presumably, did not alter the computer in any manner, ComputerStore is entitled to indemnity only from Compco. Choice **A** is wrong because there is no right of indemnity against MiddleManCo. Choice **C** is wrong because the

retailer ordinarily has a right to indemnity only against the manufacturer of the item unless the distributor has altered it in some manner. Finally, choice **D** is wrong. On these facts, ComputerStore should be able to obtain indemnity from Compco.

77. **D** The sudden emergency doctrine reminds a jury that when people act in emergencies they may act differently from the way they would act in the absence of an emergency, but it does not compel or preclude findings of negligence in typical factual situations. The rescue doctrine satisfies a rescuer's required showing of causation in a suit against one who created an emergency, but it does not protect a rescuer from being characterized as negligent if the rescuer's conduct was unreasonable under the circumstances. Choice **A** is a mistaken description of the effects of the sudden emergency doctrine. Choice **B** is a mistaken description of the effects of the rescue doctrine. Therefore, choice **C** is wrong because it states that both **A** and **B** are correct.

78. **D** One who engages in an abnormally dangerous activity is ordinarily liable to those suffering personal injury or property damage as a consequence of the peculiar risk associated with that conduct, but will not be liable if either (1) the harm is not that which can reasonably be anticipated from that conduct or (2) a superseding cause leads to the damage or injury. The peculiar risk associated with fumigation is the escape of noxious gas—not an explosion caused by a stranger who recklessly lights a match. Choice **A** is wrong because the peculiar risk associated with fumigation is the escape of a noxious gas, not the flammability of that gas. Choice **B** is wrong because although the fumes may have been a contributing cause, Kevin's reckless conduct was a superseding cause. Finally, choice **C** is wrong because both the abnormally dangerous activity doctrine and the principles of negligence allow an aggrieved plaintiff to recover for property damage as well as personal injury.

79. **D** The only loss Edgar claims is an economic loss related to the information Dr. Clark gave him. Dr. Clark's conduct did not cause any physical harm to Edgar. In these circumstances, recovery for "mere economic loss" would likely be rejected. Choices **A** and **B** are both wrong because Dr. Clark had no duty to protect Edgar from mere economic losses. Choice **C** is wrong because the zone of danger theory has no application in mere economic loss cases.

80. **B** A contractor that engages in an abnormally dangerous activity is liable to those suffering personal injury or property damage as a

consequence of the peculiar risk associated with that activity, even if the defendant acted with due care. Since Danco was involved in an abnormally dangerous activity (blasting alongside a highway), it would be strictly liable for Carl's injuries. Contributory negligence by the plaintiff is not normally a defense in a strict liability claim, especially when the plaintiff's negligence consisted of inattentiveness. The fact that Carl may have been negligent in failing to notice the sign does not relieve Danco of liability. It's usual for people who blast to place flagmen on the road to warn motorists under these circumstances. Choice **A** is wrong because Danco's liability arises from the strict liability placed upon those who work with explosives, not from negligence or lack of care. Choice **C** is wrong because one cannot assume a risk without having actual knowledge of it. Because he failed to notice the sign, Carl cannot have had any knowledge of the danger posed by the blasting. Finally, choice **D** is wrong because, even if Carl was contributorily negligent, he could nevertheless recover against Danco under strict liability principles.

81. **A** The owner of a domestic animal that has not previously exhibited dangerous or violent propensities is not strictly liable if that animal unexpectedly causes harm to another. Because Doggy was docile and Susan had no reason to suspect that she would ever bite anyone, Cindy cannot recover from Susan. Choice **B** is wrong because it states the wrong reason for precluding Cindy's recovery. The fact that she may have been engaged in an improper act is not a defense *per se* in a case involving the dangerous propensities of an animal. Choice **C** is wrong because dogs are not considered dangerous animals unless and until they exhibit dangerous tendencies. Finally, choice **D** is wrong, because Susan's failure to obtain a license does not constitute negligence *per se*. There was no direct link between the lack of a license and the bite.

82. **C** Because the power saw malfunctioned in use and was defective for its purpose, Steve is able to recover in strict product liability. Any commercial supplier who, in the regular course of business, provides a defective product is liable to the purchaser or user for personal injury or property damage resulting from the defect, even when that supplier has exercised due care. Because Wecut Company, the Max Brothers, and Tom's Hardware Store are all commercial suppliers in the chain of delivery to Blue, they are all liable to Steve under a products liability theory. Choices **A** and **B** are wrong because they fail to recognize that liability extends to each level of the chain of supply. Finally, choice **D** is wrong because the facts specifically

recite that there is no evidence that the power saw was negligently manufactured and the law does not require proof of negligence because Wecut is strictly liable for its defective product.

83. **D** Choice **A** is wrong because only a ***merchant with respect to goods of that kind*** can be liable for breach of the implied warranty of merchantability. Also, the warranty is not usually extended to used goods and the car had been used by Andrew when he sold it to Charles. Choice **B** is wrong because strict liability for defects in products is applied only to sellers who are regularly engaged in the business of selling the product at issue. Because Andrew was not a commercial supplier of cars, it is unlikely that Charles will recover from him under a strict liability theory. Choice **C** is wrong because the facts offer no support for a finding that Andrew was negligent in any way. He drove the car without problems for an entire week. Choice **D**, stating that Charles has no theory to support recovery, is therefore correct.

84. **B** A commercial supplier who, in the regular course of business, provides a defective product is liable to the purchaser or user for personal injury or property damage resulting from the defect, even when the defendant has exercised due care in the item's production. Although Drugco provided the pills to Dr. Frank gratuitously, it did so with the intent that Dr. Frank should in turn offer them to her patients. Drugco's purpose was to encourage commerce in its product. Although the courts are sometimes reluctant to apply strict products liability in the case of prescription drugs, the injury here seems so severe and unforeseeable that strict liability should be imposed. Choice **A** is wrong because Dr. Frank regularly provides services, rather than products. She is not a supplier of drugs in the normal chain of supply. Choice **C** is wrong because Dr. Frank is not a merchant (someone who ordinarily deals in items of this type), and therefore would not come within the purview of UCC implied warranties. Finally, choice **D** is wrong because Alex can probably recover against Drugco for implied warranty of merchantability in most courts. The lack of privity between Alex and Drugco is not likely to prevent recovery, in a case involving a consumer and the manufacturer of a defective product.

85. **B** This question concerns the liability of a merchant for injuries to someone who is neither the purchaser nor a member of the purchaser's family. It also requires examination of the difference between strict products liability and liability for implied warranty of merchantability. The correct answer is choice **B**. Even though Margaret

was a bystander, she was a foreseeable user. The product in question was a toy to be played with by children. Children often play with other children, who use their toys. Although Jolson's Toy Store sold the toy rocket to Brett, it was intended for use by James and his friends. Margaret's guardian can successfully sue Jolson's under a products liability theory. Choice **A** is wrong because there is no evidence that James's parents were negligent. James had been utilizing the toy rocket without incident for a whole month. Choice **C** is wrong because the lack of privity is no longer regarded in most courts as an obstacle to recovery for breach of the implied warranty of merchantability. Finally, choice **D** is wrong because, as explained above, although Margaret may have no claim against Brett, it is likely that Margaret can successfully sue Jolson's Toy Store in products liability.

86. **A** An eight-seat airplane is obviously intended to be used by eight passengers. Because the victims were all foreseeable users, their executors will all be able to recover in strict product liability against the merchant who sold the plane to John if the plane was defective and the defect caused the plane to crash. Because the plane's engine malfunctioned on its first flight, it was clearly defective, and Equinox will be liable to their executors. Choice **B** is wrong because, even if the evidence shows that the pilot performed his duties in a negligent manner, his negligence will probably not overcome the strict liability of Equinox. Choice **C** is wrong because, although Equinox did not ordinarily sell aircraft, it still provided planes to lessees or buyers on a regular basis. It was in the business of dealing in airplanes. Its liability for defects in its planes extended equally to planes it sold and planes it leased. Finally, choice **D** is wrong because even if it exercised due care, Equinox will still be liable in products liability.

87. **D** The characterizations of invitee, licensee, and trespasser are applied by most courts in actions between land entrants and landowners or land occupiers. When a tenant sues a landlord, the tenant is treated as a tenant and not as an invitee, licensee, or trespasser. Landlord-tenant cases are governed by doctrines different from those in typical landowner-land entrant cases. Choices **A, B**, and **C** are therefore wrong because they refer to legal categories that have no role in landlord-tenant cases.

88. **B** Trespass is an intentional tort for which a defendant is liable if he enters or causes an entry on the plaintiff's land, regardless of the defendant's beliefs about property rights or the defendant's overall

reasonable conduct. Choices **A, C,** and **D** are wrong because each is a variation of types of reasonableness that Remodeler might have manifested. Regardless of how reasonable Remodeler was, if he meant to put the expansion where it wound up, and it wound up on Nextdoor's land, Remodeler will be liable for trespass.

89. **A** When a plaintiff is injured by a defendant's activity, and the activity is classified as one for which strict liability applies, the plaintiff is excused from the usual tort requirement of proof of unreasonable conduct. Choice **B** is wrong because regardless of the basis for establishing that a defendant has breached a duty, a plaintiff must still show that there was a causal connection between the defendant's conduct and the plaintiff's harm. Choice **C** is wrong because the quality of the defendant's care is not relevant in a strict liability suit. Choice **D** is wrong because *res ipsa loquitur* is a negligence, not a strict liability, concept.

90. **C** This statute is an example of a "50 percent rule" modified comparative negligence statute. It allows a negligent plaintiff to recover as long as the plaintiff's share of responsibility is ***not greater*** than the share assigned to the defendant. Where a plaintiff is 50 percent responsible and a defendant is 50 percent responsible, the plaintiff's share is ***not greater*** than that of the defendant, so a proportionally reduced recovery would be permitted. Choices **A, B,** and **D** all misinterpret the statute.

91. **D** A commercial supplier that, in the regular course of business, provides a defective product is liable to the purchaser or user for personal injury or property damage resulting from the defect, even when the defendant has exercised due care with respect to the item. The injured plaintiff many sue any or all of the firms that have been a part of the chain of distribution—manufacturer, distributor, and retailer. If she recovers against one, the defendant may be entitled to indemnity from another firm in the chain. Yattle is liable to John under the products liability doctrine, but can obtain indemnity from Xavier, the manufacturer, and the seller to Yattle. The correct answer is choice **D.** Choice **A** is wrong because products liability is a strict liability theory. Yattle is liable under this theory even if it exercised due care in handling the set. Choice **B** is wrong because (1) John was probably a foreseeable user (rather than a mere bystander), and (2) even bystanders are, in most jurisdictions, permitted to recover under a products liability theory. Choice **C** is wrong because Zerio did not sell the sets to Yattle (the distributor).

Index

Deceit
See Fraud and misrepresentation

Defamation
Generally, E17, E18, E20, E21, E24
Common interest privilege, E24
Criminal behavior, allegation of, E20
Damages, E17, E18, E20, E24, M70
Defamatory statement, E18, E20, E25, M72
Intoxication, allegation of, E25
Malice, E20
Media defendants, E19, E20, E25, M33
"Of and concerning" plaintiff, E19, E20, E24, M70, M72
Opinion, expressions of, E19, E25, M32
Pecuniary harm, E19, E20
Protection of property, privilege, E17, E18
Public figures, M33
Slander per se, E17, E19, E20, E24
State of mind, E17
Truth as defense, E21
Vicarious liability, E19

Defense of others, assault and battery, E1, E3, E6

Defense of property
Assault and battery, E6, M54
Wrongful death, M6

Defenses
See also Assault and battery; Consent; Conversion; Necessity; Negligence; Products liability; Self-defense
Privacy, invasion of, E21, E23

Disparagement
Generally, E24
Common interest privilege, E24

Domestic animals, injuries caused by, M11, M12, M81

Druggists, duty of care, M62

Electric shock devices, defense of person or property, E2

Employer and employee
See Respondeat superior; Vicarious liability

False imprisonment
Generally, E4, E17, E18, M5, M39
Consent as defense, E4, E17
Damages, E18
Shopkeeper's privilege, E17

False light, invasion of privacy, E20, E23

Fitness for particular purpose, implied warranty of, E15

Foreseeability
Assault and battery, E1
Intentional torts, E1, E2
Negligence, E3-E10, E13, E14, E18, M8, M22, M62
Trespass, E4

Fraud and misrepresentation
See also Negligent misrepresentation
Generally, E19, E23, M34
Contributory negligence as defense, E19
Damages, E19
Products liability, E14, E16
Strict liability, E14

Good faith, trespass, E4

Gratuitous aid or assistance, negligence, E10, M9, M23

Guest statutes, motor vehicles, M1, M4

Indemnification
Generally, E13, M13, M74, M76
Conversion, M10
Intentional torts, M13
Products liability, M76, M91